Reality and Representation

PHILOSOPHICAL THEORY

SERIES EDITORS
John McDowell, Philip Pettit and Crispin Wright

For Truth in Semantics
Anthony Appiah

The Dynamics of Belief: A Normative Logic
Peter Forrest

Abstract Objects
Bob Hale

Conditionals
Frank Jackson

Reality and Representation
David Papineau

Reality and
Representation

DAVID PAPINEAU

Basil Blackwell

Copyright © David Papineau 1987

First published 1987

Basil Blackwell Ltd
108 Cowley Road, Oxford, OX4 1JF, UK

Basil Blackwell Inc.
432 Park Avenue South, Suite 1503
New York, NY 10016, USA

British Library Cataloguing in Publication Data

Papineau, David
    Reality and representation. —
    (Philosophical theory).
    1. Realism
    I. Title   II. Series
    149'.2   B835

    ISBN 0–631–15517–1

Library of Congress Cataloging in Publication Data

Papineau, David, 1947–
    Reality and representation.

    (Philosophical theory)
    Bibliography: p.
    Includes index.
    1. Thought and thinking. 2. Reality. 3. Realism.
    4. Representation (Philosophy)
    I. Title. II. Series.
    B105.T54P37   1987   149'.2   87–5151
    ISBN 0–631–15517–1

Typeset in 11 on 13 pt Baskerville
by Opus, Oxford
Printed in Great Britain by T. J. Press Ltd, Padstow

Contents

For Rose

Introductory Preface

Most academic books have a 'Preface', containing various personal details and acknowledgements, and an 'Introduction', giving a chapter by chapter summary of what is to come. This 'Introductory Preface' will combine something of both these functions, and will also locate my views in the space of current philosophical positions.

This means that this is not necessarily the best place for all readers to start. In the main text I have aimed at a reasonably accessible style, and have tried not to introduce specialist terms without explaining them, except in the sections explicitly labelled 'Digressions', and in the footnotes. But here I want to explain where I stand to readers who already have some familiarity with the terrain of contemporary philosophical debate. Others might do better to go ahead to the beginning of chapter 1, perhaps returning to this Preface later.

NATURALIZED REALISM

This book is about thought and reality and the questions which arise in trying to analyse their relation. I develop a *naturalized* view of these matters. That is, I take the view that human beings are normal inhabitants of the natural world, and I try to develop philosophical theories that respect this natural status. In particular, I avoid theories that attribute any special status to human minds. I do not place minds outside the natural realm, nor do I assume that they generate a privileged kind of awareness, whereby humans are 'given' incorrigible access to their own mental states.

My view of the relation between thought and reality is also a *realist* view. I hold that reality is independent of thought, in the sense that there is no conceptual link between how things are and how humans take them to be.

Some readers will perhaps have doubts about whether a naturalized view can be realist in any full-blooded sense: if I think of humans as natural parts of the natural world, then won't I at best be an 'internal realist', in Hilary Putnam's phrase, not a 'metaphysical realist'? That is, won't my reality inevitably be reality-as-we-conceive-it, not reality-as-it-is-in-itself 'out there' beyond all conceptualization?

But I want to show that even a naturalized realism can be perfectly full-blooded. Even if I start with the idea of humans as part of the natural world, I argue for an analysis of human mental states, and of the way that they represent the natural world, which implies that the way humans conceive the world is one thing, and the way the world is, quite another. In particular, I show that it is entirely possible for human judgement to be in error, even radically in error.

Of course this naturalized realism is different from traditional, 'Cartesian' realism. I don't have the human mind as a self-intimating mental realm, with the problem then being whether the 'outside' world corresponds to the 'internal' image. But this isn't because my realism is less than full-blooded. It's because I think the Cartesian picture of self-intimating 'insides' contrasting with inaccessible 'outsides' shouldn't still be on the philosophical agenda thirty years after Wittgenstein's private language argument and Sellars's attack on givens.

NATURALIZED EPISTEMOLOGY

Realism has two parts. The first is the thesis that reality is independent of the way it is represented in human judgement: it is always possible that thought gets the world wrong. But the realism needs a second epistemological part to meet the implicit sceptical challenge: it needs to show how the danger of divergence between thought and reality can be averted.

I try to develop a naturalized solution to this problem too. The idea is simple enough. Human beliefs are the outputs of natural psychological processes. Some such processes are *reliable* for producing true beliefs, others are not. People who take pains to ensure that all their beliefs come from reliable processes will succeed in avoiding error.

That's easy enough to say. But the details are needed to show that it is a story worth telling. They will come in what follows. At this stage, however, I would like to explain how my use of the notion of reliability relates to the kind of reliabilist analysis of knowledge developed recently by Alvin Goldman and others.

I take my approach to complement such analyses of knowledge. A common reaction to the idea that knowledge is belief produced by a reliable process is that this suggestion says nothing about the central normative concern of epistemology, namely, telling us how to avoid error. But I try to show that, veiwed from the right perspective, a reliabilist epistemology can indeed tell us how to avoid error, precisely by recommending that our beliefs should come from reliable processes.

This has implications for the normative authority of epistemological prescriptions. The recent revival of interest in Wittgentstein's views on 'rule-following' manifests a concern with the nature of the norms governing human judgement. From the perspective of this book there are no such norms, or at least none that do not reduce to *conditional* imperatives of the form: *if* you want to have true beliefs, *then* you ought to embody such-and-such mental processes, since they are reliable for producing truths. (The arguments of this book are all subordinate to the assumption that true beliefs are desirable. I offer no arguments against such possible views as that our beliefs should be comforting, or unsubversive, or exciting, before they should be true, apart from the obvious point that actions based on true beliefs will succeed.)

While I think my epistemological arguments complement reliabilist analyses of knowledge, they do not overlap with the existing literature to any great extent. Most existing work in this area is concerned, first, to analyse the *concept* of knowledge, and, secondly, to show that this analysis blocks scepticism, considered as the claim that there is not (or cannot be) any knowledge. I manage to avoid the concept of knowledge almost entirely, by thinking of epistemology explicitly as the science of how to avoid error. The question I ask is not, 'How can we *know*?', but simply, 'How can we avoid error?' Correspondingly, when I examine sceptical arguments, I do not consider them as threats to *knowledge*, but simply as threats to our ability to avoid error.

SUMMARY OF THE BOOK

Much of the positive argument in this book, and in particular the naturalized epistemology just described, comes in the second half, in chapters 7 to 10. The first half is concerned rather with the first component in realism, with showing that reality is independent of thought.

In the first chapter I argue for a certain way of conceiving the issue between realism and anti-realism. Once we have rejected Cartesian 'givens', it is unhelpful to think of the issue as an ontological one, with anti-realists denying the existence of certain classes of putative entities, and realists affirming their existence. Rather the fundamental issue is what the analysis of representation implies for the relation between judgement and reality in general. Anti-realism is the thesis that the analysis of representation yields an *a priori* argument for holding that at some level judgement and reality must fit each other. Realism is the denial of this thesis. I point out that, on this way of conceiving the matter, anti-realism is committed to the further thesis that at some level there is no possibility of human thinkers adopting incompatible modes of thought.

In chapter 2 I consider an analysis of representation that promises to ground a relatively strong version of anti-realism. This is the Davidsonian view that the notion of meaning is best understood via the idea of a theory which ascribes truth conditions to the sentences in a language. This Davidsonian view has the prima facie implication that the assertions made in any interpretable language must be largely true. I point out that some of the refinements necessary to defend the Davidsonian approach to meaning weaken it as a basis for such an anti-realism. (Perhaps it seems odd to count Davidson as an anti-realist. But remember that my anti-realism does not require the rejection of some category of existents, or a commitment to assertibility conditions in the theory of meaning, but simply some kind of *a priori* argument against the possibility of error.)

My discussion of Davidson leads me to consider the notion of belief, and in chapter 3 I start analysing the representational powers of beliefs. Most of this chapter is devoted to showing that if we assume the standard functionalist account of belief, the representational powers of beliefs are more puzzling than they might at first seem.

In chapter 4 I put forward a positive theory of how beliefs represent, which I call 'the teleological theory of representation'. This is a fully 'naturalized' theory: it takes beliefs to be functionally identified states of natural beings, and analyses their representational powers in terms of their biological purposes.

In chapter 5 I show that the Davidsonian defence of anti-realism collapses entirely once we adopt the teleological theory of representation. It is quite possible for human conceptual schemes radically to misrepresent reality. In this chapter I also argue that the objections to the Davidsonian view of representation provide a strong argument for a functionalist view of belief, and therefore make it difficult to avoid the teleological account of representation.

In my terms Michael Dummett and the later Hilary Putnam are both anti-realists, in that they argue against conceptions of 'reality' which make the possibility of error ineliminable. But they allow more room for error than Davidson. They allow that actual beliefs can generally be false. Their view is only that the norms by which judgements are evaluated cannot but lead us to the truth. In chapter 6 I argue that any view of this kind presupposes universal adherence to certain patterns of rational thought, and I claim that there is no good argument for this presupposition.

In chapter 7 I turn to the idea of a 'naturalized' epistemology. I argue that we can perfectly well evaluate our methods of belief-evaluation themselves, by reflecting on their reliability for producing truths which correspond to reality. The upshot of such reflections will be *actions*, aimed at improving the reliability of our methods. Cartesian authority makes us think that epistemology is essentially to do with *inference*. I argue for a more general view of epistemology, as the practical pursuit of truth.

In chapter 8 I emphasize that this is a *realist* epistemology, by contrasting it with the kind of epistemology we would get from a coherence conception of truth. I point out that a realist epistemology is not available for mathematics and morality, and accordingly I suggest that we should adopt a fictionalist view of these areas.

Chapter 9 extends the idea of reliability-evaluations to our inferential methods of deduction and induction. In connection with deduction I appeal to Dummett's account of the justification of deduction. This leads to further discussion of Dummett's anti-realism and of mathematical truth. In connection with induction I argue that the naturalized perspective allows a kind of self-supporting defence of induction, and I consider some of the details of such a defence. This chapter also contains further discussion of moral judgements.

In chapter 10 I face up to the complaint that reliability-evaluations will always be informed by our existing beliefs about the natural world and how we fit into it. I maintain that this is no argument against the effectiveness of naturalized epistemology as a programme for avoiding error. This chapter also considers whether the history of science, or the underdetermination of theory by evidence, or traditional sceptical arguments, yield arguments against our ability to avoid error.

EPISTEMOLOGY AND CAUSATION

In the course of writing this book I realized that much of what I had to say boiled down to a simple formula: realism requires that beliefs should be caused by the facts they are about. This was not how I started off thinking about these matters. My original problem was simply: error is possible, and so what can we do to avoid it? It was only later that I realized that my answer came down to: we must arrange for our beliefs to be reliably caused by the relevant facts.

Once my position is put explicitly in causal terms, various new questions emerge. Exactly how should causation be analysed? And does that analysis support the claim that various kinds of belief (perceptual, scientific) are caused by their truth conditions, while others (mathematical, moral, modal) are not?

These are relevant questions. But I do not address them explicitly here, even though my remarks implicitly commit me to certain answers. No doubt when they are addressed directly, it will turn out that various of my theses need altering. But it will satisfy me if the arguments of this book make you agree that these are the questions that epistemology ought to be focusing on.

THE TELEOLOGICAL THEORY: BACKGROUND

The two central ideas which underly the argument of this book are the teleological theory of representation, and the idea that we can avoid error by reflecting on our belief-forming processes and adjusting them in pursuit of reliability. It might be helpful to say something about the source of these ideas.

The teleological theory first. As I develop it, this theory is built on the view that everyday psychology (or something like it) is a causal theory which implicitly defines beliefs (and other mental states) as serious explanatory entities. This view has always seemed to me to be justified by everyday psychology's evident ability to predict both 'rational' and 'irrational' human actions. Some years ago I tried to show in some detail why everyday psychology deserved respect as a serious predictive theory (*For Science in the Social Sciences*, 1978, ch. 4).

But at that time I had no clear ideas about representation as such. I was inclined to focus on sentences rather than beliefs, and took it that sentences' meanings (and hence the identities of the beliefs they expressed) were fixed by something like their Sellarsian 'role', that is, by the perceptual and inferential regularities governing their use. (Cf. my *Theory and Meaning*, 1979, chs 1–3.) On the question of 'aboutness', I simply assumed, in what now seems to me an excessively verificationist spirit, that words referred to those entities, if any, that the regularities governing their use would lead them to be applied to.

These commitments made me uneasy with approaches to meaning, like Donald Davidson's, that started with truth conditions. An obvious difficulty arose in connection with culturally distant notions like, say, *phlogiston* or *taboo*. Judgements involving such notions seemed to have perfectly well-defined Sellarsian roles, but to lack individuating this-worldly truth conditions. (Davidsonian enthusiasts would often suggest, in conversation anyway, that such notions could always be defined, along the lines of a definition of 'unicorn', in terms that did have legitimate this-worldly contents. My response was to point out that theoretical concepts can't in general be defined in observational terms.)

However, I worried about the Davidsonian approach to meaning. Hartry Field's 'Mental Representations' (1978) was a liberating influence. (And I think I was primed by Putnam's 'Reference and Understanding', 1978a.) Field showed that the *causal role* conception of belief can be separated from the idea that beliefs *represent* their truth conditions, and indeed that, from the naturalistic, causal role point of view, it is not at all clear what work the latter, representational conception does.

For some time I was attracted to the view that the notion of representation was *not* in fact needed for anything naturalistically important. (Cf. Leeds, 1978.) Its significance was entirely pragmatic: a Davidsonian theory ascribing truth conditions to sentences was simply a device helping us to draw inferences about the world from the utterances of others, but of no real naturalistic significance. (Cf. Field himself, 1978, pp. 48–9.)

But while thinking about the details of this position (and also while failing to persuade a single person to share it, so far as I could tell, despite delivering versions to about twenty different audiences), I came to realize that there was, after all, a naturalistically acceptable explanation of representation: namely, that the *biological purpose* of beliefs was to occur in the presence of certain states of affairs, which states of affairs therefore counted as their truth conditions.

This was clearly an idea whose time had come by the early eighties. I read a paper on it at the APA Eastern Division meeting in 1982, and a longer version of this was published as 'Representation and Explanation' in 1984. At the APA meeting Ruth Garrett Millikan told me she had developed some similar ideas, and her *Language, Thought, and Other Biological Categories* came out in 1984 too. Jerry Fodor's 'Semantics, Wisconsin Style' also appeared in 1984, arguing that if causal theories of representation like Dennis Stampe's and Fred Dretske's were to work, they needed to become more explictly teleological.

In a way the teleological theory of representation is a natural upshot of the recent switch in philosophical attention from sentences to beliefs. If you start with sentences, it is natural to think of their significance as deriving from *norms* specifying when they *ought* to be used. And then it is easy, in that vaguely verificationist spirit, to think of sentences as being about the situations in which it is right to utter them. Most recent thinking about beliefs, however, takes beliefs to be identified by their causal roles, not by norms governing their proper use. But causal roles will include situations in which beliefs ought not to be held (that is, where the beliefs are false) as well as cases where beliefs ought to be held (and are true). So something – the teleological theory – needs to be added to a purely causal role conception of belief if it is to account for the relationship between beliefs and their truth conditions.

EPISTEMOLOGY AS THE PRACTICAL PURSUIT OF RELIABILITY: BACKGROUND

The other central idea, that we can avoid error by adjusting our belief-forming processes in pursuit of reliability, was brought into focus by Richard Rorty's attack on epistemology in *Philosophy and the Mirror of Nature*. It appeared to me that Rorty's refusal to evaluate beliefs was particularly vulnerable in connection with observational beliefs. This might seem a surprising point at which to press Rorty, for at first sight observation looks like a stronghold for epistemological quietism: surely the findings of our senses have to be taken as an unquestioned basis for our view of the world, however critical we might later become about the superstructure. But my interest in the arguments surrounding the 'theory-dependence' of observation in science made me aware that there was nothing automatic about the authority of observation. And I felt that unless that authority could somehow be grounded we would always be open to radical relativism.

In *Theory and Meaning* I briefly aired the suggestion that we should appeal to our theories about ourselves as observers to decide which observations are trustworthy. This idea had intuitive appeal, but at that stage I had difficulty thinking it through, and indeed got into something of a tangle in the process (*Theory and Meaning*, pp. 100–3). I returned to the idea in 'Is Epistemology Dead?' (1981), and it became clear to me that the only way to develop it without appealing to incorrigible introspection at some point, was to think of epistemological evaluation as focused on our observational *processes*, rather than on the beliefs that emerge from such processes. The corollary was the picture of epistemology as a *practical* enterprise, concerned to ensure that the processes we embody are reliable for truth, as opposed to a purely theoretical enterprise within the realm of belief.

This led me to consider whether our belief-forming processes in general, including our inferential methods, could similarly be assessed and practically adjusted for reliability. Chapter 2 of Bernard Williams's *Descartes* then helped me to see how this general practical approach was a legitimate alternative to traditional Cartesian epistemology. Williams also enabled me to see how this practical approach related to reliabilist accounts of knowledge like Goldman's.

One important corollary of the practical conception of epistemology is worth mentioning at this point, given that I ignore it in what follows. On the traditional Cartesian conception, epistemology is essentially an *individual* concern, since it has to do with argumentative moves made within conscious minds. But once we switch to the idea that the aim of epistemology is to ensure the reliability of belief-forming processes in general, including processes whose operations lie outside consciousness, there is no reason why epistemology should continue to be restricted to processes that can be embodied in a single individual. We can perfectly well direct epistemological attention to, say, the social processes by which information gets transmitted from one person to another, or the social processes by which beliefs become part of the established consensus in a community. I think these topics are important, particularly to the philosophy of science. But, as I said, I shall not address them here, and shall instead confine myself to the kinds of processes that are familiar to philosophers.

ACKNOWLEDGEMENTS

Parts of this book, and of papers which preceded it, were delivered at seminars in various places, and I would like to thank all the philosophical friends and acquaintances who made comments on those occasions. I can particularly remember being helped by remarks made by Anthony Appiah, David Armstrong, Ned Block, Jim Brown, Myles Burnyeat, Edward Craig, Mark Fisher, Danny Goldstick, Jane Heal, Hugh Mellor, and Trevor Pateman. I have also had many helpful conversations with Nick Jardine, Robert Nola, and Chris Wright.

I am especially grateful to Ian McFetridge and Philip Pettit, both of whom read complete drafts at different stages. Their criticisms did much to shape the final version (though not as much, I suspect, as either would have liked). Jeremy Butterfield and Philip Percival were also kind enough to read sections of the typescript and suggest significant improvements.

I would also like to thank my sister, Sarah Papineau, for the examples of the Dzongkha language used in chapter 2.

1

Realism and Anti-Realism

1.1 THE DIFFERENCE BETWEEN REALISM AND ANTI-REALISM

This book is an essay in epistemology. I take epistemology to be a normative, practical discipline, which aims to guide us in our formation of beliefs. The reason for doing epistemology is that we human beings are prone to error in our beliefs. Epistemological reflection promises to advise us how to avoid such errors. (This isn't everybody's idea of epistemology. Some philosophers think of epistemology as primarily to do with the analysis of the concept of knowledge, and only incidentally, if at all, as about the practicalities of avoiding error. But I find it simpler to remove the concept of knowledge from centre stage, and to discuss the problem of erroneous belief directly. Let me bypass this problem for now by simply stipulating that 'epistemology' is the science of how to avoid error.)

My own account of how we can best avoid doxastic error (that is, error in our beliefs) is elaborated in the second half of this book, from chapter 7 onwards. But the first half is devoted to a different, preliminary task: namely, that of showing that there really is a danger of doxastic error, and that epistemology really is needed to help us avoid it. I engage in this preliminary task because there are philosophers who deny my starting-point. Such philosophers argue that the danger of erroneous belief is much exaggerated, and that a proper analysis of the nature of human judgement will show that, by and large, judgement and reality are *predetermined* to agree. According to these philosophers, then, epistemology is based on a mistake: there is no reason in the first place for the anxieties that epistemology is designed to assuage.

We can usefully think of the view I shall be defending, the view that epistemological anxieties are indeed worth worrying about, as *realism*; correspondingly, the thesis that epistemological anxieties are misplaced can be thought of as *anti-realism*.

This terminology might seem a little surprising. Aren't 'realism' and 'anti-realism' *metaphysical* views about the nature and constitution of the world itself, rather than *epistemological* views about humans and their beliefs?

But think of it like this. Intuitively, realists are philosophers who accept that there is an independent reality which is as it is independently of human judgement. But because they think of reality and judgement as separate in this way, realists think there is always a possibility that our judgements might fail to represent the world as it is. And so realists, unless they are to subside into scepticism, on which more shortly, will feel that there is a need for us somehow actively to ensure that our beliefs do get the world right. The force of saying that realists believe in an 'independent' reality is precisely that realists have reason to be concerned about whether or not our beliefs get the world right.

Anti-realists are philosophers who deny that it makes sense to think of reality as it is in itself in abstraction from the way it is represented in human judgement. They maintain that the nature of the relationship between 'reality' and human judgement is such that they cannot help but fit each other. And so anti-realists deny that there is any real need for us to exert ourselves to ensure that our beliefs fit the world. The force of saying that anti-realists deny any 'independent' reality is precisely that anti-realists *don't* think there is always a danger of human judgement and the world diverging.

Anti-realists of course need an argument to show that judgement and 'reality' are predetermined to fit each other. We shall be looking at various such arguments in detail in what follows. But while I am still painting with a broad brush it will be worth making one general point. No anti-realist of any degree of sophistication will want to collapse the distinction between appearance and reality entirely. Anti-realists won't want to maintain that the mere occurrence of a belief, in a particular person at a particular time, can ever be enough to make that belief correct. Rather they will equate correctness in a belief with something like: consensus on the belief throughout the community, or its coherence with other beliefs, or its having been arrived at in some authorized way, or some combination of such requirements. So anti-realists will have some initial distinction between good and bad beliefs (those beliefs which are, and those which aren't, consensual, or coherent, or properly arrived at, or whatever). But once a belief has satisfied the initial standards (of consensus, or coherence, or authorized provenance, etc.), then, so anti-realists will argue, there is no further sense to the idea that it might be mistaken, that it might still, so to speak, get the world wrong.

So according to the anti-realist there is a certain point beyond which the idea that our beliefs might still be mistaken loses all content. And at that point further demands for justification of our beliefs ought to stop.[1]

1.2 INSTRUMENTALISM, IDEALISM, AND 'GIVENS'

My main concern, then, will be this debate between realism and anti-realism. But before proceeding it will be helpful to distinguish this debate from two rather more traditional debates about 'realism'.

Many contemporary philosophers, especially those trained in the philosophy of science, think of realism as the opposite of 'instrumentalism'. Instrumentalism is the doctrine that scientific theories about such 'unobservables' as atoms and electrons are merely convenient fictions, useful for making observational predic-

---

[1] In the influential writings of Michael Dummett the issue between realism and anti-realism is often represented as the question of whether sentences can have 'verification-transcendent' truth conditions. (See, for example, Dummett, 1978a, p. 146; see also the other papers in his collection *Truth and Other Enigmas*, 1978b.) There are obviously affinities between this and my characterization in terms of the possibility of judgemental error. But Dummett's formulation involves various more specific commitments which I would prefer to steer clear of at this stage. I shall discuss Dummett in chapters 6 and 9 below. Philosophers who more obviously fit my characterization of anti-realism include Richard Rorty (1980) and recent Hilary Putnam (1981).

tions, organizing observational data, and so on, but not to be taken at face value as reporting on some real world of unobservable entities. The 'realist' alternative to instrumentalism is, then, the view that statements about scientific unobservables should be construed as literal claims about things that really exist.

There is also the rather older debate between 'realists about the external world' and their 'idealist' opponents. In this debate 'idealism' denies that *any* judgements about a world beyond the ideas of conscious experience should be taken at face value, not even judgements about such everyday medium-sized physical objects as sticks and stones. 'Realism' is, then, the view adopted by Dr Johnson and common sense, according to which such judgements answer straightforwardly to a non-mental reality.

I shall not be concerned with either of these debates, at least not in the terms in which they are traditionally framed. This is because both these traditional debates between 'realists' and their opponents take it for granted that there are *some* judgements which are quite unproblematic. In the realism–instrumentalism debate these are the observational judgements that record the data to be organized and predicted. And in the realism–idealism debate they are the judgements about ideas that are given directly to conscious experience. In both cases it is by contrast with such unproblematic 'givens' that the dubious judgements – about unobservables, about physical objects in general – are called in question.

I shall have no truck with such givens in this book. For I don't accept that there are any automatically privileged judgements. I take it that all judgements are fallible, and that no judgement gains its authority just from being made. At its simplest the argument against givens can be put like this. Any judgement, properly so-called, must lay claim to something, must answer to something for its correctness. But then its authority cannot be guaranteed by the mere fact of its occurrence. There must be a difference between being right and seeming right. In other words, there must be a gap, in conceptual principle at least, between the occurrence of a judgement, and the obtaining of the circumstances that make it correct. (Cf. Wittgenstein's remarks on sensation in his *Philosophical Investigations*, 1953, sections 244–80, especially 258: 'One would like to say: whatever is going to seem right to me is right. And that only means that here we can't talk about "right".' See also Sellars, 1956.)

Although this issue of 'givens' is centrally important to much of what follows, I do not intend to add to the intricate literature on this topic. Instead I want to take the arguments against givens for granted, and explore the epistemological issues that remain once we give up the distinction between what is given and what is not. In a sense this whole book could be thought of as aiming to develop an account of the relation between thought and reality which is free of any explicit or implicit commitment to givens.

Note in particular in this connection that *anti-realism*, as I am using the term, is *not* committed to givens. While my anti-realists want to narrow the gap between judgement and reality, they don't want to do away with it entirely. They have some further standard (consensus, or coherence, or provenance, or whatever) beyond mere occurrence to which belief has to answer.

So my anti-realism isn't to be equated with instrumentalism or idealism. It doesn't favour some set of immediately given judgements in opposition to certain disputable further beliefs which tempt the realist. Indeed my anti-realism, unlike traditional instrumentalism or idealism, isn't recommending that we *reject* any beliefs at all. It isn't recommending that we *restrict* our doxastic commitments to a sub-class of our existing beliefs. On the contrary, my anti-realist thinks that, by and large, statements about unobservables and physical objects are as good as any others, and ought to be respected accordingly.

Perhaps putting it like this might make it unclear what real substance there is to my debate between realism and anti-realism. The anti-realist rejects any supposed contrast between givens and epistemologically suspect judgements, and so endorses the general run of our beliefs. But so too does the realist: the realist also hopes to uphold our beliefs in general. True, the realist will say that belief aims at truth, in the sense of correspondence to an independent reality, whereas the anti-realist will resist such talk of independent realities, and urge that truth in the end comes down to a kind of honorific title that we attach to our more serious beliefs. But, still, is this a real disagreement, or just a matter of philosophical style?

It is possible to suspect that the apparent conflict between realism and anti-realism only arises because we are in the grip of some bad imagery. Perhaps we are thinking of a believer as a person locked inside a room (inside a mind, perhaps) looking at images projected on to the wall of the room. And then we feel, in a realist spirit, that the important question is whether the images inside the room accurately represent what is going on outside. But then we start worrying about this picture. If the believer is permanently locked inside the room, if the believer can *never* go round the back to see how things really are, then wouldn't we get a better picture by rubbing out the outside and the walls, and leaving just the believer and the images? And then we feel, in an anti-realist spirit, that reality isn't something different from the way things appear to human believers, but simply the view that humans receive.

However, these contrasting pictures are *not* how I want to think about realism and anti-realism. These are bad pictures. In particular, the second picture is quite as bad as the first. If it is wrong to think of believers as locked inside rooms, then it is wrong to think of them as looking at images at all. Both these pictures are premised on the 'myth of the given', on the assumption that the primary access of believers is always to the data of consciousness. If we reject the given, then we must reject this whole sequence of metaphors, and stop thinking in terms of 'inside' and 'outside', in terms of a secure 'internal world' opposed to a problematic 'external world'. We shouldn't think of believers as people who live inside mental rooms looking at images, but as people who live in the world itself, and are looking at things in it in the normal way.

But we can say all this, and still be left with a substantial conflict between realism and anti-realism.[2] As I have characterized this

---

[2] Here I am disagreeing with the position adopted by Arthur Fine in his (1984) and (1986). Fine argues, quite rightly, that instrumentalism, even in its more sophisticated modern versions, mistakenly takes it for granted that observational judgements are epistemologically unproblematic and non-observational judgements inherently dubious. (Cf. esp. 1986, pp. 167–8.) But he also claims that once we adopt the 'natural ontological attitude', and accept electrons along with tables, then there is no further issue about realism. My concern in this book is precisely to show that even within the 'natural ontological attitude' there is room for a substantial debate about the nature of representation and its epistemological implications.

conflict, it doesn't rest on any misconceived metaphors of 'inside' and 'outside', with realists and anti-realists in substantial disagreement about whether we are entitled to beliefs about what is 'outside'. Rather it is a debate about the extent to which human belief in general is susceptible to error, and about what if anything should be done about this. Realists, believing in an independent reality, regard such errors as an ever-present danger; while anti-realists, in denying any 'independent' reality, think that at some point this danger dissolves. This is a real dispute, even if it doesn't immediately show up in any substantial disagreement about the acceptability of any specific category of belief. The issue isn't whether we can get beyond what's 'inside' to what's 'outside', but simply how far it is possible for human judgements, of any kind, to be mistaken.[3]

1.3 THE DIVERGENCE OF HUMAN BELIEF

It will be helpful at this point to consider how the *variability* of human belief systems bears on the debate between realism and anti-realism. Let us use the term 'divergence' for the thesis that different people in different times and places can have incompatible beliefs about the natural world. (In due course it will be necessary to call this claim divergence of *belief*, to distinguish it from various other divergences. But divergence *simpliciter* will do for now.)

[3]Colin McGinn in his (1979) says that it is not feasible to be a realist or an anti-realist *tout court*: the issue can only arise with respect to some specific type of subject matter. But that is because he sees the issue as that of whether statements about specific subject matters can (anti-realism) or cannot (realism) be reduced to statements about their evidential basis. Implicit here is the thought that the evidence statements themselves are somehow 'given', and so not themselves subjects of the debate between realism and anti-realism. (See in particular McGinn's arguments on p. 117, p. 125, p. 127.) Without such givens, the fundamental question is not whether special subject areas can be made epistemologically accessible by being collapsed into givens, but what model we should have of the relation between judgement and reality in general. This is not to deny, of course, that when this general issue has been resolved, there might remain specific reasons for non-standard interpretations of specific subject matters. Thus I myself defend realism overall, but argue for a kind of fictionalism for specific areas like mathematics and morality (cf. chapters 8 and 9 below).

At first sight there might seem to be some affinity between divergence and anti-realism. Both can be thought of as raising doubts about whether our beliefs correspond to reality. But on closer examination this turns out to be somewhat misleading. Indeed, as I am using the terms, it turns out that realism is rather more at home with divergence than anti-realism is.

The realist, remember, takes the view that we need somehow to ensure that our beliefs correspond to the world. But precisely because the realist is interested in the possibility of ensuring such correspondence, there is a natural response for the realist to make to the divergentist thesis that different communities can have conflicting beliefs: namely, that at most one of those communities will have succeeded in ensuring that its beliefs are true.

Of course, realists will have their work cut out if they are to show that some favoured community (our own community, perhaps) has indeed succeeded in taking appropriate steps to avoid error. But even suppose that they fail in this task. Suppose that they cannot back up their general thought, that at most one of the conflicting alternatives is true, with any further demonstration of the epistemological superiority of our own or any other belief. Even then the realist position is straightforward enough: if nothing ensures that any of the conflicting beliefs is true, then we ought to suspend judgement between them.

One question which arises here is whether such sceptical suspension of belief will be local or global. Global scepticism is indeed an untenable position: as I shall explain in the next section, we cannot rest with a philosophical position that advises the total rejection of belief. But the unacceptability of global scepticism still leaves room for the realist to be sceptical on more specific issues.

So in the first instance realists can respond to divergence on some issue by observing that at most one of the conflicting beliefs can be true. Realists then face the challenge of vindicating some specific one of those beliefs. But realists don't necessarily have to meet this challenge in all cases, provided they can at least sustain belief on a manageable range of issues.

Perhaps this mightn't seem to leave the realist all that well-placed to deal with divergence: after all, it has yet to be shown that the realist will be able to vindicate any beliefs at all as corresponding to reality. But now consider what kind of response the *anti*-realist can make to divergence. The anti-realist, remember, holds that after a certain point it becomes inappropriate to think of belief as answering to an 'independent reality', and therefore inappropriate to engage in the project of ensuring that our beliefs do correspond to such a reality. But what then is the anti-realist to say in the face of divergence? The realist response, that only one of the divergent alternatives is true, does not seem open to the anti-realist. If anti-realists deny the need to ensure that our beliefs correspond to reality, and thereby hope to side-step the philosophical difficulties involved in satisfying this need, they can scarcely attribute the deficiencies of alternative views of the world to the fact that they haven't been vindicated as corresponding to reality.

The appropriate strategy for an anti-realist is to try to block divergence at source. That is, anti-realists should deny that variation in human judgement is possible. They should argue that, despite initial appearances, there isn't really any problem, because there isn't really any possibility of different humans having conflicting views about reality in the first place.

At first sight this might seem an unlikely line for anti-realists to take. But consider it in this light. Anti-realists claim that beyond a certain level it is inappropriate to continue asking for a justification for our views, since it follows from the nature of judgement that those views cannot but fit reality. But if that goes for us, then presumably it goes for anybody. So at a certain level the judgement of any believer can't but be right. From which it seems to follow that at the level in question it is inevitable that all believers agree in judgement.

It might seem as if anti-realists can avoid the need to deny divergence by simply taking a leaf out of the realist's book, and saying that judgement should be suspended in areas where human thought is variable. But while this strategy is certainly possible (and will be discussed further in chapter 6) it doesn't affect the basic point: namely, that in areas where judgement *is* upheld, the anti-realist needs somehow to show that conflicting human beliefs are impossible, and not just that, among the conflicting beliefs, one is preferable. Realists can uphold belief in the face of competition by arguing that one of the competitors is a superior representation of reality. Anti-realists have to uphold belief by showing that such competition cannot arise.[4]

We can put the argument of this section more graphically, if less precisely, in terms of the contrasting ways realists and anti-realists talk about 'reality'. Realists, as we have seen, think of 'reality' as something which exists independently of human judgement, to which judgement is striving more or less successfully to conform. And because of this, when realists are faced with different communities with conflicting beliefs, they can happily say that all but at most one have things wrong, all but at most one have beliefs that fail to correspond to reality. Anti-realists, on the other hand, suggest that at some point 'reality' simply *is* the picture presented by human judgement, not some unreachable abstraction we are perpetually striving to grasp. But then anti-realists cannot allow that at that point different humans can have different views. For to do so would commit them to the apparently absurd conclusion that different humans live in different realities.

I know that historians and anthropologists arguing for the variability of human belief sometimes talk in terms of different peoples 'living in different worlds'. But the point I am stressing is that, while realists have room to read this metaphorically, anti-realists have no option but to understand this as a literal, and therefore absurd, claim. Realists can take the talk of different communities 'living in different worlds' as merely a colourful way of conveying the differences between different people's *beliefs* about the world. Anti-realists, however, can't take talk of people 'living in different worlds' in this merely metaphorical way. Because anti-realists want to collapse the gap between judgement and reality, divergence forces them to the unacceptable conclusion that 'reality' itself, and not just the way people take it to be, is different for different peoples. Which is why, once more, anti-realists need to deny the possibility that different people can end up with different views of the world.

[4]Note in addition that, in areas where anti-realism *is* forced to suspend judgement, it also needs to 'suspend reality'. The realist who is forced to suspend judgement thinks that there is a fact of the matter that we can't find out about. But anti-realists, since they reject the ideea of an epistemologically inaccessible reality, have to say that there just aren't any facts of such matters.

1.4 DIGRESSION ON TOTAL SCEPTICISM

Let me explain why I take total scepticism to be untenable. The first thing to note is that once we have rejected givens, and accepted that all beliefs are initially on a par, as corrigible claims about things other than themselves, then total scpeticism, properly so-called, will leave us with no views whatsoever, not even views about our own mental life. We won't even be left with the appearances, for once givens have gone, there is nothing to stop total scepticism going, so to speak, all the way down. (In this respect total scepticism needs to be distinguished from traditional Pyrronist scepticism, as discussed, for instance, in Burnyeat, 1983.)

Because it suspends all belief, including belief in the appearances, total scepticism would leave our actions without any guides whatsoever. It would stop us believing, for instance, that bread is more likely to nourish us than arsenic, and beer more likely to make us drunk than water. It is because of this practical nihilism that total scepticism is untenable. Think of total scepticism as a prescription: it says we ought to believe nothing at all, and so implies that we should do what we can to get rid of all our beliefs. But we unperturbedly continue to believe that beer will make us drunk and that bread will nourish us, as our actions make manifest. So we are committed to rejecting total scepticism.

We can put this as a kind of practical syllogism, on the pattern of *modus ponendo ponens*. If we were to accept total scepticism, we would be committed to a certain course of action, namely, ridding ourselves of all beliefs. But we do not embrace this course of action. So we don't accept total scepticism.

There is nothing *impossible* about somebody living total scepticism, and striving to suspend belief across the board. No doubt it would be a hard and short life. But that doesn't matter. The important point is that, since *we* aren't going to do it, *we* are practically committed to the rejection of total scepticism. To profess total scepticism, and yet to do nothing to stop ourselves believing (that bread nourishes and arsenic poisons, etc.), would be a kind of practical inconsistency. I have nothing against the total sceptic who really does suspend belief. But those of us who aren't prepared to take this hard path need to find some less strenuous epistemological stance. And so from now on I shall take the avoidance of total scepticism to be a boundary condition of the overall debate.[5]

1.5 DIFFERENT KINDS OF ANTI-REALISM

As I explained earlier, anti-realists hold that 'beyond a certain point' further questions about correspondence between judgement and reality become inappropriate, that 'at a certain level' human judgement cannot help but fit reality. It is high time that this complication was brought more explicitly into the story. These phrases conceal important differences between different versions of anti-realism, and by running them together there is a danger of making anti-realism seem far less serious than it is.

Different versions of anti-realism put the point at which further questions about reality become inappropriate in different places. Thus while a strong form of anti-realism will deny that there is any serious question about conformity to reality for almost any human judgement, weaker forms will only claim this for certain general beliefs or principles of judgement, allowing that in the light of such general beliefs or principles we can sensibly ask whether classes of other human judgements 'conform to reality'. But the general connection between anti-realism and the denial of divergence remains: wherever a given version of anti-realism claims that justification stops, at that point it will need to deny the possibility of divergence.

In what follows I shall distinguish, and examine at length, two

[5]To those philosophers who advocate the sceptical thesis that we *know* nothing, but maintain that, even so, it is perfectly reasonable for us to believe what we do (cf. Unger, 1971), I would say that I am not interested in attributions of knowledge – or lack thereof – that carry no implications for what we ought to believe. To those who think that there might be a sense in which we oughtn't to believe what we don't know, but which doesn't imply that we should try to *stop* believing, I would say that I don't understand any such sense of 'ought'. And to those who doubt that our beliefs are sufficiently under our control for questions about what we ought to believe to be taken seriously, I would suggest reading on to chapters 7–10.

forms of anti-realism. The first, which I shall call *anti-realism of belief*, is the strong claim that almost all humans beliefs cannot help but fit reality and are therefore in no need of justification. Anti-realism of belief is therefore committed to the denial of divergence in a strong form: scarcely any of the beliefs of different communities can ever be in conflict.

This strong position might seem extremely implausible. Even so, it has its defenders, most notably Donald Davidson, and I shall devote much of the first half of this book to an examination of issues related to anti-realism of belief. Although I shall be arguing that it is fundamentally flawed, anti-realism of belief goes hand in hand with an influential and seductive view of the nature of judgement, and a number of important and interesting issues will arise when we examine this view of judgement.

The second form of anti-realism I shall call *anti-realism of method*. This will be the weaker thesis that the principles by which people *arrive* at beliefs are in no need of justification. According to anti-realism of method it is possible for people to adopt false beliefs, and therefore perfectly sensible to ask, at that level, whether one person's beliefs are more correct than another's. But anti-realists of method insist that there is no sense to questions as to whether the standards by which people decide such questions are themselves legitimate as good methods for arriving at correct beliefs. Correspondingly, while anti-realists of method will be prepared to allow divergence at the level of belief – different communities can have conflicting beliefs – they will deny it at the level of standards – it makes no sense to suppose that different communities adhere to different principles for evaluating beliefs. I shall return to anti-realism of method, and to a discussion of such figures as Michael Dummett and Hilary Putnam, in chapter 6.

2

An Argument for Anti-Realism

2.1 CONCEPTS AND OPINIONS

We have seen that the denial of divergence is the other side of the anti-realist coin. Anti-realists have to deny divergence. More specifically, anti-realists of belief have to deny divergence of belief, and anti-realists of method have to deny divergence of methods.

As I said, I am now going to discuss anti-realism of belief, and the Davidsonian defence thereof, at some length. But before getting started on this it will be helpful to make one further distinction, between two versions of divergence of belief. Anti-realism of belief and Davidson deny both these versions. But some of the arguments we shall be concerned with will treat the two versions rather differently, and we shall save time by distinguishing them at this point.

The first, more straightforward, version (which I shall call divergence of *opinion* henceforth) restricts itself to the simple claim that different people can have different beliefs about the world. The other thesis (divergence of *concepts*) maintains in addition that such differences are sometimes due to people having different concepts. According to divergence of concepts, it is not just the beliefs themselves that differ across times and places, but the very components out of which people build their beliefs.

The best way of illustrating the contrast between divergence of opinion and divergence of concepts is in terms of attitudes to the history of science. Some writers, most famously Karl Popper, hold that new scientific theories characteristically contradict old ones: where the medievals held that force is proportional to velocity, we post-Newtonians take it to be proportional to acceleration; where seventeenth- and eighteenth-century scientists generally took light to consist of corpuscles, we now view it as a kind of radiation; where Daltonian chemists took the atom to be indivisible, we now think it can be split; and so on. Somebody who so views science in terms of the new contradicting the old is in my terms a divergentist of opinion about the history of science. (See, for example, Popper, 1959.)

But then there are writers, such as T. S. Kuhn and Paul Feyerabend, who argue that developments in the history of science aren't just a matter of succeeding theorists contradicting the assertions of their predecessors, but of their introducing radically new *ways* of thinking. It's not just a matter of the medievals measuring force by one number and our now measuring it by another. Rather the medieval *concept* of force was itself quite different from the concept we now have. The medievals had in mind a quantity inhering in any moving body, which caused its continued motion and which could be transferred to another body in impact. We think of force as something external to a body, applied from without, which causes a change in motion, and which, in Newton's words, 'consists in the action only, and remains no longer in the body when the action is over' (1687, p. 3). Somebody who thinks that science characteristically displays this kind of conceptual shift is in my terms a divergentist of concepts about the history of science. (See Kuhn, 1962; Feyerabend, 1975.)

For the divergentist of concepts the fact that we and the medievals might use the same *word* 'force' is something of a misleading accident. There isn't a single quantity, called 'force', about which we and the medievals disagree. They used the term to stand for something quite different from the quantity we call 'force'.

And similarly, a divergentist of concepts is likely to say, with the other examples: the concepts are quite different, even if the words are the same. It's not just that we disagree with our predecessors as to whether or not radiation is what light is made of. The difference goes deeper than that, in that what we mean by 'radiation' – namely, phenomena describable by the equations of quantum mechanics – is quite different from what they meant – namely, periodic variations in the density of some medium. Again, we don't just differ from Daltonians as to whether atoms can be split. We differ on the very meaning of the word 'atom': where they had in mind the smallest units of matter, the building blocks out of which all material things are made, we think of 'atoms' as a certain kind of stable arrangement of fundamental particles, not as the fundamental particles themselves.

The conceptual divergentist is in effect denying the possibility of word-by-word translations between the languages of different scientific communities. In so far as the concepts of two such communities are different, there will be no equating words on point of meaning across their two languages. This is of course most easily recognized when the two sides actually use different words, such as, say, the Latin 'vis' and our modern English 'force'. But, as we have seen, even in examples where the words are typographically identical, the conceptual divergentist will view this identity as simply a misleading coincidence, obscuring the fact that the two scientific communities are expressing quite different meanings.

Note now that divergence of *opinion* does not automatically involve divergence of *concepts*. That two parties disagree on which assertions involving some term should be accepted, does not immediately imply that the two parties have different concepts in mind when they use that term. (This, after all, is probably how most people think of scientific conflict: they accept Popper's divergentism of opinion, but balk at Kuhn's and Feyerabend's divergentism of concepts.)

However, while conceptual divergence is in this sense stronger than divergence of opinion, we cannot simply suppose that the former thesis is a straightforward extension of the latter. Indeed, conceptual divergence is altogether a rather less straightforward doctrine than it might seem.

Note that divergence, of whatever kind, isn't just the thesis that different people have different views *about different subject matters*. We wouldn't want to count it as a case of divergence that medieval thinkers had views which we lack about, say, the virtues of different kinds of sandstone as building materials, while we have views which they lacked about, say, seasonal variations in the world's ocean currents. This kind of difference need be due to nothing more than the communities in question focusing on different topics. If either side did have the interest and opportunity to acquire the views they lacked, there would be no difficulty about their simply adding those views to their existing stock of judgements.

If divergence is to be interesting, it needs to be a matter of different people having *incompatible* views, views which are competing alternatives, in the sense that they cannot simply be conjoined with each other. It is only when faced with such incompatibility that we are confronted with a question as to *which* alternative is correct, and so it is only divergence in this sense that the anti-realist, who wants to avoid such questions, is concerned to resist.

The difficulty with divergence of concepts is that it is not at all clear how concepts as such can be incompatible. Kuhn and Feyerabend talk of 'incommensurable' concepts, and this is intended to convey a kind of incompatibility. But what exactly is supposed to be involved here? It is obvious enough how opinions can be incompatible – one can negate what the other asserts. But since concepts as such don't actually *assert* anything – what does the concept *atom* assert? – how can they be incompatible?

Indeed, there is reason to think that any kind of incompatibility requires *non*-divergence of concepts. Two opinions are incompatible, as I have just said, if they contradict each other about some matter. But does this not then require some common concepts to identify the common subject matter? If the concepts behind the two opinions are different, as the divergentist of concepts wants to claim, then aren't the two sides just talking about different things? If the medievals and ourselves really do mean different things by 'force', what makes our respective judgements about 'forces' any more incompatible than our respective judgements about limestone and sea currents?

I think that this way with divergence of concepts is too quick. That is, I think that good sense can be made of different people having incompatible concepts, where this is a kind of incompatibility that goes beyond mere inconsistency of opinion. But this will have to wait until section 5.3. My purpose in this section has simply been to draw attention to the prima facie difference between divergence of concepts and divergence of opinion.

Before proceeding, it is worth observing parenthetically that the difference between conceptual and opinion divergence can usefully be put in terms of the distinction between 'type' and 'token' beliefs.

Divergence of opinion claims that the particular *token* beliefs of different people are inconsistent. Divergence of concepts claims that the general belief *types* available to different people are incompatible. The difficulty with conceptual divergence is the difficulty of seeing how 'available belief types' can be incompatible, given that the mere *availability* of a belief type doesn't *commit* anybody to anything.

The reason one naturally puts a thesis about belief types in terms of 'concepts' is that the range of belief types available to someone presumably derives from a finite stock of belief components ('concepts') together with a finite number of ways of putting them together. Talk of 'concepts' thus simultaneously refers to a repertoire of available belief types and recognizes that that repertoire will stem from a finite base.

2.2   THE TRANSCENDENTAL ARGUMENT TO END ALL TRANSCENDENTAL ARGUMENTS

I have just mentioned one possible reason for doubting divergence of concepts. Anti-realism of belief, however, wants to reject more than just divergence of concepts. It wants to side-step awkward questions about possible failures of correspondence between belief and reality altogether. So it needs to deny divergence of opinion as well.

It might seem surprising that anybody should be prepared to deny divergence of opinion – surely it has to be admitted that different communities can have contradictory beliefs? But, even so, there is a line of argument which promises to deliver just this denial. This argument proceeds in two stages. The first stage dismisses divergence of concepts. But the manner of this dismissal then gives rise to an argument against divergence of opinion itself. (The argument I shall present is inspired by Donald Davidson's 'On the Very Idea of a Conceptual Scheme', 1974. But I have simplified the argument in various ways and put it in my own terms. Some of the relevant refinements will be reintroduced later; in particular, the suggestion that Davidson reifies truth conditions will be corrected in 2.6 below, and the suggestion that he is committed to unqualified charity will be corrected in 2.7.)

The first stage, then, is to rule out divergence of concepts. We want to show it is impossible for another community to have a conceptual scheme incommensurable with ours. The argument goes as follows. If we suppose that another community are making judgements at all, then surely we must suppose that their judgements have content, that they say something about the world. But then it ought in principle to be possible to specify what the contents of those judgements are, what aspects of the world those judgements are about. We ought to be able to specify what facts those judgements lay claim to, what the truth conditions of those judgements are.

But when we give such a specification, we will of course do so by using our own concepts to identify the relevant conditions. If the aim is to specify what facts the alien community's judgements answer to, then we will need to use those concepts of our own which pick out the same facts. Or, to put it at the level of language, we will specify what their words say about the world by using words from our language which say the same thing. So the very idea of another community making judgements seems in itself to preclude the possibility of their having concepts different from ours, of their language being untranslatable into our own.

Perhaps this dismissal of divergence of concepts seems too quick. Might there not be an alien people able to think and talk about things which we simply lack concepts for? What about the Eskimos, with their thirty-odd words for different kinds of snow, or the Bedouin, with their similar prolixity about sand? Whatever the anthropological accuracy of these familiar tales, surely they can't be ruled out *a priori* simply on the grounds that *we* don't make those distinctions.

The opponents of conceptual divergence clearly need to leave room for the Eskimo and Bedouin examples. But still, they can say, when we suppose that the Eskimos' judgements are specifically *about* different kinds of snow, aren't we thereby recognizing that our conceptual repertoire could be *extended* so as to enable us to identify the contents of the Eskimo judgements? And doesn't that give us a perfectly good sense in which their language must be in principle translatable into ours?

You might think that this weakens the denial of conceptual

divergence beyond interest. Is it so surprising that we will be able to translate any alien language, if we are allowed to *extend* our own language to do the job? But anodyne as this form of the denial may be, it is quite enough for the anti-realist's purposes. For it suffices to rule out the possibility of an alien community having concepts that are *incompatible* with ours.

The point about the Eskimos and the Bedouin is that they are much more *interested* in snow and sand than we are. That's why they have concepts that we lack. And so the underlying reason for the qualification about conceptual extensions is simply that different communities have different focuses of intellectual concern. But, as we saw in the last section, the notion of different communities being interested in different subjects is a long way from any disturbing conclusions about different communities having *incompatible* ideas. And the argument at hand does seem to preclude any such substantial divergence. For, to repeat, if the alien judgements are in any sense claims about the world, it must be possible to specify what aspects of the world they are about. Even if we currently lack the conceptual resources to do this, even if we don't yet have words with those contents, this will only indicate a lack of interest or opportunity on our part, not any principled impossibility. Indeed, if their judgements really are about something, what principled barrier *could* there be to our specifying what that something is?

Now for the argument against divergence of opinion. Given that the content of alien judgements must somehow be specifiable using our concepts, let us now ask what makes it the case that a given alien judgement type has the *specific* content that it does. Consider this question from the position of a 'radical interpreter'. Suppose we are faced with a completely alien community which cannot be presumed to have any historical or cultural affinity with ours. What makes it right to interpret their judgements in a certain way, to pair sentence *s* of their language with sentence *t* of ours?

Let us start with 'occasion sentences', such as 'It is raining' or 'He is asleep', whose truth conditions depend on the place, time, and source of the utterance. The obvious answer for such sentences seems to be that a pairing of alien *s* with our *t* will be accurate if the circumstances which characteristically obtain when alien speakers assert *s* are the same as those that obtain when we assert sentence *t*.

That is, for occasion sentences it seems that we should aim for charitable interpretation – for an interpretation of alien judgement types that makes all actual alien assertions come out true. For if the content of any given type of occasion sentence, the truth condition of that alien judgement type, is to be given by a sentence of ours that picks out a circumstance that normally obtains when the aliens accept that judgement, then we can't help but conclude that whenever they accept that judgement they are judging truly: for, after all, we have identified what is required for such truth by finding some condition which is present in all those cases.

Charity seems also to be a sound principle when we proceed to interpretation in general, including the interpretation of 'standing sentences', like 'Grass is green' or 'There is no greatest prime number', whose truth conditions do not vary with the circumstances of utterance. For even in this general case, what other test of the translation of alien *s* by our *t* is there, apart from the requirement that such translations should succeed in making the judgements that the aliens actually accept come out as truths about the world?

But now we have an argument against divergence of opinion. Since the checking of a translation will in practice always depend on our opinions as to what is true about the world, the commitment to charity means that we can't help but end up representing the *alien's* actual judgements as being ones that *we* share. So it seems to follow from the very idea of a judgement type having a given content that all actual human judgements, in whichever alien community, must agree with our judgements, and therefore amongst themselves – that is, it seems to follow that divergence of opinion is not a coherent possibility.

You might or might not find this pair of arguments persuasive. But it should at least be clear how this Davidsonian line of argument promises to support anti-realism of belief. If successful, it shows that any community that makes judgements cannot possibly have beliefs about the world incompatible with ours. Or, to put it in a way that more accurately reflects the thrust of the argument, neither they nor we can possibly have beliefs incompatible with the world. At a stroke we are shown that all epistemological anxieties are misplaced, that there is no need to go on worrying whether our view of the world corresponds to the facts. As Richard Rorty has put it, Davidson's argument is a 'transcendental argument to end all transcendental arguments' (1979, p. 78).

2.3   EXTRINSIC AND INTRINSIC NOTIONS OF JUDGEMENT

Before going on to a more detailed examination of the argument of the last section, I want to make one general point. Note that the argument (and in particular the initial step which denied divergence of concepts) relied crucially on the assumption that the identity of a judgement depends on its truth condition, on what possible circumstances in the world it answers to. The argument proceeded by assuming that any judgement, properly so-called, must answer to some aspect of the world, and that identifying a judgement is therefore a matter of identifying its truth condition.

This is not the only possible view. Instead of thinking of judgement identity relationally, in terms of a judgement's *extrinsic* relationship to some truth condition, one might somehow attempt to identify judgements *intrinsically*. That is, one might somehow try to identify judgements in terms of their properties as represent*ers*, rather than in terms of what they represent.

There are various possible ways in which this might be done. If we assumed that the most basic representers were psychological states, then we might hope to identify them empathetically, in terms of some grasp of what it was *like* to have those states. Or we could, in a more materialist spirit, hope to identify psychological states in terms of the way they entered into the causal workings of the brain. Alternatively, we might prefer to think of the basic representers as sentence types, rather than as psychological states. In which case we might aim for an intrinsic identification of such sentential representers in terms of patterns of word use in the relevant linguistic community.

As it happens, I am going to defend a materialist version of the psychological option: I shall eventually take the view that the primary representers are beliefs, and that they should be identified in terms of their causal roles in our cognitive workings. But such details are not yet important. At present I only want to point out that the Davidsonian argument rests on an extrinsic view of judgement identity, and therefore that the adoption of any intrinsic approach to judgement threatens to block the Davidsonian argument. For, if we can somehow identify the judgements of an alien community in terms of the way their psychological states, or their sentences, operate, it will no longer be possible to argue directly that recognizing their judgements requires that we identify what circumstances those judgements answer to. On an intrinsic view of judgement identity we can identify alien judgements, and yet leave open the question of whether those judgements answer to circumstances that we recognize as part of the objective world. Of course intrinsic accounts of judgement may give rise to their own arguments against divergence. But if they do allow us to rule out divergence, it will have to be by a more roundabout route than Davidson's.

In the rest of this chapter I shall examine the Davidsonian extrinsic account of judgement identity. The difficulties facing this view will lead naturally to a discussion of alternative approaches to judgement identity, and in chapters 3 and 4 I shall develop the view that the primary representers are intrinsically identified beliefs. The question of whether this latter view of judgement itself yields an alternative route to the denial of divergence will be resolved in chapter 5.

2.4   TARSKI'S T-THEORIES

These last remarks have raised the question of whether the primary medium of representation is mind or language. Let us begin with linguistic representation. In particular, let us examine Davidson's own account of meaning in natural languages. We shall be led back to mental representation soon enough.

The starting-point for Davidson's theory of meaning is Tarski's work on truth. Not that Davidson is here particularly interested in truth as such, nor indeed in Tarski's account of it. But Tarski provides a technical apparatus that is central to Davidson's account of meaning.

In the 1930s Tarski showed how it was possible to construct, for any suitable language, a 'theory' which would specify the truth conditions of all the sentences of that language (Tarski, 1949, 1956; see also Platts, 1979, ch. 1, and Blackburn, 1984, ch. 8). Such theories – let us call them *T-theories*, for Truth and Tarski – would deliver, for each sentence s of the language in question, a 'T-theorem' of the form

s is true if and only if p.

Thus, for instance, if the language we were studying were Italian, and one of its sentences was 'La neve è bianca', then we would have a theorem like

'La neve è bianca' is true if and only if snow is white.

For the moment, let's not worry about what T-theories are good for, but just accept that they are theories that deliver a T-theorem for each sentence in the relevant language. The hard part of constructing T-theories is to do with non-finite languages, languages where there are an indefinitely large number of sentences. If you were dealing with a finite language, you could straightforwardly, even if tediously and unilluminatingly, list the requisite T-theorems one by one. A large but finite set of axioms, which took the s's one by one and simply stated the truth condition of each, would still be a T-theory which specified the truth conditions of all the sentences of the language.

But of course all serious languages are non-finite. We can talk about 'the father of Jim', and 'the father of the father of Jim', and 'the father of the father of the father of Jim', . . . Or, again, we can say 'I know who did it', and 'I know you know who did it', and 'I know you know I know who did it', . . .

And so the tedious 'list' strategy for constructing T-theories will be unavailable in most cases. Tarski dealt with this by focusing on the internal *structure* of sentences. Even if there are an infinite number of sentences in a language, there will be only a finite number of words (dictionaries come to an end) and a finite number of ways of combining them. The infinitariness of the language will be entirely due to the fact that many of the ways of combining words can be iterated indefinitely, as in the above examples. And so it is in general possible to construct T-theories for infinite languages by discerning structure in complex sentences, and specifying the truth conditions of those sentences as functions of that structure. More precisely, one can state a finite number of axioms for the words, and the ways of combining words, which specify what contribution such components make to the truth conditions of any complex sentences they occur in. Repeated use of the axioms will then enable one to 'build up' the truth condition of any complex sentence as a function of its components and the way they are combined.

2.5 EMPIRICAL AND PHILOSOPHICAL THEORIES OF MEANING

Tarski thought that by showing how to construct T-theories he had shown how to give a philosophical account of the concept of truth. I shall say a bit about this in a moment. But more important for our immediate purposes is the way Davidson uses Tarski's constructions to analyse meaning.

A T-theory is a theory with a finite set of axioms which nevertheless specifies truth conditions for all the sentences in an infinite language. Davidson points out that, whatever we might want to say about *truth*, there are good reasons for thinking of such a T-theory for a given language as a theory of *meaning* for that language. Does not such a theory specify what each sentence of the language claims about the world, what it answers to, what it says – in short, what it *means*? And, moreover, does it not do so in a way which accounts for the ability of human beings, which after all are only possessed of finite brains, to cope with an infinity of sentences? For by building up the truth conditions of complex sentences from the contributions made by their parts, does not a T-theory show how an infinity of meanings can be derived from a finitely stored amount of information about the workings of sentential components? (See in particular Davidson, 1967.)

Many people are initially suspicious of this idea. How *could* a

T-theory in the style of Tarski amount to a theory of meaning? Such a theory doesn't seem to get to grips with any of the philosophical difficulties surrounding the concept of meaning. After all, philosophical puzzlement about meaning stems, in the first instance at least, from the mysterious circumstance that words carry significance, that they stand for things other than themselves. We want an account of meaning somehow to *explain* this mystery. But a T-theory, far from explaining it, seems simply to take it for granted. When a T-theory, via its theorems ('*s* is true if and only if p'), purportedly tells us about meanings, it simply *uses* words from the theorist's language to specify what things the object language sentence *s* answers to. Yet surely, we feel, a theory of meaning ought to be explaining the ability of words to stand for things, not just taking advantage of this ability.

At this point we need to distinguish between two kinds of theory of meaning: *empirical* theories of meaning, and *philosophical* theories of meaning. (Cf. Sainsbury, 1979.)

An empirical theory of meaning is a theory which tells us what all the sentences of an actual natural language mean. It is the kind of theory that we would look for from an anthropological linguist – from somebody, say, who had spent five years with the Dzongkha speakers of Bhutan and was now going to write a manual telling us which sentences they used to say what.

Philosophical theories of meaning, by contrast, are not concerned with the meanings of particular words in particular languages. They do not seek to identify meanings in that sense. Rather they are philosophers' theories, seeking to explain the *nature* of meaning, seeking to explain what it is for *any* word in *any* language to have the meaning it does.

What now about Tarski-style T-theories? Certainly one can see how they might be argued to provide a model for empirical theories of meaning. A T-theory for a given language will specify what each sentence of that language says, and will do so in a way which exhibits how the meanings of complex sentences depend on the meanings of their parts. And certainly when T-theories are viewed in this way it will be no complaint that the meaning-theorist 'simply *uses*' his or her own words to specify what the foreign sentences stand for, without explaining how words *can* stand for anything. For the anthropological linguist, as an 'empirical meaning-theorist', is not interested in the phenomenon of meaning as such, but simply in such things as what, say, the Dzongkha sentence 'Chhu-bom' means.

But doesn't this now show why T-theories are not *philosophical* theories of meaning? Precisely because they are concerned with particular facts about particular languages, they seem to say nothing general, nothing philosophical, about meaning as such.

However, it is a misunderstanding of the Davidsonian approach to read it as claiming that a Tarski-style T-theory in itself amounts to a philosophical theory of meaning. Rather the idea is that we can get a philosophical grasp of meaning *through* an understanding of how Tarski-style empirical theories work. As John McDowell puts it, 'If there can be such a thing as a [empirical] theory of meaning for any language, meaning cannot be anything but what any such theory is a theory of' (1976, p. 42).

The suggestion here is that we should explain what meaning is by explaining the nature and workings of an empirical theory of meaning. After all, many theoretical concepts in science have to be explained in this way, via our grasp of how they slot into the relevant theories. Thus compare the situation of somebody philosophically puzzled about meaning with that of a physics student puzzled about the notion of *force*. Suppose we explained to the student how empirical theories of forces worked. We explained that there were theories stating that certain forces (frictional, gravitational, electromagnetic) are present in certain circumstances, and that they have effects in accordance with Newton's second law. And we pointed out how these theories generated various predictions, by means of which they could be tested. If, after we had explained all this, the student still remained puzzled (What *are* forces? What is the *nature* of force?) there would be nothing more to say. For what is force, but what an empirical theory of force is about?

And similarly, the idea is, with meaning. Once somebody has been shown how an empirical theory of meaning specifies the meaning of each sentence in the language under study, and has thereby been shown how we can test such theories, what more is there to say about meaning? In effect the notion of meaning will have been implicitly defined by a specification of the role it plays in empirical theories of meaning.

It is worth observing at this point that this implicit definition approach to the concept of meaning provides the basis for the initial step in Davidson's anti-divergentist argument, the step that rules out divergence of concepts. For Davidson's approach to meaning, as explained so far, forces us to an extrinsic notion of judgement identity: our grasp of the notion of meaning is supposed to come entirely from our understanding of how an empirical theory of meaning works, and an empirical theory of meaning is a recursive specification of truth conditions. So the idea of a sentence being meaningful just is the idea of its having a specifiable truth condition. And then of course the argument against divergence of concepts follows straight away: any alien sentence, if it is indeed meaningful, must answer to some truth condition in principle specifiable by us.

2.6   DIGRESSION ON THE CONCEPT OF TRUTH

Tarski thought that T-theories solved the philosophical problem of truth because they were tantamount to (and indeed, given a bit of set-theoretical apparatus, could be explicitly converted into) an eliminative definition of truth, a specification of a condition (albeit an extremely complicated one) satisfied by all and only the true sentences. But, as Hartry Field has pointed out, the 'definitions' one gets from Tarski's work are language-specific, in the sense that the condition common to all the true Italian sentences, say, is quite different from that common to all the true German sentences. Tarski does indeed show us how to construct a predicate coextensional to *true-in-L* for given L. But Field's point makes it clear that this in itself does not amount to a philosophical account of truth (Field, 1972).

However, might not defenders of Tarski's approach to truth respond to Field's criticisms by adopting the line that Davidsonians adopt about meaning? That is, can't they argue that, although the construction of a predicate coextensional to true-in-L for some given L yields only an empirical definition for a particular language, and not a philosophical account of truth, what does amount to such a philosophical account is a general understanding of how such empirical constructions are possible and authenticable? In effect this would be to think of truth as a kind of second-order property, namely, the property of satisfying an empirically accurate definition of true-in-L for the relevant L. And this would then give us a notion of truth applicable across languages: a sentence in any language is true just in case it has the property of being true-in-the-language-it-belongs-to.

Fair enough. But it should be noted that when we come to explain what makes an hypothesized 'definition' of the first-order property of being true-in-L empirically accurate, we will need to appeal to 'Convention T', to the requirement that the 'p's in the theorems of our recursive theory of true-in-L should *translate* the object language *s*'s. Of course, the 'definition' of true-in-L itself will make no mention of the notion of translation. But we are not now concerned with such empirical definitions as such, but with the second-order 'philosophical' definition which appeals to a notion of what makes a first-order definition of true-in-L empirically accurate. And in this context the reference to translation is essential.

All of which is not necessarily to say that a philosophical theory of truth along the lines suggested is unviable, but simply to point out that it stands in need of supplementation by a philosophical account of meaning, to provide the requisite explanation of the notion of translation.

On the other hand, it should be noted that most philosophical theories of meaning will offer quicker ways of explaining truth philosophically than by pointing to the possibility of empirical definitions of true-in-L for variable L and then building a second-order property on this basis. Thus consider any theory of meaning which thinks of the possession of meaning as a matter of having truth conditions, and which reifies truth conditions as possible states of affairs or as sets of possible worlds. Such a philosophical theory of meaning will no doubt *imply*, in conjunction with the relevant facts about any suitable L, a recursive T-theory for that L. But, given any such theory of meaning, truth itself could be explained much more directly, without going via the possibility of recursive definitions of truth-in-L, by simply saying that a sentence is true if and only if its truth condition obtains.

While on this topic, I should warn readers that the overall position developed in this book will argue against any commitments to such abstract entities as sets of possible worlds or possible states of affairs. This issue will be discussed in 9.4 below. One implication of this discussion will be that I ought, strictly speaking, to explain truth by the long route, via the possibility of empirical definitions of true-in-L, not by appeal to the idea of a truth condition obtaining. And, more generally, the implication will be that I ought not, strictly speaking, to depend in any context on talk of truth conditions as reified possible states of affairs.

However, it is not always convenient to speak strictly, and so I shall allow myself, as I have been doing so far, to make free with the terminology of truth conditions. I believe that in principle it would be possible to eliminate such references to reified truth conditions from my discussion. But to do so would greatly hamper the exposition.

This point is particularly relevant to my exposition of the Davidsonian approach to meaning. I have talked of T-theories as 'ascribing truth conditions' to sentences. Here too I would like to be understood as adopting a convenient mode of speech. I am aware that the construction '*s* is true if and only if p' does not refer to a truth condition on the right-hand side, but merely uses the sentence 'p', and that, moreover, many philosophers regard the consequent avoidance of reified truth conditions as a major virtue of the Davidsonian approach to meaning. But, even so, it is far easier to explain the Davidsonian approach with the help of the terminology of truth conditions. None of my criticisms of Davidson will hinge on this simplification.

Perhaps one further feature of the way I talk about truth needs defence. I have assumed at a number of points that from a realist point of view truth is a matter of 'correspondence'. And this notion of correspondence will be explicitly appealed to in a number of my arguments, especially in chapter 8. But it might seem that any such notion of correspondence presupposes the idea of a truth condition as a possible state of affairs or set of possible worlds: for what is correspondence but a matter of the possible state of affairs associated with a sentence obtaining in the actual world, or the actual world being included in the set of possible worlds associated with a sentence, or some such?

But consider again the idea that truth is a kind of second-order property, the property of being true-in-L for the relevant L. Two features of this approach to truth are relevant here. First, this approach does not require us to *explain* truth in terms of correspondence and reified truth conditions. And yet, secondly, in the light of this approach we can see that there is a perfectly natural sense in which a sentence's being true is a matter of its corresponding to the world, a sense which does not involve any ontology of truth conditions. To see this, note that for a given L, the property required for a sentence x to be true-in-L is in effect a long disjunctive property along the lines of '$x = s_2$ and p_1, or $x = s_2$ and p_2, or . . .' So if x *is* true-in-L for the relevant L, this will be because, for some n, x is s_n, and p_n. In this sense, for example, 'La neve è bianca' is true because snow is white, and, in general, any true sentence is true because the non-linguistic world is independently a certain way. This seems to me to make it quite natural to say that truth is a matter of a sentence corresponding to the facts. That, anyway, is how I want to be understood when I talk about correspondence.

2.7 TESTING T-THEORIES

Our present concern is not with truth, but with Davidson on meaning, and in particular with the idea that the concept of meaning can be explained via the possibility of empirical theories of meaning. I want now to look more closely at the idea of an empirical theory of meaning. In particular, I want to ask exactly how we are supposed to *test* such a theory.

But first a preliminary point needs dealing with. I propose to simplify things from here on by assuming that the theorems of our empirical T-theories have the form

s means that p.

Davidsonians, I know, prefer the formulation

s is true if and only if p.

But this way of putting things seems to me responsible for a great deal of confusion. For its suggests that understanding empirical theories of meaning requires the concept of truth. And this then invites the perfectly reasonable complaint that the concepts of truth and meaning are too close for one to illuminate the other.

But we oughtn't to be seeing things this way. Given the Davidsonian approach, we can, speaking loosely, think of an empirical theory of meaning as pairing each sentence of the object language with some condition. The relation between the sentence and the condition can be expressed as a matter of the former 'meaning' the latter, *or* of its 'being true if and only if' the latter obtains (or of its 'standing for' the latter, or 'signifying' it, or 'laying claim to' it, or 'answering to' it, or whatever). But *whichever* expression is used, including 'is true if and only if', the idea ought not to be that we can understand theories of meaning because we understand that expression, but rather that we understand that expression because we understand how theories of meaning work. All of which will be much clearer if we simply stick to the formula '*s* means that p', and remember the analogy with theoretical concepts like force.[1]

Now for the question of how to test an empirical theory of meaning for a given natural language. It is all very well for a theory to *claim*, say, that the Dzongkha sentence 'Chhu-bom' means that the river is full. But what is supposed to show that this claim, and the theory behind it, is indeed true? A theory of physical forces it testable because it makes predictions about accelerations. What is supposed to correspond in the case of an empirical theory of meaning?

Presumably the answer will be something to do with the

---

[1] Davidsonians argue that we need 'is true if and only if' rather than 'means that' in our theorems because only the former is an extensional connective which will permit the substitutivity of co-referrers when deriving the T-theorems from the axioms. But this is by no means a compelling argument. The issue hinges, *inter alia*, on the question of whether speakers know T-theories for their own languages and on the possibility of substitutional quantification. For further discussion of this complex issue see Sainsbury (1979), Taylor (1982), and section 5.6 below.

linguistic behaviour of the people who speak the language. Clearly finding out what words mean must somehow hinge on noting who says what on what occasions. But beyond this the story can be filled out in a number of different ways.

The simplest approach is to adopt the charitable strategy outlined in section 2.2 above. On this account we test an attribution of meaning to occasion sentences (such as 'Chhu-bom') by seeing whether the ascribed truth condition (the river is full) normally obtains when speakers utter those sentences; and, more generally, we test the attributions of meaning to sentences in general by seeing whether those attributions make all actual alien judgements come out true.

It was this commitment to a principle of charity in interpretation which in 2.2 gave rise to the argument against divergence of opinion: if the right way for us to check a proposed interpretation of an alien language is to see whether it makes everything the aliens actually say come out true by our lights, then it is inevitable that all alien assertions will be ones that we share, and hence inevitable that different communities will always have compatible opinions about the world.

Note in this connection that where the argument against divergence of opinion depends on the specific idea that empirical T-theories should be tested as dictated by the principle of charity, the argument against divergence of concepts depends only on the general idea that the notion of meaning is to be grasped implicitly via a grasp of the possibility of a theory which ascribes truth conditions to all the sentences in a natural language, and independently of how exactly we decide that theories ascribing such truth conditions should be tested.

Let us now look more closely at the principle of charity. It is not hard to see that as so far stated it is far too crude. The principle of charity seems to commit us to the conclusion that every human utterance is true. But surely people do sometimes say false things. There must be something wrong with an approach to interpretation which rules out this perfectly normal possibility *a priori*.

As an initial response to this complaint, Davidsonians can point out that the need to have a *uniform* interpretation of each utterance type for different speakers and times, and the need to derive such interpretations from a *finite basis*, both mean that the aim of perfect charity in interpretation is an unattainable ideal. However we adjust our interpretations, these two constraints will inevitably force us to portray some alien utterances as false. We will never be able to find a perfect fit between the world itself and the way our interpretation suggests that the aliens see the world. At best we will be able to optimize ascription of truth to alien utterances, not to make *all* alien utterances come out true. (Cf. Davidson, 1967, p. 27; 1973, p. 137; 1974, p. 168. Page references here and throughout are to the collection, *Inquiries into Truth and Interpretation*, Davidson, 1984.)

There are questions which can be raised about why interpretations should *have* to be uniform and finitely based. (Cf. Sainsbury, 1979.) But suppose we let that pass, and allow that in practice even the most charitable interpretation will always involve some ascription of falsity. Even so, there is still something seriously wrong with the charitable approach to interpretation. For, despite the above refinements, the charitable strategy still views false utterance as a kind of peripheral 'noise', something that arises only because we cannot make the fit between interpretational scheme and true utterance perfect. Falsity is still something to be *minimized* by interpretation, even though we recognize that the best interpretation will inevitably leave us with a fair amount of it. But is even this a defensible attitude to charity?

Suppose, for example, that we see a group of Dzongkha speakers chance upon a film set in nearby northern India, and that they there see some life-size papier-mâché oak trees, which lead them to utter 'Shing'. Or, suppose again, that we have noted that the Dzongkha speakers are led to utter 'Gyem sguk rim' by meeting a succession of tall, and only tall, foreigners. A natural reading of the situation is to conclude that 'Shing' means *tree* and 'Gyem sguk rim' that *all foreigners are tall*. But this then implies that the particular Dzongkha utterances in question are false. Now, it might be arguable that these falsity-attributing interpretations are forced on us by the constraints of uniformity and structure, despite the fact that they imply the Dzongkha speakers to be saying false things. But I think we should first ask here why we need to be *forced* to an uncharitable interpretation in this way.

Given the circumstances as described, it is scarcely a *deficiency* in the interpretations *tree* and *all foreigners are tall* that they impute falsity to the particular Dzongkha utterances in question. Such imputations of falsity are scarcely something to be *minimized*, in some spirit of charity. For the false utterances in question are just what the suggested interpretation would *predict* the Dzongkha speakers would say in the circumstances. So surely they should count in favour of the suggested interpretation despite their falsity, rather than as the kind of defect that the best interpretation ought to minimize.

The moral here is that if we can *understand* why some alien people should accept the judgements our interpretation attributes to them, those attributions should count positively in favour of our interpretation, even if the judgements in question are false. It makes perfectly good sense that the Dzongka speakers should be asserting the presence of trees and the tallness of foreigners, for, as I have told the story, the presence of trees and the tallness of foreigners are just what we would expect them to believe in.

This line of argument suggests a different approach to testing T-theories. If we want to know whether a particular utterance counts for or against an interpretation we shouldn't just look at the objective circumstances obtaining on that occasion. We should also consider the speaker's likely beliefs. The charitable strategy in effect assumes that utterances are direct indexes of external circumstances, for it tests the claim that *s* means p by seeing whether p normally obtains when people utter *s*. But it makes rather better sense to see utterances as in the first instance manifesting speakers' beliefs, and to test the interpretational claim that *s* means p by seeing, not whether p obtains, but whether the speakers could plausibly believe that p.[2]

---

[2] Davidson occasionally endorses this latter strategy for testing interpretations (see, for example, 1975, p. 169). But more often he simply stands by the maximization of charity. The difference between the two strategies is of fundamental importance for my overall argument. I suspect, however, that from the perspective of Davidson's philosophy of mind the difference is fairly minor. For more on this point see section 5.5 below.

2.8   THE SWITCH TO HUMANITY

So now we have an alternative to the charitable strategy for interpreting alien sentences. Instead of noting what objective circumstances obtain when *s* is uttered, we consider what beliefs the speakers could plausibly have on those occasions. Let us call this the 'humanitarian strategy' (cf. Grandy, 1973). Where our original strategy urged charity, advising us to interpret so as to make as much as possible of what the aliens say come out true, this new strategy requires only humanity. We can interpret the aliens so as to make their judgements false, as long as we represent them as having the kind of beliefs that we would expect humans in those circumstances to have.

The switch to humanity is an important development. It brings mental attitudes like belief explicitly into our philosophical story. Let me pause to point out some of the consequences of this.

If our philosophical analysis of meaning did *not* appeal to such psychological notions as belief, then it would perhaps have been possible to analyse belief in terms of meaning. We might, for instance, have analysed believing that p as being disposed to assert some sentence that meant that p.

But once the Davidsonian approach is thought of as incorporating humanity rather than mere charity this possibility disappears. Given the general Davidsonian implicit definition approach to meaning, our philosophical grasp of the concept of meaning is supposed to come from knowing how an empirical theory of meaning ascribing truth conditions works. Part of that is knowing how such an empirical theory is tested. But now it turns out that it is necessary to bring in the concept of belief to explain this. So we can scarcely any longer hope to turn round and explain belief away in terms of meaning.

Some philosophers, such as H. P. Grice (1957), favour the converse approach of explaining meaning in terms of belief. But that is a further step. Even if we admit that belief has to enter our story as an independent notion somewhere, we can still stick to the general Davidsonian strategy of approaching meaning via an implicit characterization in terms of the way empirical theories of meaning ascribing truth conditions work. The notion of belief then comes in only when, in giving this characterization, we come round to the specific question of how to test such theories.

I shall have more to say about the alternative Gricean approach in the next chapter. But for the moment let me just spell out exactly why belief has to be granted at least some independence from meaning, for the point will be of some importance for my subsequent arguments. Given the Davidsonian implicit definition approach to meaning which we are currently assuming, sentence meaning is a matter of answerability to truth conditions. So to regard belief as reducible to an independent notion of meaning would be to think of the identity of beliefs in turn as constituted by their answerability to certain truth conditions. But in order for humanity to be substantially different from charity, there must be more to belief than such answerability to truth conditions. There must be extra strands to the notion of belief, if the humanitarian requirement that interpretation should lead to the ascription of plausible beliefs is to be any different from the charitable requirement that interpretation should attribute truth to utterances.

After all, the reason for switching from charity to humanity in the first place was to allow for the possibility of explicable *falsity*. So the switch from charity to humanity presupposes that we have some grasp of the ways in which humans can be seduced into false beliefs. We could say that the concept of belief has been introduced precisely because of those strands in this concept which allow us to judge whether attributions of false belief are plausible or not.

Does the switch to humanity make any difference to the transcendental argument against divergence? Let us take divergence of concepts first. The relevant point here is that the switch to humanity is still a move *within* the Davidsonian programme of implicitly characterizing meaning, and not yet a commitment to some explicit reduction in the style of Grice. A sentence's being meaningful is still a matter of its having a truth condition specifiable by an empirical theory of meaning. And so the argument against divergence of concepts still stands. The concepts embodied in any one meaningful language must always in principle be expressible in terms of any other meaningful language.

All that has changed with the switch to humanity is our account of how to *test* an empirical theory of meaning (namely, by seeing whether it leads to a plausible attribution of beliefs to alien speakers). But this modification lies, so to speak, 'outside' what such an empirical theory itself *says*. And so it is irrelevant to any argument, like the argument against the divergence of concepts, that hinges entirely on what kind of *content* such a theory has.

On the other hand, the argument against divergence of opinion *is* now called in question. For this did depend on how empirical theories of meaning are tested, and not just on what they say. Crucial to the argument against divergence of opinion was the idea that an adequate empirical theory of meaning is one which interprets the actual utterances of alien speakers as true.

Though we didn't note it at the time, the initial refinement mentioned in the previous section, that an interpretation should make *most*, rather than all, utterances come out true, already implied some weakening of the argument against divergence of opinion. However, this initial move did still require an adequate empirical theory of meaning to *minimize* imputations of falsity: it was precisely in order to ensure that our interpretation made the general run of utterances come out true that we were prepared to tolerate a little local falsity. And, correspondingly, even if *some* disagreement between intellectual communities was thereby allowed to be possible, it would only have been against a background of overall agreement in the general run of their judgements.

But all this is now changed by the switch to humanity. There is no longer any demand at all that most alien utterances should come out true. We are now to choose that empirical theory of meaning which best succeeds in making the aliens understandable, which best succeeds in attributing to them beliefs we would expect human beings to have. There is no obvious reason why this should ensure that any particular proportion of alien beliefs should be true. We have already seen examples where false beliefs (there's a tree, all foreigners are tall) were perfectly explicable, given the circumstances in question. What is to stop a given community being in circumstances which make *most* of its beliefs both false and explicable?

Perhaps there are further arguments to show that the idea of a community having mostly false beliefs is still incoherent. This is a question to which I shall return, for I shall have much more to say about the concept of belief. But for the moment let us just note that somebody who still wants to dispute divergence of opinion stands in need of such arguments, for there is nothing obvious in the principle of humanity, by contrast with the principle of charity, to constrain the extent of false belief.

3

Belief and Representation

3.1   THE GRICEAN PROGRAMME

At the end of the last chapter I pointed out that the switch to humanity did not yet amount to a reduction of meaning to belief. But some of you might have wondered what motives there are for continuing to resist such a reduction, given that we have had to bring the notion of belief into the story to some extent.

Reductions might not be mandatory. But they are nice if you can get them. It would have been a great achievement, for instance, if physicists had succeeded in reducing all forces, including gravitational and electromagnetic forces, to action by material contact. True, this reduction turned out to be impossible, and in the end physicists had to settle for an implicit characterization of the concept of force in terms of its theoretical context. But in philosophical semantics we already have the Gricean programme offering us an explicit definition of meaning in terms of belief and such allied notions as intention and convention. Why shouldn't we accept this offer of an outright reduction of meaning?

According to the Gricean programme a sentence *s* means that p just in case the members of the relevant community are mutually aware that speakers use *s* when they desire their hearers to believe that p. (Cf. Grice, 1957, 1968, 1969; Schiffer, 1972.) There are hidden complications here. For example, mutual awareness needs to be a rather complex state (I believe that you believe that I believe . . .) if the proposed definition is to capture the *overtness* characteristic of full-fledged communication, yet it seems implausible that speakers really do have such complex attitudes. And there are other complications. But I do not propose to pursue such issues here (though I shall say a bit more about complex mutual awareness in 5.6 below). I refer the interested reader to Blackburn (1984), chapter 4, for a thorough recent discussion. Let me simply assume for now that the Gricean programme offers us an initially cogent way of defining meaning in terms of psychological notions like belief.

There remain, however, general objections to the whole Gricean idea of explaining meaning in terms of belief (as opposed to internal difficulties of how exactly to formulate the Gricean definition). The Gricean explanation of meaning in terms of belief is intended as a full-blooded philosophical reduction. By way of analogy, consider the reduction of temperature to molecular motion, or of colour to electromagnetic reflectance, or of economics to individual psychology. In each such case there are two levels of description. On the one hand there is the reduc*ing* level, where we speak of molecular motion, or electromagnetic radiation, or individual psychology. And then there is the reduc*ed* level, with talk of temperature, colours, price movements, and so on.

The point of this kind of reduction is to show that the reducing level is in principle adequate to specify all the facts there are. What a reduction shows is that the terms in the reduced language are merely shorthand for picking out certain complex facts in principle already specifiable in the reducing language. Thus we are shown that temperatures are really *nothing but* mean kinetic energies; colours *nothing but* reflectance profiles; price rises *nothing but* changes in the behaviour of buyers and sellers; and so forth.

The reduced facts are thus explained away – not in the sense that they are shown not to be there at all, but in the sense that they are shown not to be there *in addition* to facts specifiable in the reducing language. And so, the Gricean would have it, with meaning and belief. Meaning is to be explained away – not of course by being shown not to be there at all, but by being shown to be nothing over and above a certain complex of facts about the beliefs of the linguistic community.

Reductions are *philosophically* illuminating when they show us how better to understand certain prima facie problematic concepts. Reductions show that the world has a rather smaller inventory of contents than we previously supposed. Instead of temperatures and molecular motions there are just molecular motions. Instead of meanings and beliefs there are just beliefs. And so on a conceptual level a reduction means that any obscurities peculiar to the reduced notions will have disappeared. Nothing remains to be understood about temperatures, given our understanding of molecular activity. Nothing remains to be understood about meanings, given our understanding of belief.

But this now makes it clear that a reduction will only be philosophically significant if the reducing language does not itself incorporate the kind of concept we are trying to explain away. It would not be much of a reduction of temperatures to molecular activity if we had to make essential reference in the reducing language to the temperatures of molecules. True, we would have done something: we would at least have explained away macro-temperatures in terms of micro-temperatures. But we wouldn't have explained away temperatures as such. And consequently any conceptual difficulties attached to the notion of temperature would still be with us.

Of course that's not how the reduction of temperature to kinetic theory actually works. But it is possible to harbour just this kind of suspicion about the reduction of meaning to belief. That is, one can well argue that such reducing concepts as belief already covertly incorporate the essential features of the concept of meaning.

As I had occasion to observe in the last chapter, philosophical puzzlement about meaning stems in the first instance from the mysterious fact that arbitrary sounds or marks can *represent*, can stand for things other than themselves. But once we stop to think about it, is there not just as much of a puzzle, indeed just the same puzzle, about the fact that beliefs represent? The natural way to think of beliefs is as some kind of internal state of the mind, or of the brain. But if that's what beliefs are, then how come *they* manage to stand for things other than themselves?

I shall be exploring this question at length in this chapter and the next. It is far more important for my purposes than any internal details of the Gricean proposal. For, even if the internal details can be ironed out, the Gricean reduction won't decide any of the general philosophical issues I have raised unless it is conjoined with an explicit analysis of how beliefs represent.

At first sight the Gricean reduction might appear finally to undermine the anti-realist argument discussed in the last chapter. That argument, remember, had two strands: the denial of divergence of concepts, and the denial of divergence of opinion. The argument against divergence of opinion was called in question once we switched from charity to humanity as principles of interpretation. But the argument against divergence of concepts remained unscathed as long as we continued to suppose that the notion of meaning derived from our grasp of empirical theories ascribing truth conditions. The Gricean reduction, however, opens up the alternative possibility of identifying alien judgements intrinsically, in terms of the identity of the beliefs involved, and thereby promises to free us from the need to see such judgements as answering to objectively available truth conditions.

But these issues are by no means finally decided. Whether the Gricean reduction really allows untrammelled divergence of concepts, and indeed whether the earlier switch to humanity allows untrammelled divergence of opinion, depends on the nature of belief, and in particular on how beliefs work as representers. There might yet be alternative routes to the Davidsonian conclusions. The idea of reducing meaning to belief means that the Davidsonian argument does not work as it stands. But a final verdict will only be possible once we have an analysis of the representational powers of beliefs.

3.2 PHYSICALISM AND FUNCTIONALISM

I said a moment ago that the natural way to think of beliefs is as internal states of the believer. Can we be more specific?

One possibility here is to identify beliefs with physical states of the brain. On this suggestion, having a given mental state simple *is* a matter of one's brain being physically arranged in a certain physical way.

Adopting this line would of course only aggravate the problem raised at the end of the last section, about the representational powers of beliefs. How can an arrangement of molecules, or some similar physical state, stand for something other than itself? The idea of molecules representing is, if anything, even more puzzling than the idea of sounds or marks doing so.

But let us postpone the topic of representation for a minute. For the idea that each type of mental state is identical with a certain type of physical state can scarcely be literally true. It is surely grossly implausible to suppose that President Mitterand, and myself, and a South Sea Islander must all have the same type of arrangement of molecules somewhere in our head, just because we all believe, say, that the earth is round.

And if that is not enough of an argument, consider the possibility of artificial brain parts. It is not beyond imagination that medical science should develop the technology for replacing damaged bits of brains. Presumably people with such replacements could also believe that the earth is round. But by hypothesis their brains wouldn't have the same type of physical make-up as the rest of us.

These objections have led most contemporary philosophers with physicalist sympathies to opt for a rather weaker doctrine than the outright identification of types of beliefs with types of physical states. Instead of maintaining that two people who share the same belief-type must therefore share some physically describable type of state, they suggest that what is common between President Mitterand and the South Sea Islander and myself, such that we all believe that the earth is round, is that we all have *some* type of state which plays the same *role* in our respective cognitive workings.

This doctrine is known as functionalism. The central idea of functionalism is that the identity of beliefs and other mental attitudes is a 'second-order' matter, a matter of being-in-a-state-which-plays-a-given-causal-role. Functionalists view descriptions in 'first-order' terms, such as physical descriptions of brain states, as in themselves unimportant. What matters is not what the mental state is made of, but simply that it can be produced by any of a certain range of causes (including, most importantly, perceptual causes) and will in turn produce a certain range of effects (including behavioural effects). (See the papers in Block, 1980, part 3.)

Consider, by way of analogy, the notion of, say, a *carburettor*. I take it that a carburettor can be characterized as something that mixes air together with petrol, and in particular does so in response to movements of the accelerator and choke. Given that it satisfies these specifications, a carburettor can be made of many different materials, and in many different designs. Thus it seems that what it takes to be a carburettor is the right set of causes (accelerator and choke movements) and effects (mixing air with petrol), and not any particular physical make-up.

A more sophisticated analogy is provided by the modern digital computer. Consider what it means to say that a computer instantiates a certain programme. To say this is to say that the computer is such that, for any of a given range of inputs, it will go through certain computations and thereby produce a certain output. But note that nowhere in this is there any mention of what the computer needs to be *made of*. It might be more convenient to make it out of little silicon chips, but even if it were made of old-fashioned valves, or even of revolving metal gears, it would still be running the same programme, provided that its physical arrangement *somehow* ensures that it will go through the operations required to produce the requisite effect in response to any of the given range of causes. Here again it seems that the exact physical make-up of the computer does not matter, as long as it instantiates a certain structure of causes and effects.

Thus also, according to functionalism, with mental states. A given mental state is a state, any state, that gets produced by a certain range of causes, including perceptual causes, and gives rise to a certain range of effects, including behavioural effects. The identity of the mental state does not depend on its physical realization, but purely on its having the right causal role.

An important part of functionalism (and what distinguishes it from its historical predecessor 'behaviourism') is the recognition that the causal roles of mental states are both complex and interdependent. Thus, for instance, the behavioural output of a given belief will depend on what other mental states are present – most obviously, on what other desires the agent has. And, again, on the input side, which perceptual causes will give rise to a given belief will characteristically depend on what other beliefs the agent has.

So the functionalist supposes that our notion of a given mental state is constituted by our assumptions about its possible causes and effects, and also holds that many of these assumptions will make essential reference to the presence or absence of other mental states. Of course these other mental states will themselves be similarly defined. But this process taken as a whole need not be circular, since terms for the relevant perceptual inputs and behavioural outputs can be supposed to be independently understood. The idea is to characterize the full gamut of mental states simultaneously – as a set of things which-bear-certain-causal-relations-to-each-other-*and*-to-perception-and-behaviour.

As some readers will be aware, functionalism is a special instance of Ramsey's attitude to theoretical terms. Ramsey held that theories involving unobservables could be reformulated by replacing all theoretical terms by existentially quantified variables. Theories about unobservables could then be read as saying: there exist various unobservable entities which bear the following causal relationships to each other, *and* to observables (Ramsey, 1931). The functionalist thinks of mental states as Ramsey did about unobservables, with perceptual inputs and behavioural outputs playing the role of his observables. What plays the role of the relevant theory for the functionalist is not always so clear. I shall say something more about this in the last section of chapter 4 and in chapter 5, sections 4–5.

3.3 SYNTAX AND SEMANTICS

Let us now return to the question of representation. If we adopt the more sophisticated functionalist view of mental states, rather than simple physicalism, does it become any easier to understand how beliefs and other mental states can stand for things other than themselves?

In fact it isn't clear that functionalism is of any help here. The functionalist thinks of mental states as causal intermediaries between perceptual inputs and behavioural outputs. This is an advance on thinking of them simply as physical states. But, for all that, functionalism still presents mental states as part of a system of causal pushes and pulls inside the head. And there still isn't any obvious place in this picture for any conception of mental states as *representing* anything. As Brian Loar has put it, once we have specified a set of 'horizontal' relationships between perceptions, mental states and behaviour adequate for our explanatory purposes, why should we need in addition any 'vertical' relationships between mental states and the things we intuitively think of them as standing for? (Loar, 1981, p. 57.)[1]

In the study of logics one distinguishes between the *syntax* and the *semantics* of a logical system. The syntax specifies the shapes of the symbols and how they can be combined into strings, and gives a set of rules for moving from given well-formed strings to others. From the point of view of the syntax the symbols may as well be counters in a game, and the rules a set of allowable moves. It is the semantics that then attributes representational significance to the symbols, that tells us that they are words which refer to certain objects or classes, that they are sentences which are true or false, etc. And the semantics then allows us to think of the rules, not as arbitrary moves in some game, but as principles designed specifically to take us from old truths to new ones.

One can usefully think of functionalism as giving us a purely 'syntactic' view of mental states. Of course, since functionalism has already abstracted from the physical descriptions of mental states, there is nothing in the analogy corresponding to the syntactic specification of the shapes of symbols. But the more important part of a logical syntax is the system of moves for going from one string to another, and here there is indeed a close parallel to the functionalist specification of how a given mental state will causally derive from, and give rise to, other such states. The functionalist concentrates on the links between mental states, on the possibilities of moving from one mental state to another, and has no overt concern with any relationships between those mental states and any non-mental things they might represent. And so, just as the syntax of a logical system can be studied independently of any

[1] Note here that there is nothing in functionalism as such to require that the 'first-order' realizations of functional states be *physical*. One could be a functionalist and a dualist. But even this wouldn't help with the problem of representation. A dualist functionalist would still be thinking of mental states as things embedded in a set of causal relationships, and would still have a puzzle about the source of their representational powers.

semantic considerations, so also the functionalist specification of mental states seems to be independent of representational questions. (Perhaps the analogy is even closer. It is arguable that the syntactic study of logics itself abstracts from physical realizations, in just the way that functionalism does. For a system to instantiate the propositional calculus, say, it doesn't matter what *symbols* are used, provided we have the right structure of rules of inference.)

A number of philosophers have argued in recent years that there are two *aspects* to our notions of belief and other mental states. (See in particular McGinn, 1982.) On the one hand we have the idea of states with certain causal roles, states which are postulated in order to account for our behavioural responses to our surroundings. And on the other we have the idea of states which represent, which are *about* something. The point I have been making in this section is that functionalism, by concentrating entirely on the first aspect, makes it puzzling why there should be the second, representational aspect to mental states at all.

3.4 LABELLING AND CONTENTS

Some of you might perhaps have been finding it difficult to understand how an account of belief *can* leave us with a problem of representation. After all, consider how we identify beliefs in our everyday thinking, as the belief that *the earth is round*, the belief that *all foreigners are tall*, the belief that *there's a tree in front of me*. Surely we identify beliefs in the first instance by reference to their 'contents', by reference to the states of affairs they represent. But if so, then how can an approach which quite ignores representation be an account of *belief* at all?

Moreover, this query can be raised in a way that is particularly pressing for functionalism. Functionalists think of mental states in terms of their causal roles. So presumably they have in mind some set of generalizations linking mental states to other mental states and to cognitive inputs and outputs. But if there are such generalizations, surely they will 'quantify over contents'. Surely they will be about all the beliefs with a certain kind of truth condition, and not just about some specific belief. That is, surely we won't just have

For any x, if x believes that *it is raining* and x believes that *the sun is shining*, then x will believe that *it is raining and the sun is shining*.

Rather we will have something like

For any x, p, and q, if x believes that *p*, and x believes that *q*, then x will believe that *p and q*.

Again, we won't just have

For any x, if x desires *to be cooler* and believes that *opening the window will bring this about*, then, other things being equal, x will desire *to open the window*.

Rather it will be something along the lines of

For any x, p, and q, if x desires *q* and believes that *p will bring q about* then x will desire *p*.

So it seems that functionalists, by appealing to the existence of psychological generalizations, are already implicitly invoking the idea of the states of affairs – the p's and the q's – represented by beliefs and other mental states. (Cf. Fodor, 1986, pp. 1–4.) How then can I maintain that the functionalist account of belief leaves representation out of the story?

The key here is to recognize that functionalists needn't think of 'content clauses' like 'that the earth is round', 'that p', 'that q', etc., as doing anything more than *labelling* causal roles. (Cf. Dennett, 1978b, pp. 26–7.) Functionalists think of beliefs as bearers of causal roles. And so in the first instance they can construe our everyday ways of identifying beliefs as ways of indicating what the causal roles of those beliefs are. That is, instead of thinking of content clauses as picking out beliefs as the beliefs-that-represent-such-and-such, they can think of them as picking out beliefs *directly* as beliefs-with-such-and-such-causal-roles. We could say that for functionalists the 'content' of a belief, the thing that individuates the belief, and which its content clause is about, is in the first instance its causal role, rather than anything it represents.

The most graphic way to bring out this point is to note that from the functionalist point of view there is no reason in principle why we shouldn't use a rather different system of labelling, say a system of numbers, to pick out beliefs. The functionalist assumes that on the one hand we have a set of possible causal roles that beliefs can bear, and on the other a system of labels to pick out those causal roles. So, if we were familiar with an adequate mapping from numbers to causal roles, there would be nothing to stop us picking out beliefs as belief-743, belief-93,654, etc.

Of course such an alternative system of labelling would need to be properly *systematic*. There are an indefinite number of possible beliefs-as-causal-roles, just as there are an indefinite number of meaningful sentences in any natural language. And so any workable mapping from numbers to causal roles would have to discern certain structural features of the numbers (their prime factors, say) and then build up causal roles in a way that depended on that discerned structure. Such an alternative system would undoubtedly be awkward and unfamiliar. But from the functionalist point of view there seems no principled reason why it shouldn't be possible.

This then shows how functionalists can understand psychological generalizations that 'quantify over contents'. Instead of reading them as generalizing over all beliefs that stand for given states of affairs, they can read them as generalizing over all beliefs that have a certain kind of label. Thus

> For all people x, and all labels 'p', 'q', if x has a belief labelled by 'p' and a belief labelled by 'q', then x will have the belief labelled by 'p and q'.

And similarly with the belief–desire generalization:

> For all people x, and all labels 'p', 'q', if x has the desire labelled by 'q', and x has the belief labelled by 'p will bring q about', then x will have the desire labelled by 'p'.

(Though if we had a system where we labelled by numbers, instead of our actual system, we wouldn't have 'p and q' or 'p will bring q about' involved here, but a reference to some numerical function of the numbers labelling the atomic beliefs and desires.)

3.5   DIGRESSION ON OUR ACTUAL LABELLING SYSTEM

We don't in fact use numbers to label our beliefs. How does our actual labelling system work?

There is a tendency among some functionalist writers to argue that we identify the causal roles of beliefs by means of a mapping that depends on the *syntactic* properties of content clauses: they suggest that the causal role of the indicated belief is a function of the *typographical* structure of the 'that p' phrase. (See, for example, Loar, 1981, ch. 7. Also see Stich, 1983, ch. 8: Stich doesn't acknowledge beliefs as legitimate theoretical entities, but he does assume that labels for any respectable cognitive entities would have to function in this typographical way.)

This seems to me an implausible view, fostered by far too enthusiastic a commitment to the idea that functionalism is independent of semantic considerations. It is true that functionalism as such does not require us to think of beliefs as representational. And for those who hold, as I am inclined to, that the representational powers of words derive from the representational powers of beliefs, this will then mean that functionalism as such will fail to account for the representational powers of words. But all this does not mean that we should deny representation absolutely. If functionalism doesn't account for representation, the moral is simply that we should look for further philosophical considerations which will. And a further moral is that there is thus no absolute requirement that we should view the words in 'content clauses' labelling functional roles as purely syntactic objects without representational powers.

After all, even our hypothetical system of labelling causal roles by numbers required us to understand the symbols in the subscripts as *numerals* which had *numbers* as their referents. And in general understanding a labelling system requires us to see the *words* in the identifying phrases as standing for certain structured objects, with a mapping then taking us from those structured objects to the entities labelled.

Now, I suppose it is possible in principle that the words used in labelling phrases should be 'homoreferential', standing for themselves as typographical entities, and thus themselves playing the role of the labelling objects. Indeed Brian Loar has shown in some detail how such a system might work for labelling the causal roles of beliefs. But the above reflections show that there is no reason, as Loar himself admits (1981, p. 144), why labelling systems should *have* to work this way. And certainly in the case of beliefs it seems to me highly implausible that they do.

Let me now say something positive about our actual labelling system. This is a complicated and well-trodden area, and I shall restrict myself to some general comments. Frege had it that when words were used in content clauses to identify thoughts, those words referred to their own senses, rather than to their normal referents. This is not entirely dissimilar to the idea that content clauses refer to causal roles. For there are analogies between the causal roles which are supposed to give beliefs their functional identities, and the senses which the mind is supposed to grasp when it has a thought directed on an object. In particular, the phenomenon of 'referential opacity' is explained similarly by both the Fregean and the functionalist stories: since words in content clauses refer to senses (Frege), or to causal roles (functionalism), and since two words with the same referent can have different senses (Frege), or can label different causal roles (as seems plausible given functionalism), both accounts give the same explanation of why co-referring terms can't be substituted *salva vertitate* in content clauses.

But it would be a mistake simply to identify causal roles with Fregean senses. For one thing, causal roles shouldn't be thought of as things which are internally graspable by conscious minds. Causal roles are second-order identifications of entities introduced in order to explain the responses of humans to their environments, and there is no reason to suppose that such explanatory constructs are internally available to consciousness. And, in any case, Frege really only gives us a sketch of how to account for the workings of content clauses. He indicates the general lines of an explanation of referential opacity. But more remains to be said about the structure of senses, and in particular about our ability to label a potential infinity of senses by a potential infinity of content clauses.

Some writers adopt a more abstract approach to the question of content, and start from the idea that contents are some kind of function from possible worlds and other entities to truth values. To some extent how this works depends on how we build our possible worlds. But on any such account it is clear that the content of a belief has to be more than *just* its truth condition, in the sense of the set of possible worlds in which that belief is true. For that wouldn't cope with opacity, nor with necessarily true beliefs. The belief that Cicero was assassinated and the belief that Tully was assassinated are different beliefs, but they will be true in just the same possible states of affairs. And all beliefs in necessary truths have the same truth condition, for all necessary truths are true in all possible states of affairs. So in order to get the 'contents' by which beliefs are identified coming out more 'fine-grained' than mere truth conditions, the abstract approach invokes such things as 'modes of presentation' (different for Cicero and Tully), and 'intensional structures' (different for different mathematical truths), in order to distinguish beliefs with the same truth conditions. Truth conditions themselves can then be thought of as 'coarse-grained' contents. (Cf. Lewis, 1972, section V.)

This notion of 'fine-grained' abstract objects being used to individuate beliefs does not neccessarily conflict with the view that beliefs are individuated by causal roles. For there is nothing to stop us construing 'fine-grained contents' as themselves labels for the causal roles of beliefs. True, this is probably not how most philosophers who deal in possible worlds think of them. And there would certainly be work to be done in making this idea explicit, and in particular in spelling out the structure of the causal roles being labelled. But, even so, it seems clear that the reason for admitting 'fine-grainedness' is the recognition that even truth-conditionally equivalent beliefs can have different causal antecedents and consequences. What will lead to the belief that Cicero was assassinated is in general different from what will lead to the belief that Tully was assassinated, and so also is what will be inferred from these beliefs. Similarly with the beliefs that $2 + 2 = 4$ and that

$d/dx\ (e^x) = e^x$. That is, we need to attribute 'fine-grained contents' to beliefs to just the extent required to ensure that identical beliefs behave identically in recognitional, inferential, and action-guiding contexts.[2]

If we do think of fine-grained contents as labels for causal roles, then identifying a belief will require us to refer to more than its truth condition. But we will still need to refer to that truth condition *inter alia*. It is important to recognize, however, that by accepting this we have not yet resolved any philosophical puzzles about 'aboutness'. The mere fact that y's play a part in labelling x's does not necessarily mean that x's are about y's. Houses don't refer to their street numbers, nor (a closer analogy) do sentences refer to their Godel numbers (except of course in the very special case of the Godel sentence). And so, even if we *invoke* the idea of representational relations between beliefs and their truth conditions to explain the workings of our labelling system, we won't thereby have *explained* that idea, and any philosophical problems that it raised will still remain to be answered.

3.6   THE MEANING OF SUCCESS

As I pointed out in 3.4 above, functionalism certainly 'quantifies over contents', in that it generalizes about beliefs of certain types. But this in itself didn't establish that functionalism makes use of the notion of 'aboutness' (and so failed to cast any philosophical light on the general philosophical problem of representation). For 'quantification over contents' as such left it open that functionalist generalizations can all be construed as about beliefs-with-a-certain-kind-of-causal-role, rather than about beliefs-with-a-certain-kind-of-truth-condition.

---

[2] As a number of writers have recognized, the desire that beliefs should be discriminated just as far as is demanded by their explanatory role can also lead to the *equating* of beliefs with *different* truth conditions. Indexical beliefs, such as the belief that *I am cold*, will have different truth conditions when thought by different people, but will nevertheless play the same causal role in each. Nor are such beliefs eliminable with respect to the explanation of action. See Dennett (1982), sections I–III, for a discussion of the issues involved here.

But still, mightn't there be further features of the functionalist framework which do cast light on aboutness? In particular, even if the identification of beliefs as such doesn't force functionalists to recognize aboutness, mightn't it still be that certain more specific generalizations recognized by functionalism *do* quantify over truth conditions? And won't this in itself then give us a philosophical hold on 'aboutness'? The approach here would be analogous to Davidson's implicit definition approach to meaning. Just as Davidson hoped to give us a philosophical grasp of meaning by showing how the notion of meaning was important to certain empirical theories of language, so here we might hope to get a philosophical hold on mental representation by seeing how the relationship between beliefs and their truth conditions was important to certain empirical (functionalist) generalizations about mind.

One possible such line of argument appeals to the close relation between the truth of belief and the success of action. At its simplest, we have the principle that an action guided by a true belief succeeds in its goal. And this connection carries over to more complicated cases. Doesn't this now give us a set of generalizations which do involve truth conditions? Thus we have (the simplest case)

For any x and p, if x believes that p, and p obtains, then actions based on that belief will succeed.

Here the reference to 'p's obtaining' makes it clear that 'p' is a variable ranging over truth conditions, over the states of affairs represented by beliefs, rather than a variable ranging over labels for causal roles. Which, of course, is just what we should expect. For, after all, it is precisely the *truth* of people's beliefs that allows us to explain, and even on occasion to predict, the success of their actions.

It is true that this principle, that true belief ensures success, commits us, unrealistically, to the assumption that choices of actions are always rational. However, it would complicate the exposition unnecessarily to incorporate an explicit discussion of rationality, and so I shall for the most part skip over this point. Full rigour would also require discussion of decisions under uncertainty, but this too I shall omit.

So let us now consider the following general account of representation: the truth condition of a given belief type is that circumstance whose presence guarantees the success of actions based on that belief.[3]

The difficulty here is that, although the connection between truth and success gives us a kind of generalization in which reference to truth conditions is indeed essential, we cannot rest with this as an adequate philosophical explanation of the notion of representation. The reason is that we haven't yet explained the notion of *success*. So far I have been taking this notion for granted. But note that, for an action to succeed, it is not enough that any old satisfactory effect ensue. What is required is specifically that the action should produce a result that *satisfies the desire* behind it.

But the notion of satisfaction, for desires, is closely analogous to that of truth, for beliefs. And, in particular, it is a notion that raises just the same conceptual problems about representation.

Thus suppose we start with a functionalist notion of desire, according to which desires, appropriately labelled, play certain causal roles in our cognitive workings. Given that we have such a conception of desires as elements in our mental mechanisms, why do we need to go on to think of them as things which point to further states of affairs, as things which *represent* the circumstances that would satisfy them? These are just the questions that we are having difficulty answering for belief and truth. We can scarcely take it as given that they have a solution for desire and satisfaction.

That truth guarantees sucess is a joint constraint on the attribution of truth and satisfaction conditions that any account of representation ought to observe. But without a further story about success this joint constraint does not amount to an adequate philosophical account of representation.

---

[3] Perhaps this suggestion seems too much like Bertrand Russell's straw version of pragmatism (1946, book 3, chs XXIX–XXX). Surely we don't want to count a belief as true just because it 'works', just because the action it prompts has satisfactory results? But the suggestion isn't that it is enough, for the truth of a token belief, that a particular action, prompted by the particular token in question, should succeed. The idea is rather that we should have a condition that *guarantees*, for *all* tokens of the relevant belief *type*, that ensuing actions will be successful.

Perhaps the best way to make this clear is to observe that the joint constraint in itself is consistent with any number of absurd pairings of beliefs with truth conditions and desires with satisfaction conditions. For instance, suppose, for the sake of argument, that we considered the desire we normally *call* the desire 'for warmth' to be satisfied, say, by the presence of noise. (What is there in the joint constraint to preclude this?) Then we could correspondingly construe all the beliefs we normally label as being 'about warmth' to have truth conditions involving noise. For when somebody acts, as we normally describe it, 'to get warm', because they 'believe it is warm over there', their action, construed instead as aimed at *noise*, will be 'successful' just in case it is *noisy* over there.

If we are to understand what it is in our notion of aboutness that makes these pairings wrong, we will need to do something more to tie down the notion of success. If the notion of success were well understood, then certainly we could account for truth as something needed to explain success. But we can scarcely account for truth in this way if our philosophical hold on success is as weak as our hold on truth.

3.7 REPRESENTATION AS CAUSATION

I want now to consider a rather different way in which the psychological generalizations presupposed by functionalism might be thought to bring in truth conditions for beliefs.

As we saw earlier, functionalism thinks of beliefs as states which can be caused by a certain range of perceptual circumstances. That is, functionalism assumes that there are generalizations relating beliefs to their perceptual antecedents. Why then shouldn't we simply think of the truth condition of a belief as the presence of one of those possible perceptual causes? (True, this suggestion only promises an immediate solution for more or less observational beliefs, beliefs whose production is relatively insensitive to the presence of other beliefs. But it would be a start, and might perhaps lead on to a solution for non-observational beliefs.)

Perhaps we could try a similar idea with satisfaction too. Perhaps we could think of the satisfaction condition of a desire as those effects which are behaviourally produced by it. (Again, this suggestion would clearly work best for immediately realizable desires, desires which always lead to a given bit of behaviour, independently of the presence of other mental states. But, once more, it would be a start.)[4]

There is a good reason and a bad reason for thinking this causal explication of representation won't work. Let us get the bad reason out of the way first.

Some philosophers, most notably Jerry Fodor (1980), hold that theoretical psychology ought to be 'methodologically solipsist', in the sense that it ought not to concern itself with anything outside people's heads. Fodor argues that the proper subject matter for psychology is the *internal* workings of our cognitive mechanisms, since there is no possibility of any serious scientific generalizations linking up internal cognitive states with external circumstances.

Anybody who takes this line will think of the 'perceptual causes' and the 'behavioural results' by which functionalists tie down their characterizations of mental states as *peripheral states of the body*. That is, they will think of the 'causal input' as patterns of stimulation of the sense organs, and the 'output' as physically characterizable bodily movements. And clearly if we do construe functionalism in this way, there will be no possibility of thinking of the truth condition of a belief as the causes specified by its functionalist characterization, for in nearly all cases (beliefs specifically *about* peripheral stimulations being the exception) the functionalist characterization will simply not mention what we naturally think of as the belief's truth condition. And the same difficulty arises for the suggested account of the satisfaction conditions of desires, for (exceptional cases apart) we don't want to think of all our desires as aimed at physically specifiable bodily movements.

---

[4]The suggestion here isn't so much that we have functionalist generalizations 'quantifying over contents' as such, which thereby allow an implicit Davidson-style definition of representation, but rather that we have a whole lot of once-off generalizations, one for each observational belief type and realizable desire type: for example, 'For any person x, whenever a tree is present, x will believe that there is a tree there', and, again, 'For any person x, whenever x desires to walk, x will walk.' It is because it deals in such once-off generalizations that the suggestion will only give us truth for observational beliefs, and satisfaction for realizable desires, and won't explain truth and satisfaction in general.

But should functionalists be 'solipsists' in the first place? Despite Fodor's arguments, I don't think that they can. It is true that functionalists think of mental states as 'internal', in the sense that they take them to be causal intermediaries inside the head. But the whole point of functionalism is that it doesn't identify such states in terms of their inherent physical properties, but in terms of their causal relations to other states. And so it doesn't follow, from the idea that mental states are inside the head, that the causal network in terms of which they are identified can't extend outside.

The important question is not whether the mental states themselves are internal (of course they are), but whether the 'inputs' and 'outputs' which tie down the functionalist characterizations of mental states should be internal (or at least limited to the bodily peripheries). And here I think the answer should be negative. For peripheral bodily states are conceptually in very much the same boat as internal mental states. If there are good reasons for identifying mental states functionally, in terms of their causes and effects, rather than in terms of their physical substance, then it seems to me that there are equally good reasons for identifying sensory stimulations and bodily movements in the same way. And this then means that peripheral states cannot be the appropriate point for functionalist characterizations to stop. For if peripheral states are themselves functionally characterized, we will need some further set of antecedently understood notions to tie down those characterizations in turn.

My point here is this. The underlying principle of functionalism is that a given mental state can be thought of as the bearer of a certain causal role, even though we don't know how to identify it in physical terms, and even allowing that its physical identity might be different in different people. But a moment's reflection shows that just the same principle applies to sensory stimulations and bodily movements. So the causal network invoked by functionalism cannot stop with sensory stimulations and bodily movements.

Thus consider, say, the pattern of retinal stimulation that will produce the belief that *there's a tree in front of me*. I take it that nobody knows how to identify this in terms of the activation of rods and cones, etc. Indeed I take it that the right identification in such terms will be different for different subjects (think of experiments with 'inverting lenses', etc.). But still, we take there to *be* such a pattern of retinal stimulation for any given person, just as we take there to be a subsequent belief that there's a tree in front of me. And this is because, just as with the belief, we identify the retinal stimulation *functionally*, as that pattern of stimulation which will be produced (for a given person) by that person looking towards a nearby tree, or by various other visually similar causes, and will give rise to the relevant belief. It seems that anybody who accepts functionalism at all ought to accept it for sensory stimulations as well as for 'more central' mental states, and for just the same reasons. And consequently they ought to think of the antecedently understood 'input' terms which tie down the overall characterization as being terms for the external causes of surface stimulations, like *trees*, not terms for surface stimulations themselves.

A similar point can be made on the 'output' side. Consider the bodily movements involved in *tying up a shoelace*, say, or even in *walking*. Here too I doubt that anybody knows how to identify the movements in purely physical terms. And it is arguable that any uniform such identification across subjects is doomed to failure, for different subjects have quite different ways of tying shoelaces, and even of walking. So here too it seems that bodily movements are identified functionally, as those which give rise to certain external effects (tied shoelaces, moving around, etc.) and are produced by certain desires. And here too it seems that the antecedently understood 'output' terms which anchor the functionalist's causal net are not terms for movements of appendages, but terms for such things as *tied shoelaces* or *moving around*.

So the 'solipsist' reason for resisting a simple causal explication of representation is a bad reason. We have as much reason to identify sensory stimulations and bodily movements in terms of their relations to their causes and effects as we originally had for so identifying mental states. And once we extend the functionalist causal net beyond the bodily peripheries in this way, there is no reason to think that the states of affairs we intuitively think of as represented by mental states will be left out.

Let us now turn to the good reason for resisting the suggestion that we consider the truth condition of a belief as the set of its possible causes. The real trouble with this suggestion is not that it necessarily leaves the right things out, but, on the contrary, that it probably lets too much in.

Consider once more the belief that there's a tree in front of me. Maybe, as I have just argued, the causal inputs to the functionalist characterization of this belief are normal physical objects in the external world. But this doesn't mean that they are just trees.

Remember the Dzongkha speakers and the papier-mâché trees. In the example it was papier-mâché replicas that caused them to believe that trees were present, not actual trees. And we can imagine other similar examples. After all, it is a perfectly familiar and unpuzzling fact that people can be caused to believe that trees are present by things other than trees.

Yet we don't consider the truth condition of the belief to be the disjunctive presence of a-tree-or-a-good-replica. On the contrary, we take the belief to be specifically about *trees*, and deem it false when it is produced by papier-mâché or other imitations.

One would like to say that an imitation tree is somehow an *abnormal* cause for the belief in question. But unfortunately there is nothing in the suggestion currently under consideration to warrant this. As I said, there is nothing especially unfamiliar or puzzling about the idea of illusory causes. And so we would expect an adequate functionalist characterization of tree beliefs to mention tree replicas as amongst their possible causes. But then, if the truth condition of a belief is the presence of one of its functionally identified causes, what is to stop illusory trees being as good a part of the truth condition of tree beliefs as real trees?

Similar problems arise with the idea that the satisfaction conditions of desires are the effects they produce. It is all very well thinking of desires as producing effects outside the body. But this suggestion too lets too much in. There are all kinds of effects of desires that intuitively don't count as satisfying them. Thus even desires like the desire to tie your shoelaces can have deviant effets – as when the shoelaces are too short, and you fail, or when they are too frayed, and they break.

It is of interest at this point to recall what was said about the principle of charity in the last chapter. In effect the trouble with charity was that it advised us to include, as far as possible, *all* causes of a given sentence's utterance as part of its truth condition,

including the unwanted ones that one naturally thinks of as making
the sentence false. In the last chapter we dealt with this difficulty
by switching to humanity, which, so to speak, allowed us to exclude
those causes that gave rise to the utterance only via a false belief.

We are now facing essentially the same difficulty. We are trying
to capture the truth conditions of judgements in terms of their
causes, but find that this too is too liberal to exclude unwanted
cases. But at this point the earlier solution is no longer available.
For we are no longer trying to do the trick for sentences, but for
beliefs themselves, and so can no longer deal with the difficulty by
excluding those causes that give rise to false belief. The difference
between true and false belief is precisely what we are trying to
capture.

4

The Teleological Theory of Representation

4.1 REPRESENTATION AS BIOLOGICAL FUNCTION

In the last chapter I looked at a number of possible philosophical approaches to mental representation, and I argued that none of them were satisfactory. I now want to make a positive suggestion, namely, that we should adopt an explicitly *biological* approach to the problem. More specifically, I want to argue that representation is best understood as a matter of the biological *functions* of our beliefs and desires.[1]

Thus consider again the tree replica problem from the last section of the last chapter. I would say that the reason the belief in question represents the presence of a *tree*, rather than a *tree-or-a-good-replica*, is that, although the belief is actually present more often in the latter, disjunctive, circumstance, its biological function is specifically to be there in the presence of *trees*, not tree replicas.

Or, again, consider the 'noise–warmth' example discussed in 3.6. Although it is true that the belief in question (the belief that it is warm over there) is sometimes present when there is noise in the relevant direction, and may even on occasion be caused by such noise, the biological *purpose* of that belief is to be present when it is warm there, and not when it is noisy.

A similar point can be made about desires. Take the noise–warmth example again, and in particular the desire for warmth.

---

[1] This idea is in Dennett (1969), especially section 9, though it has almost disappeared from Dennett's later writings. The present chapter is a descendant of Papineau (1984). Similar ideas can be found in Millikan (1984), especially chapter 9. See also Fodor (1984a), which criticizes Stampe's (1977) and Dretske's (1981) accounts of the representation for being insufficiently teleological.

Although the actions that issue from this desire may on occasion lead you towards noise, what the desire is biologically *supposed* to do is lead you to warmth.

So I would like to suggest the following analysis of representational notions. The biological function of any given belief type is to be present when a certain condition obtains: that then is the belief's truth condition. And, correspondingly, the biological function of any given desire type is to give rise to a certain result: that result is then the desire's satisfaction condition.

One immediate comment before we go into details. It might seem that this suggestion is already implicit in the 'functionalist' approach to mental states. After all, am I not simply recommending that we concentrate on the *functions* of mental states? And isn't this what *functionalists* have been saying all along?

But this is just an unfortunate terminological confusion. To talk about something's 'function', in the biological sense, is to talk of some effect of that thing which accounts for its being there. In the philosophy of mind, talking 'functionally' means talking in a second-order way, talking of mental states as entities which enter into a certain structure of generalizations, without commitment to any view on their first-order substance. There is nothing in 'functionalism', as a position in the philosophy of mind, to imply that the occurrence of mental states can be explained in terms of the effects they produce, or in any way to suggest that mental states have 'functions' in the biological sense.[2]

In order to avoid any possible confusion in what follows, I shall reserve 'functional' and its cognates for the doctrine that mental states are identified in second-order terms as bearers of causal roles. When I want to talk about biological explanations in terms of effects, I shall use such terms as 'teleological', 'purposive', etc.

---

[2] Which is not to say that there are no connections between the two notions. In my (1985) I argue that the functionalist denial of type–type reducibility commits us implicitly to the existence of selection mechanisms which ensure that neurophysiological states perform certain biological functions. And I am currently arguing, on quite independent grounds, that if functionalists in the philosophy of mind are to deal with the specific problem of *representation*, they need to bring in the biological functions of mental states.

4.2 THE SELECTION OF BELIEFS

The idea that representation is a teleological matter might not seem that much of a step forward. For doesn't the idea of teleology raise its own philosophical difficulties?

I favour a natural selection account of teleology. That is, I think that when we talk of some characteristic C being present *in order to* produce E, we should understand ourselves to be claiming that C is now present because of some past selection process that favoured C because it produced E.

This natural selection account is not uncontroversial, and I shall say a bit about alternative views in 4.4 below. But first I want to illustrate in rather more detail how the natural selection approach would deal with the representational powers of beliefs and desires.

Let me take beliefs first, and leave desires for the next section. The problem we came up against in the last chapter was that without an adequate account of representation we were unable to distinguish, amongst all the possible causes of a belief (noise as well as warmth, papier-mâché trees as well as real ones), those 'normal' causes which counted as its truth condition. The trouble was that tokens of the belief often resulted from 'abnormal' causes as well as 'normal' ones. I have now suggested that the 'normal' causes are those that the belief is biologically supposed to respond to. In effect this suggestion takes us beyond causal explanations of particular tokens of belief types in terms of believers' dispositions to respond to circumstances, to the question of why we are so disposed to respond to circumstances, that is, to the question of why we have those belief types in our repertoire in the first place. And the natural selection answer to this question is then as follows: we have the present disposition to form beliefs of that type because, in the past, its tokens have generally had advantageous behavioural effects, and this has led to its preservation.

Note how this natural selection explanation now gives us a substantial distinction between 'normal' and 'abnormal' causes. For it is specifically when trees, and not tree replicas, were present, that belief about trees would have had advantageous behavioural effects. And similarly, it is specifically in the presence of warmth, and not noise, that behaviour produced by a belief in warmth would have been advantageous. That is, these belief types were selected because of the advantageous effects they had when they resulted from their 'normal' causes. And so talk of 'normality' is no longer empty, as it was at the end of the last chapter, for it is specifically because of what happened in the 'normal' circumstances, and not in the abnormal ones, that the beliefs got selected.

These last remarks might have created the impression that I am taking all belief types to be genetically innate. But this is not so. There is no need to restrict ourselves to inter-generational selection here. Natural selection occurs within generations, by learning, as well as between generations, by genetic changes. We can think of learning as selecting components for our cognitive mechanisms, analogously to the way that inter-generational evolution selects genes.

Suppose our individual psychological developments throw up new possible belief types, new ways of responding mentally to circumstances, at random, analogously to the way that our genetic history throws up mutations at random. Then we would expect such new dispositions to become 'fixed' just in case the belief tokens they give rise to lead to advantageous (that is, psychologically rewarding) actions, analogously to the way that genetic mutations become fixed just in case they have advantageous (offspring-producing) results. Only some of the random possible belief types will become fixed in this way, since, being random, there is no reason in general why the circumstances that produce tokens of such beliefs should be ones in which the actions those beliefs direct will be advantageous. More specifically, only those few doxastic mutations which produce beliefs that are *usually* caused by circumstances in which the resulting actions are rewarding will get fixed.

Of course, even a new belief type which *is* 'learnt' in this way still won't *always* lead to advantageous action, for sometimes it will be triggered by 'abnormal' circumstances, circumstances other than the one that in the learning process ensured the belief had advantageous efects and which therefore led to the selection of the disposition behind it. My suggestion is that the belief should be counted as false in these 'abnormal' circumstances – or, to put it the other way round, that the truth condition of the belief is the 'normal' circumstance in which, given the learning process, it is biologically supposed to be present.

An interesting special case here is the acquiring of belief types as the result of specifically *linguistic* training. Suppose, to take a simple example, a child has a disposition to respond to certain circumstances with a mental state which leads it to utter the sound 'blue'. This disposition will get fixed, according to my suggestion, just in case the action, uttering 'blue', has psychologically rewarding results. But clearly this will happen just in case the circumstance that prompts the mental state is the presence of something blue, for it is then that parents and others will reward the child for the utterance. More generally, we can see how this kind of process can lead to the acquisition of any belief type that will enable the individual to recognize circumstances in which it is socially appropriate, and therefore rewarding, to utter certain words.

4.3 THE SELECTION OF DESIRES

Now for desires and their satisfaction conditions. I suggested earlier that we can think of the satisfaction condition of a desire as the effect it is biologically supposed to produce. In terms of natural selection this would be that effect of the desire in virtue of which it has been selected for.

But there is a difficulty. Consider the desire for sweet things. Prima facie, this desire is biologically supposed to produce, not only the taste sensation, but also the ingestion of sugar, enhanced metabolic activity, survival, and, eventually, the bequest of the genes behind the desire to the next generation. More needs to be said if we are to explain why we should count, as is intuitively desirable, the first result in this list as the satisfaction condition of the desire.

We can put the difficulty in general terms. The effects of a given desire can be 'concertinaed out' into a characteristic succession of results, each a means to the next, and so, eventually, to the bequest of genes. Sometimes this chain will break down, and we get the earlier stages (the taste, the sugar, even the survival) without any real evolutionary pay-off in terms of gene bequests. Which suggests that if we want results of desires which are *always* selectively advantageous, we will need, counter-intuitively, to count all desires as having the same satisfaction condition, namely, the bequest of genes.

But suppose, just to follow the argument through for a moment, that we did think of all desires as aimed alike at gene bequests. Then we would have to recognize lots of beliefs we didn't know we had, such as the belief that eating sweet things increases the chance of bequeathing genes, to explain why the putative 'master' desire for gene bequests gives rise to such actions as eating sweet things.

And this now shows what has gone wrong. For while people with a sweet tooth do indeed have a mental state focused on sweet things, it seriously exaggerates their rationality to say that they have the belief that eating sweet things increases the chance of bequeathing genes, rather than simply saying that they have the desire to eat sweet things: for their state doesn't respond to evidence as the relevant belief would. If it really were the belief that eating sweet things will help to bequeath genes, then their state would simply disappear given, say, information that such actions will only enhance obesity. But notoriously, and unfortunately for many people, it doesn't.

There is a sense in which natural selection as such *does* have the sole aim of bequeathing genes: natural selection favours actions according as they are an effective means to gene bequests. However, which actions are so effective depends on variable environmental circumstances. So natural selection favours organisms with cognitive mechanisms which take as input variable environmental circumstances and have as output actions that are advantageous in those circumstances. But natural selection has not 'designed' these cognitive mechanisms so that they take into account *all* possibly relevant environmental circumstances. (Apart from other difficulties, the computations involved would presumably be quite unmanageable). Instead natural selection simplifies the cognitive task by having brains 'take for granted' that different 'proxy' ends, such as sweetness (or sex, or security, etc.) are biologically advantageous, and then having brains direct actions only on the basis of circumstances relevant to the achievement of such 'proxy' ends. Or, to put it in more familiar terms, instead of our having one standing desire to bequeath genes, and our then acting on all beliefs relevant to the satisfaction of that end, we have a number of different desires for more immediate ends, and only take into account information relevant to their satisfaction. (This story could be elaborated further to take explicit account of desires which vary with circumstances, and desires which are acquired in the course of individual development. But this would take us too far afield. See Papineau, 1984, section IX, for further details.)

Let me try to be a bit more explicit, for our present aim is really to explain away familiar talk of desires being 'for such-and-such', and indeed metaphorical talk of natural selection designing brains 'to pursue proxy ends'. My suggestion, then, is that such talk is justified precisely because our cognitive mechanisms, although in general designed to ensure gene bequests, are not sensitive to evidence about such things as the connection between eating sweet things and gene bequests. The full biological explanation of somebody eating sweet things will indeed allude to the fact that such actions tend to enhance gene bequests. But it is only natural selection, and not people, that can in any sense be said to 'believe' in this connection – again, just in the sense that further information about this connection won't directly alter people's tendencies to eat sweet things.

So I would suggest the following account of satisfaction. Any particular action stemming from a desire will have a sequence of potential effects which are relevant to gene bequests. As we proceed outwards, so to speak, we will go past effects (eating this piece of food, say) which are taken to be relevant only in virtue of current beliefs, on to effects (eating sweet things, increased metabolic activity) the relevance of which is assumed by natural selection but not by the agent, and ending up, if all goes well, with gene bequests. The satisfaction condition of the desire is the *first* effect (eating sweet things) which is taken to be relevant by natural selection and not by the agent.

We can say that producing actions with that specific effect is the biological purpose peculiar to the desire. The desire isn't in any sense selected in order to produce the earlier effects, because whether it has those effects at all depends on what beliefs it is interacting with. And it isn't distinctively selected to produce the later effects, since what distinguishes it from other desires is its being designed to produce those later effects via producing the specific effect in question.

These conclusions about satisfaction conditions now show that some of my earlier remarks about truth conditions were over-simple. I talked earlier as if the natural selection of belief-forming dispositions hinged simply on those beliefs occurring in circumstances where they had 'biologically advantageous' effects. But one implication of the above discussion of desires is that beliefs will in general have biologically advantageous effects only in so far as they have effects which satisfy desires. So we ought to count the truth conditions of beliefs not simply as circumstances in which they have biologically advantageous effects, but more specifically as the circumstances in which they will have effects that will satisfy the desires they are working in concert with.

In effect we have now adopted the idea, from section 3.6 above, that truth conditions are circumstances that guarantee the success of action, but now in addition the notion of success has been tied down, as it was not in the last chapter, by evolutionary considerations. It is no longer arbitrary what result we count as making an action successful, as satisfying the desire behind it, for we have now explained how that result has to be the one the desire has been distinctively selected to produce.

Before proceeding, I would like to comment briefly on an example introduced by Fred Dretske in connection with the teleological approach to representation (Dretske, 1986). The example involves a species of marine bacteria which have internal magnets (called magnetosomes) which are aligned parallel to the earth's magnetic field, and thereby help the bacteria to move away from the oxygen-rich surface water which is toxic to them. It seems natural to say here that the purpose of the magnetosomes is to lead the bacteria away from oxygen, and thence, perhaps, to conclude that they *represent* the direction of oxygen-free environments. But, as Dretske observes, why not as well say that the purpose of the magnetosomes is to lead the bacteria in the direction of the magnetic field, and therefore that they represent magnetic direction instead? Dretske's overall conclusion is that this kind of indeterminacy disappears only in systems where a number of different processes lead to the state in question, and moreover where these processes are modifiable by learning. And so he concludes that only such complex systems can have representational states.

I agree entirely with Dretske that the bacteria in question are too simple for their magnetosomal alignments to have determinate truth conditions. Some extra complexity is needed for a state to be about oxygen-freedom rather than magnetic direction. But I would like to use my analysis so far to suggest a somewhat different diagnosis of what the bacteria lack.

The first point to make is that in order to identify the biological purpose of a putatively representational state it is essential that we consider its output (that is, its effects on behaviour) as well as its input (its perceptual causes). All biological purposes are a matter of *results*. Without considering the behavioural output of a representational state we cannot possibly identify the circumstances in which the state is working as it ought to. In Dretske's analysis the outputs of representational states receive little explicit attention. Once we do focus on outputs it turns out that Dretske's multiple and modifiable input channels are unnecessary for determinate representation.

But even if we do bring in outputs, the marine bacteria still present a difficulty. The point of emphasizing outputs is that it allows us to fix the truth condition of a representational state as *that circumstance in which the behavioural output of the state produces successful results*. The difficulty with the bacteria, as described, is that they don't have any desires by reference to which we might tie down the notion of success, either to avoiding oxygen, or to moving in the direction of the magnetic field. The only end that can sensibly be attributed to the bacteria is survival: and from this perspective their magnetosomes simply represent that the indicated direction is conducive to survival.

But if we do have a being with enough complexity to have desires, then Dretske's difficulty disappears, without our having to worry about multiple input channels, etc. For the analysis I have developed in this section explains exactly which effect is to be counted as satisfying that desire. And this then fixes which circumstances count as the truth conditions of states which inform the pursuit of that desire.

Suppose the bacteria did have a desire-like state, triggered, say, by certain internal conditions, whose purpose was to generate actions which, in so far as they conduced to survival, did so by moving the bacterium away from oxygen. That 'desire' would be about oxygen-freedom, not magnetic direction, for it would *not* have been selected for the results it produced in those (abnormal) circumstances where the magnetic field did not in fact lead away from oxygen. And consequently the truth condition of the 'belief' which, in conjunction with that 'desire', moved the bacterium in a specific direction, would be that the direction in question was oxygen-free, not that it was the direction of the magnetic field.[3]

4.4 TELEOLOGICAL EXPLANATION

From now on it will be convenient to put desires and satisfaction to one side, and conduct the discussion in terms of beliefs and their truth conditions. The suggestion I am defending, then, is that the truth condition of a belief is a matter of the belief's biological purpose, where biological purposes are to be understood in terms of natural selection.

It might seem odd that truth, of all things, should be thought to depend on natural selection. Isn't it intuitively obvious that the representational powers of an organism's beliefs depend on what that organism is like *now*, not on its ancestry and education?

Thus suppose, for the sake of argument, that you, with all your past history, had never existed, but that a being in all respects physically identical had come into being by some kind of cosmic accident a few seconds ago. Wouldn't that being have all the same

[3] When I first started thinking about the teleological theory of representation, I used just this kind of example to illustrate the difference between the teleological theory and the simple causal theory discussed at the end of the last chapter. My idea was that although the bacterium's state was *caused* by magnetic direction, rather than oxygen-freedom, its *purpose* was to lead the organism away from oxygen, not in the direction of the magnetic field. But when I said this in a talk in Sydney in 1983, David Armstrong quite rightly complained that he didn't see why the purpose of the state wasn't itself to do with magnetic direction. It was thinking about how to respond to Armstrong that led me the above account of desires (and to the recognition that, as described, the bacterium's state doesn't represent oxygen-freedom).

beliefs, and about the same things, as you in fact do? Yet my teleological account of representation seems to preclude our saying this, for, according to this account, representation depends on past histories of selection.

The first thing to note here is that nothing in my account precludes your accidental replica having beliefs with the same *causal roles* as your actual beliefs. If it were physically identical to you, then *a fortiori* it would be functionally identical, and so would have internal states with just the same causal roles as your beliefs. To the extent that talk of beliefs is talk about functional states labelled by 'that p' clauses, your accidental replica would have just the same beliefs that p as you have. (And, moreover, to the extent that it is 'like something', phenomenologically speaking, to have your beliefs, it seems likely that an identical accidental replica would feel just the same way as you do.)

But is this enough? There is still the problem that, on the argument so far, the accidental replica's beliefs wouldn't be *about* the same things as your beliefs, indeed wouldn't be *about* anything at all. And surely this in itself is counter-intuitive. Surely our intuitions aren't just that the replica would be causally structured like you, and that it would feel like you, but also that it would share your beliefs *about* such things as your immediate surroundings, the shape of the earth, the history of rhythm 'n' blues, and so forth.

I agree that the accidental replica presents a prima facie problem for my overall argument. But note that it is not so much a problem for the specific suggestion that representation depends on teleology, as for the conjunction of this with the more general thesis that teleology depends on natural selection.

As I mentioned earlier, the natural selection account of teleology is by no means uncontroversial. Some philosophers reject it, and argue instead that a teleological understanding of some item requires only that the item somehow contributes to the welfare of some larger system, not that it is the result of some past selection process. (See, for instance, Woodfield, 1976.) On this kind of view, then, the *history* of the item in question is in itself conceptually irrelevant to questions about its teleological purpose.

Such alternative accounts of teleology offer the possibility of detaching the teleological account of representation from any specific concern with past histories of natural selection. That is, we could continue to explain *representation* in terms of the fact that the biological *purpose* of beliefs is to be present when certain states of affairs obtain, but then deny that biological *purposes* are anything to do with *natural selection*. And then of course the accidental replica would no longer be a difficulty, for we could argue that its beliefs would have the relevant biological purposes, in that they would contribute to its overall welfare, even though they lacked any selectional history.

But, unfortunately for my defence of the teleological theory of representation, I am pessimistic about the prospects for such alternative accounts of teleology. By and large, such accounts either leave 'welfare of some larger system' as a vague notion in which case they end up counting too much as purposive, or they give some more specific reading, in which case they tend to be easy prey to counter-example. But I do not want to argue this general issue here. There are a number of thorough defences of the natural selection account of teleology over the alternatives (Wright, 1973; Neander, 1984), and I refer interested readers to these.

But I do at least need to say something more about the accidental replica. Even if the accidental replica raises no problems for non-selectionists, my pessimism about non-selectionist views makes it a problem for me.

Perhaps there is room to question our intuitions here. Consider a simpler accidental creature, a little green bug who coagulates by cosmic happenstance, and just happens to get a rudimentary limb suitable for putting food into its rudimentary mouth. Would one want to say that the little green limb was there *in order to* help the creature to feed itself? I would say the creature was just *lucky* to have the limb.

No doubt non-selectionists would disagree. They would say that, since the limb contributed to the bug's welfare, it had a function. And they would probably accuse me of allowing my intuitions to be shaped by my selectionist view of teleology. But then what's wrong with that? Why shouldn't my intuitions be shaped by my selectionism? There is no reason to suppose that there is some set of timeless teleological intuitions to which all theories of teleology must conform. (Even non-selectionists will have to give some account of the fact that is natural nowadays, but certainly wasn't before Darwin, to think of the male peacock's tail as being there *in order to* attract female peacocks, or to think of animal altruism as occurring *in order to* help kindred genes into the next generation.)

And this then shows what I should say about the original accidental human and its counter-intuitive lack of representational powers: namely, that we ought to change our intuitions. Just as we selectionists have allowed our theory to change our intuitions about the little green bug, so we ought to allow our theory to alter our intuitions about the accidental human.

The difference between the two cases, of course, is that it is only when conjoined with the teleological theory of representation that selectionism bears on the representational powers of the accidental human. And the idea that representation is a teleological matter is a new one. So we wouldn't expect the general influence of natural selection theory on teleological intuitions yet to have had any effect on intuitions about what does and does not have representational powers. But perhaps if the teleological theory of representation came to be generally accepted, our intuitions about representation would change, and we would come to feel that a perfect chance replica of a human being wouldn't really have beliefs *about* its immediate surroundings, etc., but was just *lucky* to have functional states that worked the same way.

Let me add one final remark for any readers with firm commitments to non-selectionist accounts of teleology. For the purposes of the rest of this book I would ask such non-selectionist readers to remember that the teleological account of representation can be detached from the selectionist account of teleology (and indeed, as this section shows, is far better off without it). If non-selectionist readers do so disengage the two accounts, there will be no reason why they should not accept most of what follows in this and subsequent chapters. Some of the details, it is true, will depend on my selectionism. But my overall line of argument depends far more on the teleological account of representation as such than on the selectionist theory by which I want to account for teleology.

4.5 THE STRUCTURE OF BELIEFS

So far most of my examples have involved beliefs that are effectively unstructured 'feature-placers' – such as the belief that *it's warm*, or that *it's noisy*, or that *trees are present*, etc. But of course most beliefs are more complex. We need somehow to accommodate the fact that beliefs have internal structures.

To start with we can introduce the idea of structured causal roles. That is, we can think of beliefs, conceived of as bearers of causal roles, as made up of various components ('concepts') combined in various ways, with the overall causal role of the belief then depending on those components and the way they are combined.

And once we do this, it seems natural to think of the truth condition for the bearer of such a complex causal role as itself structured. In particular, it is natural to think of it as involving entities, and a mode of composition, which are functions of the concepts and structure constituting the causal role in question. More familiarly, we want to think of the truth condition of a belief as containing the *referents* of its constituent concepts, with those referents then contributing to the truth condition of the belief in a way indicated by the belief's internal structure.

How might this idea of structured beliefs, with correspondingly structured truth conditions, be accommodated within a teleological theory of representation? Well, we can say that the biological purpose of any given concept is to allow us to form certain beliefs, and that the purpose of such beliefs is, as before, to be present when certain states of affairs obtain. But we can now also say that which states of affairs these are will depend in turn on the concepts and structure making up the causal role of the belief in question.

Let us put this explicitly in natural selection terms. A concept will get selected because in combination with other concepts it forms beliefs which, in 'typical' circumstances, lead to advantageous behaviour. At bottom it is the concepts that get selected, because what beliefs we form, and what circumstances they arise in, depends on our concepts and how they operate. And so we can think of the concepts themselves as having purposes – namely, to 'refer' to certain objects – which then contribute to the purposes of beliefs. But we should not forget that it is only when concepts do combine into beliefs that they have any effect on action, so it is only via ensuring that certain beliefs typically arise in certain circumstances that concepts get selected at all. Which is to say that in a sense the purposes of concepts are always subservient to the purposes of beliefs.

We should not be perturbed by the appearance of circularity here. The circularity, such as it is, is quite benign. Thus recall a familiar theme in the theory of meaning: it is only in the context of a sentence that a word has a meaning, but at the same time the meaning of a sentence depends on its constituent words. Exactly parallel, we can say that it is only in the context of a *belief* that a *concept* has a *purpose*, but at the same time the *purpose* of a *belief* depends on its constituent *concepts*.

The fact that beliefs and their truth conditions have co-ordinated structures is crucial to an important further feature of our cognitive workings: namely, our ability to move deductively from one belief to another. Since the truth conditions of beliefs depend on the structure of those beliefs, it follows that beliefs with related structures will have related truth conditions. In particular the truth conditions of beliefs with certain structures will include the truth conditions of beliefs with other, related, structures, in the sense that the truth of the former beliefs will guarantee the truth of the latter.

Thus, to take one example, consider a belief whose causal role is labelled by a clause of the form 'p and q'. Given the way the causal role of this belief is related to the causal role of the corresponding beliefs that p and that q, it seems plausible that the purpose of this belief is to be present when the truth conditions of the belief that p and the belief that q both obtain. But this then means that the truth of the belief that p and q guarantees the truth of the belief that p (and, of course, the truth of the belief that q).

Habits of thought which correspond to such deductively valid steps will tend to be preserved by natural selection. Since truth conditions are identified as circumstances in which beliefs lead to advantageous action, the teleological theory of representation implies that true beliefs are *ipso facto* biologically advantageous. And so it follows that habits of thought which generate new true beliefs from old ones will also be biologically advantageous.

Perhaps this is a somewhat unsatisfactory way of putting things. For the causal role of beliefs labelled by 'p and q' clauses is in large part constituted by the fact that we have, on the one hand, the habit of forming such beliefs when we have both the beliefs labelled by 'p' and by 'q', and, on the other hand, the habit of going from such beliefs to either of these latter two beliefs. And so our having beliefs that p and q at all is largely dependent on our having the corresponding inferential habits in the first place. Which makes it somewhat misleading to suggest that the belief that p and q *first* has a certain truth condition, and *then* natural selection finds an inferential habit that will move us truth-preservingly to this belief. One cannot really separate the purposes (and hence truth conditions) of complex beliefs from the purposes (namely, truth-preservation) of our deductive habits. But this does not invalidate the point that truth-preservation is indeed the purpose of such habits.

4.6   NON-OBSERVATIONAL CONCEPTS

Inattention to structure was not the only respect in which my earlier examples were oversimplified. I have also dealt exclusively with observational concepts. I now want to say something about non-observational concepts.

The possibility of non-observational concepts itself depends on our ability to make deductive inferences. But this is not just a matter of deductive inference on occasion allowing us an alternative route to conclusions which could have been arrived at by direct observation (as we might come to believe that Jim ate the cake, not as a result of direct observation, but because we already had the belief that either Jim or John ate it, and the belief that John didn't). Rather the interesting cases are concepts for which the possibility of indirect, inferential access is central, not just a useful auxiliary.

The most obvious examples are concepts for scientific unobservables, such as *electromagnetic wave, quark, gene*, etc. It is a familiar point that concepts like these get their identity from their roles in the relevant theories. To have the concept of a gene, for instance, you simply need to know the theory of inheritance (and hence, ideally, to be able to draw conclusions about genes from suitable observational evidence). Here the possibility of indirect inferential access to conclusions about genes cannot be thought of as auxiliary, for in the absence of the theoretical assumptions which make such inferences possible there wouldn't be any concept of a gene in the first place. One might say that the idea of a gene just *is* the idea of the kind of entity postulated by genetic theory.

But the point is not restricted to concepts peculiar to scientific theories. Both everyday dispositional concepts, like *fragile* or *soluble*, which specify what objects would do in given circumstances, and everyday multi-criterial concepts, like *length* or *mass*, which can be measured in various different ways, are in important ways akin to theoretical concepts. Neither kind of concept can happily be construed as standing for purely observational states of affairs. The only good way to understand them is as ideas of properties-which-satisfy-certain-general-assumptions. Thus fragilty, for instance, is that property such that all objects that break when dropped (including those that haven't yet broken) possess it. And length is that property which can be measured by rigid rods, *and* by the time of light traversal, *and* by various other means. (See my 1979, ch. 1, for further discussion of dispositional and multi-criterial concepts.)

Indeed it is arguable that *all* concepts are to some extent 'theoretical', in that no concepts stand for purely observational states of affairs. This is not of course to claim that no belief tokens are ever arrived at directly and non-inferentially. Such a claim would clearly be self-defeating, for there would then be no premises from which we could arrive at beliefs by inference. The argument would rather be that no belief *type* has its identity fixed purely by the possibility of such direct observational input: every belief type is at least in part constituted by the fact that it can be arrived at by inference from other beliefs. (Cf. Papineau, 1979, ch. 1.)

From the perspective of this chapter there is nothing especially puzzling about non-observational concepts. As far as causal roles go, we can simply say that it is central to the identity of such concepts that they can be applied as a result of indirect inferences underpinned by general assumptions, as well as (if at all) by direct observational prompting. And when it comes to representation, we can think of the referents of non-observational concepts, not as directly observable features of the world, but rather as properties which, so to speak, stand behind the appearances. And in general terms this accords well with the teleological account of representation: since many (if not all) of the significant features of the world aren't always immediately apparent, it is obviously biologically advantageous to have beliefs which can be triggered indirectly as well as directly.

It is worth noting in this connection how the non-observationality of concepts introduces a kind of holism into the teleological analysis of representation. In the earlier observational examples I assumed that each concept was associated with a single observational process, and that the referent of the concept was then that external property that was biologically supposed to activate that process. But with non-observationality we no longer have a distinct process for each concept. Rather the path to beliefs involving non-observational concepts will go through other beliefs, along routes indicated by the structure of our general assumptions. And so we shouldn't think of a non-observational concept as referring to some property that directly gives rise to it, but rather as referring to that property whose place in the causal structure of the world mirrors the place of the concept itself in our structure of general assumptions.

Let me put the point explicitly in terms of purposes. The purpose (and hence referent) of a non-observational concept doesn't depend on a process specific to that concept, for non-observational concepts are not governed by such 'dedicated' processes. Rather their purposes (and hence referents) depend on the biological purpose of our 'model-building' ability as such, namely, to enable us to respond to features of the world to which we only have indirect inferential access. Which is why we should think of the purpose (and hence the referent) of any non-observational concept in terms of that property whose causal role in the workings of the world matches the role of the belief itself in our mental model.

4.7 REPRESENTATIONAL GENERALIZATIONS

Let me recapitulate a little. At the beginning of the last chapter I pointed out that there is a philosophical puzzle about the representational powers of mental states. I then looked at the functionalist picture of mental states, which took mental states to be part of a system of causal pushes and pulls inside the head. But I argued that this picture left us with – indeed reinforced – the puzzle about representation. Nor did it serve to think of representation as implicitly defined by any of the generalizations that functionalism invokes.

It was only when we went beyond the structure of mental causes and effects assumed by the functionalist, and asked why we have that structure in the first place, that we got an adequate philosophical hold on representation. To understand representation we needed to look beyond the promixate causes of our current mental and behavioural responses, and to consider instead why we have dispositions to make those responses in the first place. For it was only when we asked about the purposes of those dispositions that we were forced to pick out truth and satisfaction conditions from among the other systematic causes and effects of our beliefs and desires.

We shouldn't conclude, however, that representational notions play no part at all in our psychological theory of our current cognitive workings. It is true that a functionalist psychological theory as such doesn't have to make a distinction between 'deviant' and 'normal' causes and effects of mental states. And it is true that because of this we can't analyse representation simply by appealing to its role in such a theory. But, given that representational notions *can* be independently defined, there is no reason why our psychological theory shouldn't *then*, so to speak, make use of them.[4]

Thus recall the 'truth-success generalization' mentioned earlier. My original point was that this generalization couldn't tie down the

---

[4]Here I am diverging from the position adopted in my (1984). In that paper I conflated the claim that representation needs a teleological explanation with the further, extreme thesis that everyday psychology has no use for representational notions at all.

notion of truth, if there was nothing further to tie down success. But now we have an independent way of tying down both truth and success, via the teleological theory of representation. So what remaining reason is there for not recognizing this generalization? It mightn't itself suffice for a philosophical explanation of representation. But that is no reason for rejecting it as part of a complete theory of our psychological workings.

The truth-success generalization said

(1) For any x and p, if x acts on the belief that p, and p obtains (the belief that p is true), then x's action will succeed.

As I pointed out in 3.6, this generalization certainly quantifies over truth conditions. And it is a generalization that we do appeal to in explaining why certain people's actions have certain results. Why do doctors' patients usually get cured? Why do cars in garages usually get repaired? We know that doctors want to cure patients, and that mechanics want to fix cars, and we also know that the beliefs of doctors and mechanics on the relevant matters are by and large *true*. Which, together with the truth-success generalization, then implies that the patients and cars will get better. And there is no way of eliminating the reference to truth in these explanations.

To be more specific, the truth-success generalization is ineliminable precisely when we know that certain people tend to have true beliefs on certain matters, without knowing exactly what those beliefs are. For if we did know exactly what their beliefs were, then we could think of such beliefs, together with certain desires, as 'syntactically' generating certain bits of 'syntactically identified' behaviour (adjusting a certain screw, say), and we could then add in the relevant facts p (adjusting that screw will fix the car, say), to infer that the car gets fixed. And in none of this would we have to allude to the circumstance that the beliefs in question are made *true* by those facts p. (Though it is true that, even in such cases where the truth-success generalization is in principle eliminable, we would get some *extra* explanatory illumination by bringing the result under the truth-success generalization.)

Here is another case where real quantification over truth and satisfaction conditions plays a role in our everyday explanatory practice.

(2) For any appropriately placed x and any perceptible circumstance p, if p obtains then x believes that p.

This is pretty vague, because of the necessary qualifications about 'appropriately placed' and 'perceptible', but even so I don't want to deny that this principle plays an essential part in our everyday thinking. For example, consider assertions like 'John will know what is in that room, even though we don't, because he has had a look.'

Perhaps we should also recognize, by symmetry, something along the lines of

(3) For any competent agent x, and any voluntary movement r, if x does r then x desires that r.

Again, 'competent' and 'voluntary' are vague here, but without some such principle we wouldn't be able to say things like 'I don't know exactly what gesture she made to upset him, but when we see her tonight she'll tell us why she did it.'

These generalizations (1)–(3) show that structural psychology does indeed treat mental states as 'semantic' as well as 'syntactic' entities. However, the important point for our purposes is still that semantic notions can't be *explained* purely by reference to such generalizations as (1)–(3). To get an adequate philosophical account of representation, it is still essential that we apply the teleological analysis of representation. For it is still the teleological theory that shows us why certain mental causes and effects are distinguished as truth and satisfaction conditions.

As we saw earlier, it is no good trying to characterize truth conditions simply as circumstances that guarantee success, for this by itself leaves it open what we should count as success, and hence truth. Nor is it any good trying to characterize truth conditions as those circumstances that cause beliefs, and satisfaction conditions as those circumstances that result from desires, for these characterizations also let far too much in.[5] The only satisfactory way to get representation into the philosophical story is to start off with the psychological structure into which our beliefs and desires enter, and then use teleological thinking to fix the notions of truth and satisfaction. (After which, of course, we can make perfectly good philosophical sense of such ideas as that truth guarantees success, or that appropriately placed people believe what is perceptibly true, or that competent agents desire what they voluntarily succeed in doing.)

All this matters because it shows that we can't do without an *intrinsic* notion of belief identity. We can't think of beliefs purely extrinsically, simply as states-which-answer-to-such-and-such-truth-conditions, for, somewhat paradoxically, this would stop us getting an adequate philosophical account of representation in the first place. The only good philosophical route to representation, and hence to an extrinsic notion of belief, is first to think of beliefs intrinsically, as items which enter into a certain structure of causes and effects, and then to apply teleological considerations. I shall return to the larger implications of adopting this intrinsic approach to belief identity in the next chapter.

4.8 DIGRESSION ON THE GENESIS OF FOLK SEMANTIC NOTIONS

So far I've been deliberately vague about where the psychological theory 'assumed by the functionalist' comes from. Implicitly, though, I've been thinking of our 'folk psychology' as playing this role. That is, I've been surreptitiously assuming that it is the common-sense psychology of contemporary society that specifies the 'causal roles' of mental states.

I shall have a bit more to say about this issue in the next chapter. But we don't need details to recognize a fairly obvious problem. Whatever folk psychology contains, it doesn't stretch to the

[5]Note that generalizations like (2) say that the obtaining of an observable truth condition is sufficient for the corresponding belief, not that it's necessary. It is the possibility of alternative sufficient conditions (remember the papier-mâché trees) that stops us defining a truth condition as whatever causes the belief.

teleological theory of representation. Most people don't even know there is a philosophical problem of representation, let alone the teleological solution. But everyday psychology does *use* representational notions, as in generalizations (1)–(3). And, more generally, everyday psychology has no apparent difficulty in pairing mental states with the states of affairs they represent. How does this sit with my claim that it is only *after* one applies teleological considerations that one can have an adequate grip on representation?

I agree that this is a prima facie difficulty. But it is by no means conclusive. In the first place, note that the teleological theory of representation is supposed to tell us what representation *is*, not what most people think about representation. There is no reason why the philosophical essence, so to speak, of the representational relation should conform to most people's conception of it. (It is not a good objection to materialism about the mind, for instance, to say that most people are intuitively dualists.)

But that is only part of the answer. Everyday thinking about representation isn't just an idle cog, something that people go in for only in their more reflective, lay-philosophical moments, as dualism about the mind arguably is. As I have just observed, everyday thinking also recognizes a systematic pairing of beliefs with truth conditions, and uses that pairing in such generalization as (1)–(3). If the 'essence' of that pairing is teleological, then how come everyday thinking, which is ignorant of that essence, embodies a working notion of such a pairing?

This is a somewhat delicate issue. There is a temptation here to think of lay thinkers as somehow pairing up beliefs and truth conditions physically, as a nursery school teacher might pair up children with their overcoats, and to start worrying about how they manage this. But this of course would be a mistake. What lay thinkers do is have certain meta-beliefs to the effect: the belief that p is about the state of affairs that p.

Such beliefs can be thought of as involving three concepts: (a) the concept: the-belief-that-p, (b) a concept of aboutness, and (c) the concept: the-state-of-affairs-that-p.

I take it – this is the problem I am dealing with in this section – that the latter notion, the notion of aboutness, is a primitive in lay thinkers' minds, an unanalysed relation between beliefs and their truth conditions. But if we concentrate on the other two components in the relevant meta-beliefs we can see why this primitiveness doesn't really generate any problem.

The reason is that the meta-beliefs by which lay thinkers 'pair up' beliefs with their truth conditions cannot really fail to be true. Think of it from the point of view of an interpreter of those meta-beliefs. Such an interpreter will take it that the right-hand side of such a meta-belief refers to a certain state of affairs, namely, that state of affairs referred to by the concept: the-state-of-affairs-that-p. But, now, which state of affairs is that? There are various long stories that might be told here. For instance, I myself would like to tell some story involving the biological purpose of the concept: the-state-of-affairs-that-p. But it is surely a boundary condition on any such story that the *state of affairs* it deems to be the referent of this concept should be identical to the *truth condition* of the belief referred to on the left-hand side of the meta-belief by the concept: the-belief-that-p. The close relationship between the concept: the-state-of-affairs-that-p and the concept: the-belief-that-p surely means that, however exactly we analyse them, we shall want the referent of the former to coincide with the truth condition of the belief referred to by the latter. Which is just to say that the everyday meta-belief 'The belief that p is about the state of affairs that p' cannot but be true.

The only real puzzle here is why everyday thinkers have the practice of identifying beliefs by using a construction so closely related to the construction they use to refer to (non-mental) states of affairs. But there is no special difficulty in thinking of possible answers to this historico-genetic question. Thus consider the following story. Once upon a time our evolutionary ancestors simply uttered and responded, without thought. Then they started to recognize that these sounds reliably indicated things, as smoke reliably indicates fire. In a rudimentary sense of 'about', they had beliefs of the form: sentence *s* is *about* the state of affairs p. But then they would have realized that the sounds were by no means perfect indicators of the things. Sometimes *s* was uttered but p didn't obtain. At this point it would have become worth while to start thinking of certain people as being in a certain internal state (namely, being disposed to utter *s*), so as better to anticipate and discount cases where they are caused to be in that state by things other than p. The natural way to identify such states would be to think of them as about the state of affairs p, like the sentences which manifested them.

Now, unlike Field (1978), I don't think that this story yields a coherent philosophical account of the modern notion of aboutness. (See Papineau, 1984, section III, for why not.) But, even so, it might well explain why people identify internal states with given causal roles (that is, beliefs) by using a construction ('the belief that p') which is so closely bound up with the apparatus for referring to states of affairs.

Here's another story (which could well be told in tandem with the first). Suppose our ancestors weren't so much rudimentary linguists as rudimentary psychologists. Suppose they started off with crude, extrinsic notions of mental states. Beliefs were identified simply as internal reflections always present in such-and-such circumstances, and desires simply as internal precursors always present given such-and-such results. Together with some assumptions about the stability of desires, and about decision procedures, this would have allowed our ancestors to anticipate the results of each other's actions. But obviously they would have become much better at this once they realized that the presence of a belief's 'truth condition' was neither necessary nor sufficient for the presence of the belief itself, and similarly with 'satisfaction conditions' and desires, and noted that 'truth' and 'satisfaction' conditions were just a sub-class of the possible causes and effects of beliefs and desires.

By which stage there is a philosophical question as to why any special significance should still be attached to 'truth' and 'satisfaction' conditions. And to this question I would give the teleological answer. But this parable too offers an explanation why everyday thinking identifies beliefs in terms so similar to the way it identifies states of affairs.

5

The Possibility of Error

5.1 DIVERGENCE OF OPINION AGAIN

Recall the transcendental argument against divergence of opinion. This was designed to show that most of anybody's beliefs had to be true, and, consequently, that most of the beliefs of any two communities had to be consistent.

This argument hinged on the principle of charity, on the assumption that the test of an interpretation was that it should make as many accepted judgements as possible come out true. But this assumption was called in question once we switched from charity to humanity. For according to humanity, interpretation need only impute understandable beliefs, not true judgements.

Still, as I pointed out in chapter 2, this left the question of divergence of opinion somewhat open. There is no question that switching from the interpretational requirement of true beliefs to a requirement of merely understandable beliefs creates more room for falsity. For there certainly are some examples of understandably false beliefs. But it remains possible that there are still some conceptual limits on imputations of falsity. Maybe further analysis of the notions of belief and representation will show there are *limits* to the extent one community can impute false beliefs to another.

We are now in a position to resolve this question. My analysis of representation is that beliefs answer to those conditions that they are biologically supposed to represent. What limits, if any, does this place on the possibility of falsity?

We can start by noting how this analysis of representation reinforces the possibility of false beliefs. The truth condition for any given belief is that circumstance which it is biologically supposed to respond to. But, precisely because the teleological approach goes beyond the simple causal approach discussed in 3.7, the teleological theory recognizes that there are other causes for any given belief apart from its truth condition. Our belief-forming mechanisms don't always work as they are supposed to. Tree beliefs can be caused by tree replicas as well as by real trees. And in such 'abnormal' cases the relevant belief is false.

But, still, it might seem as if my analysis does place some fairly strong limits on the possibility of false beliefs. After all, haven't I now allowed that the truth condition for any belief is the 'normal' cause of that belief, in the sense that the belief is biologically supposed to arise from that cause? And, given a selectionist analysis of teleology, doesn't this then mean that the truth condition will also be the 'normal' cause in a statistical sense? On my story, beliefs get naturally selected because of the good results they produce when they are (as we say) true. And this seems to imply that beliefs must at least *usually* be true, even if they aren't always so. For surely, if they didn't usually produce good results, they wouldn't be favoured by natural selection in the first place.

The trouble with this argument is that it only implies that any given belief type will usually have been true *up till now*. As with all natural selection stories, it's not the future production of good results that matters, but only their past production. In order for some item to be selected, and thus to have a purpose, it is only necessary that it have a *history* of advantageous results, not that it go on producing them. (Ostriches have wings in order to fly, even though they don't do so any more; and zebras have stripes in order to be camouflaged, including those zebras who live in zoos and are only made more conspicuous by their stripes.) And so, transposing the point to the teleological theory of representation, all that follows from the fact that any existing belief type must have been selected for good results, is that it will have had a history of usually being true, not that it will go on being so.

We can imagine different ways in which a given belief type might come to be characteristically false from now on. Perhaps, as with the ostrich's wings, its causal role will fall into disuse and atrophy, so that pathological false instances becomes more usual than normal true ones: for example, I'm not by any means as good at telling crows from ravens as I used to be. Or perhaps the environment might change, as with the captive zebras: thus imagine that all terrestrial trees die from some plague, but that kindly Martians, unknown to us, replace them all with lifelike replicas.

Perhaps these examples seem oversimplified. After all, even simple concepts like *tree* or *crow* aren't just single-criterion visual concepts. We have a number of different ways, both direct and indirect, of arriving at beliefs about trees and crows. Doesn't this mean that (if we can be bothered) we can always take steps to ensure our beliefs are true? Surely even the Martian replicas will somehow have to be detectably different from real trees, to give substance to the idea that they are only replicas in the first place.

But this doesn't affect the underlying point. Certainly the Martian replicas need, by hypothesis, to be distinguishable in principle from real trees. And of course there are real differences between crows and ravens, by which sufficiently sophisticated investigators can distinguish them. The question at issue, however, isn't whether such discriminations are in principle possible, but whether there is anything in the very idea of a belief type answering to a state of affairs which guarantees that tokens of that belief type are usually true. And here I still want to say that my belief does answer to *crows*, even though I'm wrong more often than not. And my belief would still answer to *trees*, even though in the imaginary scenario I would invariably be mistaken.

The question is not whether it would be possible for some abstract, perfectly tuned investigator to get things right, but whether we, with our actual dispositions, are guaranteed to do so. And just pointing out that our actual dispositions are somewhat more complicated than I've been making them appear, doesn't really help to show that those dispositions are guaranteed to get things generally right. Perhaps I am capable of doing a bit more than I first suggested to check up on trees and crows. But there's no reason to suppose that even my full range of multi-criterial dispositions are guaranteed to be usually right. For even they could be atrophied relative to their biological purposes, or inadequate to a changed environment. And if that goes for me, then it goes for human beings in general. There is no good argument from the nature of belief to the conclusion that truth is the statistical norm for human beings.[1]

5.2 DIVERGENCE OF CONCEPTS AGAIN

Let us now turn to the transcendental argument against divergence of concepts. Perhaps we still have reason to resist divergence of concepts, even if divergence of opinion can no longer be ruled out.

The argument against divergence of concepts did not depend on the principle of charity, but, more generally, on the idea that we grasp the notion of meaning by understanding the workings of an empirical theory of meaning which ascribes truth conditions. Given this essentially extrinsic notion of judgement identity, any meaningful judgement necessarily answered to some feature of the world, and so there could never be any barrier in principle to one community's translating the language of another.

But this argument too was called in question, once we moved from the Davidsonian implicit definition approach to meaning towards an explicit reduction in terms of belief. For this raised the possibility that the beliefs involved in alien judgements might somehow have intrinsic identities incommensurable with the identities of our own beliefs.

How do the arguments of the last chapter bear on this issue? Well, the first and most obvious point is that the idea of beliefs as bearers of causal roles gives us an immediate sense in which different communities might have different concepts. For there seems no good reason to rule out *a priori* the possibility of different communities having belief components (concepts) which play different causal roles in their respective cognitive systems.

But this in itself is of limited interest. Certainly the notion of a

---

[1] In his (1984a), pp. 248–9, Fodor suggests that a teleological theory of representation implies the 'verificationist' thesis that a belief formed in 'epistemologically optimal' conditions cannot but be true. I accept that there is a sense of 'optimal' (to do with things going according to teleological plan) in which this thesis follows. But I don't see that there is anything especially 'verificationist' about it, given that the conditions in which beliefs actually get accepted might usually, or even always, be 'non-optimal' in the relevant sense.

causal role yields a way of identifying beliefs intrinsically, without reference to their truth conditions, and so yields one sense in which different communities might have different concepts. But a more interesting kind of divergence of concepts might still seem to be ruled out. For even if extrinsic identifications in terms of truth conditions are no longer the *only* way of identifying beliefs, we still *have* a notion of a truth condition, namely, the notion of that state of affairs that the bearer of a given causal role is biologically supposed to represent. And it still seems that any given belief, any bearer of a causal role, will possess such a truth condition. For won't any given belief type have been selected, in evolution or learning, because it gives rise to advantageous effects in a certain kind of circumstance? And isn't this just to say that any given belief will have a truth condition? And then, if every belief must in this sense answer to some feature of the objective world, won't the argument against divergence of concepts go through pretty much as before?

Perhaps the causal role played by the Dzongkah concept of a tree is rather different from that played by our concept of a tree. Perhaps the sensory cues that prompt their tree beliefs are different from those that prompt ours. Perhaps they differ from us on what evidence they take to decide questions about trees. But, still, their concept, like ours, is *about trees*, in the sense that trees are what their concept, and ours, are both biologically supposed to register the presence of.

A familiar response to Kuhn's and Feyerabend's 'incommensurability thesis' is that it doesn't follow, from the fact that different communities attach different *sense* to a given term (to the term 'force', say), that the term will have a different *referent* for the two communities. (See, for example, Scheffler, 1967, ch. 3.) I am making effectively the same point. Even if the features of concepts in virtue of which they have the referents they do – namely, their causal roles – cannot always be identified across communities, it doesn't follow that the referents themselves can't always be so identified.

However, let us now look more closely at our positive reason for thinking that any concept *must* have some cross-culturally identifiable reference. This hinged on the idea that any belief type will perforce have been selected to register some objective feature of the world. The trouble now is that this argument only works for observational concepts.

A non-observational concept, recall, is a concept whose cognitive role derives, not from a single process 'dedicated' to it, but from its place in a cognitive structure of general assumptions. Correspondingly, such a non-observational concept refers to that entity whose role in the causal structure of the world mirrors the role of the concept itself in the cognitive structure. Teleologically speaking, the referents of non-observational concepts depend on the general purpose of our model-building ability as such, rather than on the purpose specific to some 'dedicated' observational process.

But what now if there is a mismatch between mental model and the objective world's causal structure? What if the cognitive network embodies the assumptions of some theory which quite misrepresents the way the world actually works? What, for instance, if some alien concept ('phlogiston') is the notion of a substance present in all combustible bodies, which is given off during burning, and which can saturate the atmosphere in confined spaces? It seems natural to say that, although this concept has a perfectly well-defined causal role, there is nothing in the objective world for it to refer to.

If there are any purely observational beliefs deriving entirely from dedicated processes then they will invariably have determinate truth conditions. Of course even such dedicated processes won't always work as they are supposed to. But when they don't the upshot will simply be falsity, not non-referring concepts. But with non-observational beliefs the situation is even worse. When the model-building processes by which we construct non-observational concepts fail to work as they are supposed to, in the sense that the models involved fail to fit the world, then we end up, not just with falsity, but with non-referring concepts.

And so the argument divergence of concepts breaks down at all levels. Not only is there the straightforward possibility of different communities having concepts which play different causal roles. There is not even any guarantee that the concepts of different communities must answer alike to objectively available referents. For once we bring non-observational concepts into the picture (and it is arguable, remember, that all concepts are to some degree non-observational), we see that there is no principled reason why human concepts should have objective referents at all.

5.3 INCOMMENSURABILITY AND TRANSLATION

Let us reflect further on non-referring concepts like phlogiston, or, again, the Zande concept of an *ira mangu* (a person who possesses *mangu*, namely, a hereditary substance that can be detected *post mortem* by the presence of an inflated gall bladder, and which gives its possessors the power to wish ill on their enemies. Cf. Evans-Pritchard, 1937, part I.) In cases like these the need for intrinsic identifications of alien ideas is obvious. It seems clear enough (at least before we start grinding any philosophical axes) that we can identify and comprehend these concepts. But it is also clear that we can't do this extrinsically by naming those features of the world that these concepts refer to, for the simple reason that there aren't, so far as we're concerned, any such features to be named.

Some philosophers like to pretend that such cases present a paradox. If we don't have words to name what their words name, then surely we can't translate their words into our language. And if we can't do that, then how can we possibly identify what their concepts signify? (Cf. Davidson, 1974, p. 184.)

But the paradox, such as it is, is a shallow one. My argument so far has shown that pairing alien words with ours isn't the only strategy open to students of alien thought systems. Instead in cases of this kind we can identify alien concepts directly and intrinsically, by delineating the theoretical structure in which they play a role. That is, we can explain what other beliefs (including observational beliefs) led eighteenth-century chemists to judgements about the presence or absence of phlogiston in certain substances, or lead the Azande to conclude that someone is an *ira mangu*, and we can explain what further beliefs (and actions) will follow, for eighteenth-century chemists, or for the Azande, from such beliefs. And once that has been done, we will have explained the identities of the alien concepts.

Isn't this account belied by the fact that we do have a word – 'witch' – in our language which is normally used to translate the

Zande 'ira mangu'? And, for that matter, don't we have 'phlogiston' for 'phlogiston'? However (even if we leave to one side questions about the acceptability of such translations as 'witch' for 'ira mangu'), this scarcely disproves my claim that we are forced to identify alien beliefs intrinsically, via their theoretical role. For 'witch' and 'phlogiston' are not words that *we* actually use in a first-order way to describe features of the world. After all, we don't think there are any witches or any phlogiston. The only reason we have adopted (or kept) these words in our language is to identify and convey the thoughts of culturally distant people, like the Azande or eighteenth-century chemists. So in effect these words function in our language purely as names for intrinsic functional roles. Which is scarcely surprising – since we don't think there are any witches or phlogiston, we couldn't use these words for extrinsic identifications of alien beliefs even if we wanted to.

This now explains something left up in the air in section 2.1: namely, the slight puzzle as to how different *concepts* can in any sense be incompatible with each other. The difficulty, recall, was that mere competence with a concept, as opposed to the adoption of a belief, didn't seem to commit a thinker to any particular view about the way the world is. But we have now seen that many (if not all) concepts carry with them a commitment to a structure of theoretical assumptions. Thus only those who accept the Zande theory of *mangu* will actually use the concept of *ira mangu* to describe real people. We, on the other hand, have theoretical views incompatible with those of the Azande, and use concepts dictated by our own theory in the same situations. Given that our theory is incompatible with the Zande theory, and given that acceptance of these theories is both necessary and sufficient for the use of the relevant concepts, it seems only natural to talk of the concepts themselves as being incompatible. (Of course there is the other sense in which we do have the concept *ira mangu*, even though we reject the theory which gives this concept its identity: namely, we have a second-order concept which we use to describe Zande thoughts. But, as just explained, this is really a rather different concept, a concept-of-an-alien-concept, which gets its identity from its role in our interpretative theory of Zande thought, rather than from their theory of *mangu*.)

We can imagine a recursive specification giving the intrinsic identities of all the beliefs in an alien community's repertoire. This would start by characterizing the functional roles of their atomic concepts. Then it would add a specification of their ways of combining concepts into beliefs, and of combining beliefs into further beliefs. And thus it would give the functional roles of all the beliefs available to the alien community. This would be a kind of analogue of a recursive Davidsonian specification of extrinsic identities for all a community's judgements. But instead of systematically specifying the truth conditions for an indefinite range of alien judgements, this would specify an indefinite number of functional roles.

Of course we want to leave room for the possibility of giving a recursive specification of truth conditions for another community's judgements as well. If the community in question has theories that (we consider to) fit the world, then their beliefs will answer to features of the world, and there will be no barrier to our systematically specifying what those features are. But, even so, the specification of their judgements' functional roles will be more fundamental, in that we can always give a specification of functional roles, while it will only be in those cases where these functional roles do succeed in answering to determinate truth conditions that we will be able to specify truth conditions.

It is notoriously unclear how far a community's theories have to go wrong before we deem their concepts to lack determinate reference. Phlogiston and *ira mangu* seem clear cases of concepts without a reference. But what, say, about the medieval concept of *vis* (force)? I am inclined to say that this refers to nothing too, since there aren't any active powers within bodies which keep them moving. But at least the medievals measured their force by matter × speed. So perhaps we should deem their concept to refer to momentum. Again, consider the Newtonian concept of mass. No actual quantity fits the bill perfectly (cf. Field, 1973). But, still, we could perhaps construe it as referring to rest mass (Earman and Fine, 1977). Perhaps, indeed, we should even accept that such concepts as *ira mangu* and phlogiston have referents, and construe them as referring to people with inflated gall bladders, or to the absence of oxygen, rather than to nothing.

I don't think that much hangs on this issue. It is possible to argue that, strictly speaking, pretty much *any* mismatch between theory and the world produces failure of reference in theoretical concepts: not only do phlogiston and *ira mangu* lack reference, but so also do *vis*, Newtonian mass, and indeed any concept that gets its identity from an erroneous theory. Indeed my *Theory and Meaning* (1979) is in effect a sustained defence of just this position, at least to the extent of showing that it does not have many of the unpalatable consequences that are generally thought to follow from it.[2]

However, even if we do accept that, strictly speaking, any theoretical concept embedded in a faulty theory lacks reference, we ought at the same time to recognize that there can be good pragmatic reasons for ascribing referents to faulty alien concepts. Maybe we want to convey an idea of some alien thought, yet don't have time to spell out the whole theoretical context. Or maybe we are in a context of discussion where it doesn't matter. In such cases a rough-and-ready extrinsic identification of the alien concept could serve our purposes perfectly well. Again, perhaps we are primarily interested in what tokens of alien judgement types can most usefully be taken to indicate about the external world, rather than in the internal workings of the aliens. Here too we will be happy to identify their judgements in terms of those external circumstances that they are most reliably correlated with. But these pragmatic points are consistent with an insistence that such extrinsic identifications of concepts from foreign theoretical systems force those concepts into moulds they do not fully fit.

So far in this section I have been discussing the implications of conceptual variability across different *communities*. But to the extent that concepts are theory-dependent, we would expect there to be conceptual variation between *individuals* as well, for there are differences in sets of theoretical assumptions within communities as well as across them. This might be too much for some readers –

---

[2] As it happens, I now recognize that the overall position adopted in that book implies an untenable scepticism about all our current beliefs. But this scepticism was as much due to my acceptance of the Popperian thesis that theory failure is endemic to science, as to the further, quite independent, thesis that reference failure follows from theory failure. I still don't think this latter thesis makes things any worse than the Popperian thesis does.

surely I don't want to say that every theoretical difference between individuals creates differences in the identities of their concepts, and threatens reference failure whenever those theories are faulty. But I don't think these conclusions are as absurd as they might seem. For one thing, there are strong pragmatic reasons, over and above those already applying to inter-communal interpretation, for forcing individual concepts into a common extrinsic interpretation. (Cf. Papineau, 1986a, pp. 58–9.) And on the question of intrinsic identifications, there is a strong reason for allowing inter-individual variation in concept identity. Our central reason for attributing causal-role concepts to people is to understand the dynamics of their beliefs and actions. Individuals with different theoretical assumptions are led thereby to accept different beliefs and to perform different actions. Why then insist that such individuals have the same causal-role concepts, when the tendencies to thought and action we want those concepts to inform us about are different? (How can there be psychological generalizations, if the content of any thought is pretty much unique to the individual having it? Cf. Fodor, 1986, pp. 9–13. But recall that the interesting psychological generalizations 'quantify over belief-types': they make claims which start 'for *any* p, q, . . .' And so the fact that concepts vary across individuals doesn't pose a threat to a generalizing psychology, any more than the fact that masses vary across bodies poses a threat to a generalizing dynamics.)

5.4 THE IMPORTANCE OF HUMANITY

The Davidsonian argument against divergence of belief has now collapsed entirely. Not only are there no *a priori* limits to divergence of opinion, there seem to be no *a priori* limits to divergence of concepts either. After the initial promise of the 'transcendental argument to end all transcendental arguments' this might all seem rather disappointing. At this point I would like to pause to reconsider exactly why the Davidsonian transcendental argument breaks down.

The crucial point was the switch from charity to humanity. As I observed at the time, this step immediately made some concession to divergence of opinion: the whole point of the switch from truth to intelligibility, after all, was the intelligibility of other people's false beliefs.

But in retrospect we can see that the switch from charity to humanity has a rather greater underlying significance. For once we make the switch, it is difficult to resist the move from an extrinsic truth-conditional notion of belief to an intrinsic functionalist one.

Suppose we start off with the extrinsic idea of a belief as a mental state that in some primitive sense 'reflects' another state of affairs, namely, its truth condition. The switch to humanity then forces us to recognize that there is more to our notion of belief: namely, that for most beliefs (the belief that a tree is present, say) we are aware how that belief can be caused by something other than its truth condition (as, for instance, by a papier-mâché imitation). Again, the whole point of the switch to humanity is that on occasion we find it *intelligible* that *in such-and-such circumstances* people are likely to have *false* beliefs.

So in effect the switch to humanity contains the potential for intrinsic identifications of beliefs: humanity leads us to think of a given belief type as a state that has a certain range of causes, as a state that plays a certain functionalist causal role, instead of simply as a state which 'reflects' a certain truth condition. Of course the truth condition will as a rule be included amongst the possible causes. But once we start identifying beliefs intrinsically, in terms of their overall causal role, then the truth condition of a belief is just one among its various possible causes.

Indeed, from the point of view of the intrinsic definition in terms of overall causal role we need a philosophical theory – the teleological theory of representation – to explain why truth conditions have any special significance at all. And, as we saw in 5.2, that theory of representation in the end leaves room for certain intrinsically identified beliefs to lack truth conditions altogether. Which is to say that once we switch to humanity, and thereby open the way to intrinsic identifications of belief, we end up allowing divergence of concepts as well as divergence of opinion.

Put like this, perhaps the argument seems a bit quick. I am suggesting that, once we switch to humanity, we cannot resist the functionalist account of beliefs as bearers of causal roles, and that

then we are inevitably led, via the teleological theory of representation, to an unqualified acceptance of divergence. But does
humanity really force us to functionalism in the first place?

We can consider this as a question about the structure of folk
psychology. In the last chapter I surreptitiously assumed that a
conception of beliefs as bearers of causal roles was part of our
everyday psychological thinking. But was this reasonable? There is
no doubt, I think, that folk psychology is committed to humanity: it
is certainly part of common sense that people are likely to form false
beliefs in misleading circumstances. But can I move straight from
this to the conclusion that folk psychology conceptualizes beliefs as
functional states whose truth conditions are merely one among a
number of possible causes?

Couldn't somebody accept humanity, but still maintain that our
central notion of belief was the extrinsic notion of a state that
'reflected' some other state of affairs? That is, couldn't it be argued
that any belief is identified *primarily* in terms of what it is about, and
that our humanitarian recognition of other possible causes is *then*
grafted on, as a kind of peripheral addendum?

I'm not sure that I really want to take issue with this as an
account of folk psychology. There is clearly a sense in which folk
psychology has a firm grasp of what any given belief is *about*, by
comparison with which its hold on which misleading circumstances
are also likely to give rise to that belief are fragmentary, tentative,
and, in some cases, even non-existent. Folk psychology, after all,
names beliefs by using words which in normal contexts refer to the
things those beliefs are about. And, as I suggested at the end of the
last chapter, it is no doubt no accident, historically speaking, that
we name beliefs in this way. So it is only to be expected that our
grasp of what further circumstances, other than its truth condition,
might cause a given belief, will be a tentative addition to that
truth-conditional core.

My inclination is to say that all this is rather beside the point.
Maybe folk psychology currently has a firmer hold on truth
conditions than on further causal roles. But humanity shows that it
does pay *some* attention to such further causal roles. And if folk
psychology goes beyond truth conditions to this extent, why should
we not hope for a future psychology which gives a full and detailed

story about *all* the causes which can give rise to a given belief? Surely our ultimate concern ought to be with what beliefs *are*, rather than with how folk psychology currently thinks of them.

One possible objection at this point would be to deny that folk psychology deals in *causal* explanations at all. That psychology is about causes is something I have taken for granted throughout. But there is a significant alternative school of thought which holds that the explanation of belief is a matter of *understanding* believers as rational beings, where 'understanding as rational' contrasts with causal explanation. And from this point of view it might be possible to admit humanity, and yet, by emphasizing the possibility of rationally understanding all cases of belief, still argue that the identities of beliefs are essentially constituted by what would make them true. However, I would prefer to postpone discussion of this kind of objection until the next chapter, when I turn to anti-realism of method. So for the present I shall continue to take it for granted that folk psychology deals in causes, and thus continue to pursue the suggestion that a functionalist theory of the overall causal roles of beliefs might always be developed out of folk psychology, even if folk psychology does not at present amount to such a theory.

But what if such a future 'cognitive science' deviated markedly from current folk psychology? Wouldn't there come a point at which it should be deemed to have stopped dealing with beliefs and desires at all, and to have started postulating its own explanatory entities? Maybe so. But in the present context of argument not much hangs on this point either. For even if the explanatory states of a mature functionalist psychology differed significantly from the beliefs and desires of current everyday psychology, they would still be representational states identified in terms of causal roles, and it would still be necessary to introduce a teleological analysis of representation to account for the difference between cases where these states were fulfilling their representational purposes and those where they weren't. Which means that the general epistemological issues with which this book is concerned (as opposed to the more detailed question of the status of our current psychology) will still arise in the same way within a mature functionalist theory, even if that theory diverges significantly from folk psychology.

We can put the point the other way round. Even if everyday psychology and its explanatory states are destined to be replaced by maturer alternatives, there will still be enough similarity of underlying structure between current psychology and mature psychology to make current psychology an adequate context in which to pursue the general philosophical concerns of this book. For, to repeat the thesis of this section, the principle of humanity shows that everyday psychology recognizes causes of beliefs other than their truth conditions, and so shows that everyday psychology has conceptual space for the identification of beliefs in terms of *all* their causes and effects. Maybe, by the time folk psychology has fully filled out this conceptual space, its representational states won't look very much like beliefs any more. But even if this is how it eventually turns out, we can perfectly well assume folk psychology for the philosophical purposes of this book. For even if it has the details wrong, folk psychology is still an embryonic theory of cognitive states as bearers of causal roles, and as such is an appropriate framework for the arguments which follow.

5.5 DIGRESSION ON DENNETT AND DAVIDSON ON FOLK PSYCHOLOGY

It is perhaps worth distinguishing my attitude to folk psychology from that defended by Daniel Dennett (1971). Dennett in effect denies that folk psychology is a rudimentary version of a functionalist psychology. He allows that a functionalist psychology, based on the 'design stance', and aiming at a 'sub-personal theory' of the internal causal architecture of our brains, is possible. But he denies that folk psychology itself involves any such sub-personal theory. Rather, folk psychology takes an 'intentional stance': it explains behaviour by showing how it is appropriate to the organism's needs, not by identifying internal cognitive causes.[3]

---

[3] In his (1981) Dennett modifies his position somewhat, allowing that folk psychology might recognize some of our psychological imperfections (see especially p. 47). But he still insists that folk psychology is far more akin to an 'intentional' than a 'sub-personal' theory.

Dennett argues that the applicability of the intentional stance is guaranteed by general evolutionary considerations. We can take it for granted that any creature produced by natural selection will tend to respond to its environment in a way appropriate to its needs. No doubt there is, for any such organism, a 'sub-personal programme' which is responsible for its being able to respond in this way. But, argues Dennett, we don't need to know what that programme is in order to give folk psychological intentional explanations. It is enough to know that evolution must *somehow* have ensured that the organism will behave sensibly.

In a sense Dennett is going one better than functionalism. Functionalism says that we can ignore the physical make-up of the brain, since functional explanations lay claim only to causal structure, not causal substance. (The same structure can be realized in different materials.) But Dennett says that we can ignore the functional make-up of the brain too, since everyday explanations lay claim only to the appropriateness of behaviour, not to its structural antecedents. (The same appropriateness can be ensured by different cognitive structures.)

I think Dennett misidentifies the level at which folk psychology operates. I don't want to deny that it would in principle be possible to explain behaviour by appeal to general evolutionary considerations alone, without any assumptions about internal cognitive structure, in the way that Dennett has in mind. And perhaps sometimes we actually do this, in situations where we are quite ignorant about the cognitive and perceptual structure of some organism (as I am with slugs, for instance). But note that all that Dennett's general evolutionary considerations on their own would ever entitle us to assume is that the organism in question will tend to perform actions which in its specific external circumstances are likely to maximize its bequeathing of genes. Explaining an action at this level is thus simply a matter of pointing to various features of the organism's external circumstances, and observing that in those circumstances the action is conducive to its ability to bequeath genes.

But of course our folk psychology of human beings (and of most other animals) does much better than that. It can deal with cases where, from the evolutionary point of view, things go wrong.

Indeed it gives us a grasp of different ways in which things can go wrong, and accordingly allows us to explain and predict different kinds of biologically *in*appropriate behaviour. Most obviously, folk psychology deals with cases where agents have false beliefs: that is, where the actual external circumstances aren't such as to make the action appropriate, but where the cognitive mechanism has got into an environment-registering state appropriate to different circumstances. We also, in the last chapter, came across cases of biologically misplaced desires: cases where certain effects aren't in fact conducive to the bequeathing of genes, but where the cognitive mechanism is in an action-generating state which would be biologically appropriate if they were. And we could also mention here cases of irrationally chosen actions: cases where there is nothing biologically wrong with the organism's beliefs and desires, but where the limitations of its decision-making mechanism mean that even so its behaviour is biologically inappropriate.

So our folk psychology contains certain definite assumptions about the structure of our cognitive mechanisms. No doubt current folk psychology doesn't tell a complete story about the causal structure of our cognitive mechanisms. But it certainly goes beyond the thought that humans tend *somehow* to respond appropriately to their environments, to some kind of story about the internal structure that makes this possible. And this story then also allows us to explain what is going on in some of the cases where people behave in biologically inappropriate ways.

It would not be too much to say that the whole *point* of folk psychology, and its introduction of beliefs, desires and decisions, is to account for human error. If we were perfect biological beings, then all our actions could indeed be explained by pointing to the objective environment, and indicating how what was done was conducive to our biological needs. But of course we aren't such simple paragons. Humans get caught up in all kinds of plans and schemes, based on all kinds of wierd beliefs and outlandish desires, and if we are to understand them properly we will need to identify these internal goings on, even (or, rather, especially) when those beliefs and desires are biological 'malfunctions'.

This shows, incidentally, why humanity is an essential feature of folk psychology, rather than some optional addition to charity.

Strict charity about belief (all beliefs are true) in effect requires us to view belief as nothing more than an internal shadow cast by actual external circumstances. But then why think of actions as due to internal states at all? Why not just explain them by external circumstances? The answer, as we have just seen, is that by bringing in beliefs we can cope also with cases where beliefs *mis*represent external circumstances. But note that it is precisely the recognition of systematic human tendencies towards error that distinguishes humanity from charity. Which shows that there wouldn't be any point in bringing in beliefs at all unless humanitarian attitudes were brought with them.

There is a possible intermediate attitude towards psychological interpretation. One could resist my full-blooded functionalism, which takes folk psychology to be a theory about *how* humans register the environment, and maintain instead that folk psychology just tells us *which* features of the environment are registered. On this approach (which we might call the 'half-charitable' approach) folk psychology would do more than explain by indiscriminate reference to external circumstances, for it would restrict the range of external features about which an agent could be expected to 'have beliefs'. But, even so, it could still be committed to charity about that restricted range of beliefs, and maintain that there is a transcendental human tendency towards truth on those matters that humans do have beliefs about.

I suspect that this half-charitable approach is not far from Davidson's position. Davidson sometimes gestures towards humanity as a principle of interpretation (cf. in particular 1975, p. 167). But for the most part he is content with the idea that the best interpretation is the one that maximizes truth. This lack of concern with what I have argued to be a crucial difference is probably best understood against the background of Davidson's philosophy of psychology, about which I have said little so far. The articles in his *Essays on Actions and Events* (1980) make it clear that Davidson is highly suspicious of any idea that folk psychology contains causal generalizations about mental states. So from Davidson's point of view there is no real question of identifying beliefs via a grasp of their causal role, and then using such a grasp as an alternative to charity for evaluating interpretations. Without the causal generalizations of functionalist psychology, the notion of belief simply collapses into the notion of an internal 'reflection' of such-and-such external circumstances. Interpretations can tell us which circumstances the interpretees are psychologically equipped to register. But there is no further hold by which we can anticipate and explain their beliefs, other than by assuming that their beliefs are generally the appropriate responses to the actual circumstances. The reason Davidson doesn't worry about humanity as an alternative to charity is that from his point of view it's not substantially different.[4]

But even if there are good internal reasons for Davidsonians to uphold the half-charitable approach to folk psychology, it seems to me that it is a highly implausible picture of how folk psychology actually works. Surely our folk psychology in fact goes far beyond bare claims about *which* facts humans register, to further information about how they do so, with consequent implications about when humans will be misled. And surely there is a principled reason why this is so. Any judgements about which facets of the environment a given community of humans can register will inevitably be informed by some appreciation of the workings of their sense organs, and of the inferential patterns by which they move from observations to further conclusions. And this information will then inevitably carry with it indications of the ways in which that community can be misled about those facets of the environment.

One last point about the status of folk psychology. The issue is complicated by the fact that there are no doubt a number of different levels of possible causal-functional analysis between folk psychology and outright physical description. As well as asking how humans manage to respond appropriately to their environment (by having a structure of beliefs and desires in their heads), we could also ask how they manage to have that structure of beliefs

---

[4] One could interpret Davidson himself a bit more charitably, by crediting him with a substantial but non-causal notion of rationality, which allowed falsity as more than mere 'noise' and which therefore took humanity beyond charity, but which nevertheless placed limits on the possibility of error. But there seems to me little in Davidson himself to warrant this (especially not in early Davidson), even though this is clearly the view that most of his supporters prefer. In any case, this view is criticized in the next chapter.

and desires. At this level there are such questions as how far beliefs and desires are implicit in the design of the cognitive mechanisms, as opposed to appearing as explicit representations, or of how far mental representation is analogue or digital. And even when these questions have been decided, there are no doubt many other levels of possible causal description before one gets down to the molecules. But, *pace* Dennett, none of this means that folk psychology isn't itself a level of causal-functional description. Just because a whole hierarchy of different levels of programming description are instantiated in a single computer, it doesn't follow that the highest level isn't a programming language at all. And, similarly, just because there are many possible levels of functional theory of the brain, it doesn't follow that the highest level, everyday psychology, isn't itself a functional theory.

5.6 MEANING AGAIN

In this chapter and the last two I have been exploring a number of issues relating to the interpretation of judgement. However, I have been dealing entirely with *mental* judgements, and not, as earlier in chapter 2, with linguistic judgements. In the interests of tidiness I now want to return to the topic of language and make a few brief remarks about meaning.

Linguistic meaning has dropped out of our discussion in the last three chapters because I have been assuming, for the sake of the argument, the Gricean reduction of meaning to belief. If meaning can indeed be reduced to belief, then the interesting philosophical questions become ones about mental, rather than linguistic, representation. But at this stage it will be worthwhile having another look at the Gricean reduction.

According to the Gricean reduction, a sentence's meaning that p is nothing more nor less than the relevant community being mutually aware that they all normally use that sentence only when they desire their hearers to belief that p. However, as I pointed out in chapter 2, it is somewhat implausible to suppose that all competent language-users must have complicated beliefs about what other people believe they believe about what other people believe . . . about the desires speakers normally have when they utter a given sentence. Certainly we don't seem to be introspectively aware of any such complex beliefs.

Why not simply have it that s means that p just in case the relevant community all believe that *s means that p*? This suggestion wouldn't involve the complexities of the Gricean story, but in a sense it would still be a kind of reduction of meaning to belief, for it would still make a sentence's having a meaning nothing more than the relevant community having a certain belief.

At first sight it might seem that this suggestion will fail to explain how words manage to stand for things. Isn't it just assuming the mysterious notion of meaning, and taking it for granted that arbitrary marks and dead sounds, without any intrinsic powers of signification, can reach out and refer to things other than themselves? But we need to be careful here. In particular, we need to avoid supposing that the full-blooded Gricean reduction itself succeeds in dispelling this mystery by avoiding beliefs *about* meanings and simply appealing to the fact that people associate the words for certain things with beliefs about those things.

For, as I stressed in 3.1 above, questions about representation are not that quickly dispelled. This is because the ability of beliefs to represent things is itself in need of explanation. Not that such a further explanation cannot be given. The teleological theory of mental representation is designed to supply precisely such an explanation. But the point I am making here is that it is a mistake to suppose that the Gricean reduction itself offers an immediate explanation of representation. for it offers no explanation at all until it is supplemented by an account of how beliefs represent.

And once we are clear about this, we can see that there is no immediate objection to analysing meaning in terms of beliefs that s means that p. It's not fair to complain that this analysis doesn't *explain* how words relate to things. For without an account of how beliefs represent, the Gricean analysis doesn't do this either. And given that we do now have an account of how beliefs represent, then the suggested analysis of meaning does itself succeed in relating words to things. For the belief that s means that p is *inter alia about* the state of affairs that p. And at the same time it is also about the sentence s. So doesn't the presence of this belief in a community *per se* institute a relationship between *s* and the state of affairs that p? Why feel that no such relationship has been instituted unless 'means' within the belief in question can itself be replaced by some complex construction involving 'the belief that p'?

Of course we do need to say *something* about the appearance of 'means' within the belief that *s* means that p. Even if we don't have to reduce this 'means' away entirely, we ought at least to give some account of what it is for somebody to believe that *s means* that p. We need at least to explain what kind of perceptual evidence will lead somebody to believe that *s* means that p, and what kind of actions will follow from their believing this.

As a first attempt we could say that people will come to believe that *s* means that p as a result of observing that other speakers utter *s* when they want to *say that p*; and we could say that this will affect their actions by leading them themselves to utter *s* when they themselves want to say that p. But, still, what is it to *say that p*? It's clearly not just a matter of uttering *s* when p obtains, if for no other reason than that people sometimes say false things. Indeed isn't *saying that p* in the end just a matter of giving voice to some sentence that *means that p*? We seem to have gone round in a circle.

I agree, And I accept that at this point we need to move some way towards the Gricean reduction. We need to attribute to speakers some kind of awareness that saying p by uttering *s* is a matter of presenting oneself as wanting one's hearers to believe that p, and moreover that it is a matter of doing so in the light of the fact that speakers who utter *s* generally desire their hearers to believe that p. A speaker who didn't know at least that much wouldn't be able to appreciate the possibliity of lies, or puns, or, indeed, the possibility of somebody speaking sincerely but falsely. (Cf. Papineau, 1978, pp. 101–2.) And it seems to me that a person who couldn't understand these things could scarcely be deemed to understand what it is for somebody to mean that p by some *s*, that is, what it is for somebody to *say that p*.

But even so – and this is the main point I want to make in this section – we needn't attribute an awareness of the full-blooded Gricean reduction to all competent speakers. Perhaps some speakers do indeed think of meaning in terms of the full Gricean battery of nested beliefs. But I am sure that many simply have an irreducible notion of meaning, to which is conjoined some kind of vague awareness that speakers normally desire their hearers to believe what they mean. And no doubt there is a continuum of cases between these two extremes.

In effect this is to say that 'means' is a vague notion, in the sense that different people will understand this rather differently. But this seems to me right. After all, meaning is certainly a pretty abstruse notion, and one would expect there to be variation in the way that most lay speakers conceive of it. This doesn't of course mean that the first-order sentences in a given language have to be vague. Speakers might understand 'meaning' rather differently, and yet all agree, so to speak, that 'Le neve è bianca' means that snow is white. And provided they all have some minimal grasp of what it is for a sentence to have a meaning, this seems to me enough to say that in their language 'La neve è bianca' does mean that snow is white.

Perhaps it is disappointing to be told at this late stage that meaning is a vague notion. But it seems to me that this is the right answer to arrive at, if we are thinking of meaning as a concept that speakers have, and in particular as the concept that features in their beliefs about the relation between words and things. For surely most speakers do have somewhat sketchy notions on this matter.

This conclusion would be less palatable if the notion of meaning were needed for a central role in further philosophical analyses. But one implication of the last three chapters is that it isn't. We have seen that the representational powers of words derive from the representational powers of mental states. So questions about the relationship between human judgement and reality are best posed directly, as questions about mental representation. Linguistic representation then becomes a secondary issue, interesting enough in itself, but somewhat detached from the central concerns of epistemology and metaphysics. Which means that our overall investigations are not fated to an inconclusive end just because the analysis of linguistic representation has foundered on the complexities of social life.

Let me conclude this chapter with two relatively technical points. The first relates to the requirement that speakers should know that *s* means that p for all the sentences in their language. In a footnote in section 2.7 I mentioned the Davidsonian worry that there will be logical difficulties about inferring such an infinity of theorems from a finite basis unless the intensional 'means that' is replaced by the extensional 'is true if and only if'. I can now observe that, apart from the doubts Taylor (1982) raises about these supposed logical obstacles, this worry has little force within the context of my psychological realism. For while I want speakers to believe an infinity of theorems, I don't care how they get to do this. In particular, I see no reason to suppose that they do so by inferring the theorems from axioms. Certainly they will have to embody some appropriate generative mechanism which, for any given sentence as input, produces a belief about its meaning as output. But there is no reason to suppose that the intermediate stages in this mechanism have themselves to be representable as beliefs about words and their referential powers. For instance, we could think of the mechanism as a purely syntactic device which paired (inner representations of) '*s*'s with (inner representations of) 'p's, and which then filled in an (inner representation of) 'means that' at the last stage. Only this last stage would then need to be thought of as involving speakers' *beliefs*. (While it seems clear to me that the Davidsonian argument against the intensional 'means that' is undercut by psychological realism, I am not at all sure what attitude to psychology in general, and to speakers' relationship to theories of meaning in particular, would make it a good argument.)

The second point. I maintain that words have meaning because speakers associate them with beliefs. But do speakers here individuate beliefs as bearers of causal roles, or simply as states with a given truth condition? (We could accept the latter without collapsing back into an exclusively extrinsic notion of belief: for even if speakers identify beliefs which share truth conditions for linguistic purposes, the way that they pair beliefs with truth conditions in the first place could still be sensitive to the full functional role of those beliefs.) In some respects, and in particular when we focus on the workings of proper names and natural kind terms, it does seem that speakers are expected only to have *some* belief that picks out the relevant truth condition, whatever the causal role of that belief. But in other respects, as with qualitative predicates and indeed with non-referring names, it seems clear that the beliefs that utterances communicate are distinguished by causal role. But I shall not pursue these issues: they involve any number of detailed questions of logical analysis. (See Papineau, 1986a, part II, for a more detailed discussion.)

6

Universal Rationality

6.1 RATIONALITY AND TRUTH

Anti-realism of belief has turned out to be indefensible. It is perfectly possible for different people to hold incompatible beliefs about reality. (They can have incompatible opinions, and they can have incompatible concepts too.) This then punctures the thesis that human belief and the real world cannot help but conform to each other, for different people's incompatible beliefs cannot all be in conformity with the real world. And so there is no avoiding questions about which, if any, of those beliefs are the right ones.

But there is still scope for another kind of anti-realism, anti-realism of method. Anti-realists of method shift the focus from human beliefs to the principles by which those beliefs are arrived at and evaluated. They allow that different people can have incompatible beliefs about reality, and that there is no avoiding questions as to which such views are to be adopted. But, they will argue, there are no similar questions to be raised about human standards of belief-evaluation. There is no question as to the suitability of human rationality for generating beliefs that correspond to reality.

At its simplest, the anti-realist of method holds that 'reality' just *is* the view to which we are led by the principles of human rationality. True, the deliverances of rationality are not always immediate, if for no other reason than that our human situation forces us always to work with incomplete evidence. Which is why the actual beliefs people adopt can on occasion be in error. But there is no possibility of the eventual deliverances of rational standards and sufficient evidence being in error – for, once more, the 'right' answer simply *is* that answer that rationality in the end delivers.

There are interesting questions to be raised about the notion of the 'right answer' that one gets from anti-realism of method. Even if we accept that there are unproblematic canons of human rationality, the notion of an 'eventual' upshot to rational investigation is a somewhat dubious abstraction. How much investigation is required before we reach this upshot? How can we ever be sure that our current views approximate to it? Indeed, what guarantees that there is a point after which rational principles will 'converge' on definitive conclusions at all?

And, even if rationality does arrive at such a point of convergence, will this point have all the features of traditional 'reality'? How far does the anti-realist notion of 'right answer' recapture the structure of realistic 'truth'? It is arguably a corollary of a realist conception of the relationship between judgement and reality that every meaningful statement is either true or false: either the independent state of affairs to which any statement answers obtains or it does not. But it is by no means obvious that anti-realism of method provides any similar reason for holding that every meaningful statement must be either right or wrong: even if rational principles 'eventually converge' on definite answers to some questions, what guarantees that they will produce such answers for *all* apparently meaningful questions?

We shall return to these issues about the notion of 'right answer' generated by anti-realism of method when I discuss Michael Dummett's views about the justification of deduction in 9.2 below. But let us focus first on the conception of rationality on which anti-realism of method is based. After all, it is because of their attitude towards rationality that anti-realists of method face questions about their version of 'reality', not vice versa.

From a realist point of view, 'rationality' means ways of thinking that are good for generating truths. For the realist the rationality of a given method of belief-formation is answerable to the truth of the beliefs it generates, where 'truth' means correspondence to an independent reality. The essence of anti-realism of method is its denial of such answerability. For the anti-realist of method, 'rationality' is a primitive notion, not a derivative one. 'Rationality' is simply the basic structure of human thought, which we engage in because we are human, and not because it is a suitable means to some further end. If 'truth' means anything, it means the answers we are led to by rational thought, not some abstract correspondence to some independent reality. So, where the realist defines 'rationality' in terms of 'truth', the anti-realist of method defines 'truth' in terms of 'rationality'.

6.2 THE COMMITMENTS OF METHODISM

Anti-realism of method (let me abbreviate it as 'methodism' from now on) is a strategy for blocking epistemological worries. Where the realist needs somehow to *show*, for any favoured method of belief-formation, that it is indeed suitable for generating beliefs that correspond to reality, the methodist wants to deny that we have any such obligation. The methodist wants to claim that there is no sense to the idea that the eventual deliverances of rational belief-forming methods might fail to be true.

In due course I will comment on two arguments designed to show that the deliverances of rational methods cannot but be true: Dummett's argument that statements cannot have 'verification-transcendent' truth conditions, and Putnam's 'model-theoretic' argument that an epistemologically ideal theory must always be interpretable as fitting reality perfectly. But it will be more convenient to postpone these specific defences of methodism until various related issues have been discussed. (I consider Dummett's defence in 9.2, and Putnam's in 10.7.) In this chapter I want to look at a more general problem facing anybody who wants to adopt the methodist line.

It is not enough for a methodist to show that the deliverances of rational belief-forming methods cannot but be true. A methodist also needs somehow to show that the relevant methods do not vary across different human thinkers. Anti-realism of belief, remember, needs to deny divergence of belief. Quite analogously, anti-realism of method needs to deny divergence of method. Methodism has space for divergence of belief, because constraints of time and evidence mean that even rational belief-forming methods leave room for temporary divergence of views. But methodism cannot allow divergence of rational belief-forming methods themselves.

For, when combined with the claim that the deliverances of rational methods cannot help but get reality right, such divergence implies the absurd conclusion that incompatible things would be true for the adherents of different rationalities – that such people would literally, albeit incoherently, live in different worlds.

Neither Dummett nor Putnam has as much to say about the universality of rationality as they have to say about why the deliverances of rationality must be true. Putnam does address the question of alternative rationalities, but he doesn't really deal with it. He argues against the relativistic thesis, that different standards are right for different people, on the grounds that it is self-defeating (1981, ch. 5). However, methodism doesn't just need to show that different standards can't all be right, but, more strongly, that different standards for different people are not *possible* in the first place (cf. section 1.3 above). Putnam also suggests that humans are guided by an idea of 'cognitive human flourishing' (1981, ch. 6); but this notion is so vague (and indeed explicitly differentiated from any specific set of epistemological values) that the question of its universality becomes empty.

Dummett doesn't really address the issue at all. In Dummett's scheme of things, what I have been calling 'methods of belief-formation' appear at the level of assertibility conditions for specific statements. This seems to collapse the issue of different methods of belief-formation into the apparently uncontentious mattter of people using words with different meanings. However, as the discussion of 5.3 made clear, questions of what meanings to adopt isn't always just the uncontentious matter of which subject matter to talk about. If we consider statements whose use commits the speaker to a body of theory, there are substantial questions about *which* meanings to use: that is, about the right theoretical contexts for our statements, and hence about what assertibility conditions they ought to have. At this level the possibility of people using statements with different assertibility conditions doesn't just indicate different areas of interest, but undermines the whole idea of assertibility conditions fixing the right answer. So Dummett does need an argument for the universality of methods of belief-formation, even if his focus on assertibility conditions for statements obscures this need.

6.3 LEVELS OF RATIONALITY

So a methodist first needs to show that methods of belief-formation are universal, before they can start giving arguments to show that the deliverances of such methods cannot but be true. Let us consider the moves open to the methodist here. An initial dilemma concerns the level at which the presumed universal principles of rationality are supposed to operate. Are all actual human belief-forming dispositions supposed to be included? That is, are all human perceptual and memory habits – all tendencies to form beliefs non-inferentially in response to sensory stimulation and memory processes – and all human inferential habits – all tendencies to form new beliefs from old – to be counted as principles of rationality? Or are we only required to suppose that some more restricted class of belief-evaluating principles is universal among human beings?

The first horn of the dilemma does have the merits of simplicity and specificity. But the trouble is that it is surely quite implausible to maintain that all human beings share 'principles of belief-evaluation' in this sense. Don't different peoples often have incompatible tendencies to perceptual judgement, depending on their training, expectations, and so on? Aren't the inductive inferences of different communities often informed by different views of what constitute natural kinds? Indeed, it even seems plausible that different people can have alternative deductive habits: imagine a community that has systematic tendencies to affirm the consequent in certain circumstances.

This kind of methodological variability will be dealt with at length in what follows. But whatever else is to be said about such variability, it should at least be clear that it pushes the anti-realist of method towards the other horn of the dilemma, towards the idea that 'principles of rationality' must operate on a more fundamental level than ordinary perceptual, memory, deductive and inductive habits. If the methodist is to maintain that all humans share the same rationality, they had better not include *all* human belief-forming habits in the principles of rationality.

Now, perhaps there are indeed some general structural features of thought – some 'deep universals' of perception, memory, and inference – to which all human thought does indeed conform. Maybe certain basic patterns of perception and memory, and certain underlying modes of inference, are common to all human beings. But now the trouble is that any such universal principles operating at a level below ordinary belief-forming habits are unlikely to have enough power for the methodist's needs. For instance, they are unlikely to be powerful enough to show that Zande witchcraft theories, as opposed to our medical theories, are irrational. The methodist needs to argue here that the Zande deviation is just a temporary one, and that the transcendental rationality common to all humans will eventually move the Azande round to our point of view. But any universal rationality the second horn of the dilemma leaves us with isn't going to rule out the Zande theories, however long we wait. For what is needed to discredit such traditional theories of this kind are a critical attitude towards received beliefs, and a willingness to perform careful controlled experiments to test such beliefs. And these characteristics are certainly not universal to all human societies.

At best the universal rationality available to the methodist will lead to a widespread suspension of belief. Since neither the Zande theory nor our own is demanded by whatever rationality is common to all human beings, we ought to conclude that there isn't really any fact of the matter. The methodist equates reality with the answers given by the universal canons of rationality. So if rationality doesn't decide between our theory and the Zande one, it follows that reality doesn't contain an answer either. The corollary, then, is surely that we ought to believe neither. And the same, of course, will go for all the other questions undecided by the methodist's universal rationality.

This does not necessarily land the methodist in an entirely incoherent position. The beliefs vindicated by universal rationality might still be enough to live some kind of life by. But the methodist is certainly going to have to abandon a large range of pre-theoretically acceptable beliefs.

6.4   AN ARGUMENT FROM *VERSTEHEN*

I have just argued that a methodist is likely to end up with a widespread suspension of judgement. But suppose we let that pass, and allow that universal principles of rationality will allow the methodist to keep a minimal but workable set of beliefs. There is another difficulty facing the appeal to universal principles of rationality. If the methodist is to claim that such principles make certain answers *inevitable*, it won't suffice that those principles are *in fact* held in common by all human beings. Rather, the methodist needs some principled argument to show that human beings *couldn't* diverge on those principles. (It would scarcely validate something as a 'reality-fixing' principle of rationality if the only reason everybody agreed on it was that the human race happened to die out before anybody dissented.)

What kind of argument might be able to show that certain principles of thought are necessarily common to all thinkers? The only serious candidate is an argument which starts from the idea, touched on in 5.4 above, that the interpretation of human thought is a distinctive matter of *understanding* (or *verstehen*, to use the German term often attached to this idea). Recall the principle of humanity. According to this principle, if we find it unintelligible that people should make a certain judgement, then we must have misidentified the content of that judgement. Suppose now that we think of intelligibility as a matter of *appreciating* the judgement from the subject's point of view, of seeing how it might make *sense*, in the subject's circumstances, to believe *that*. And suppose that making sense of a subject's belief in this way depends on our being able to see how it was *rational* for the subject to adopt that belief in those circumstances. Then it would seem to follow, from the very idea of a judgement having a content, that all human thought must conform to the principles of rationality. If somebody is indeed making a judgement, then it must make sense, given their circumstances, for them to believe what they do. That is so the argument goes, it must be rational for them to have that belief.[1]

---

[1] One interesting recent attempt to defend anti-realism of method by such an argument is Jonathan Lear's (1982). Lear takes the later Wittgenstein to be arguing that, although our ways of thinking have no higher authority, there is no real alternative to our being 'minded' the way we are. Lear reads the stories about people who measure piles of wood by cross-section, or who 'go on' differently after 1,000, not to show that we could do things differently, but, on the contrary, to show that we can make no good sense of anybody being 'minded' other than we are. (See also Stroud, 1965.)

There are of course difficulties, familiar to students of the 'hermeneutic' tradition, with this argument from *verstehen*. What if an interpreter's ability to make sense of some judgement is conditioned by his or her own intellectual background? What, indeed, if an interpreter's conception of what it is rational to believe can be altered by the very activity of trying to interpret an alien culture? Clearly these possibilities threaten any attempt to derive universal rationality from a transcendental argument about interpretation. But I shall ignore these complications, since I have a rather more fundamental line of objection to the appeal to *verstehen*.

My complaint is that from the perspective of the naturalized, functionalist view of belief defended in the previous chapters, the argument from *verstehen* carries little weight. Functionalism sees human beliefs as part of the causal structure of the natural world. To explain a human belief is simply to locate it in that causal structure. There is no distinctive mode of *understanding* by which we account for human beliefs. There are simply the causal explanations that we give for natural events in general.

Functionalism doesn't necessarily deny that there is a phenomenon of empathetically appreciating another's point of view, a phenomenon of experiencing what it would be like to make a given judgement in given circumstances. But for a functionalist such empathetic phenomenology is neither necessary nor sufficient for the explanation of a belief. Once we have identified the causal workings of another subject's mind, then we are in a position to explain his or her mental states, even if we can't imagine ourselves thinking similarly. And, conversely, the fact that a certain judgement makes sense to us does not guarantee explanation, for the subject in question may not be causally disposed to respond to evidence in the same way as we are.

It may well be, the functionalist will allow, that in many cases the only feasible way to identify someone else's cognitive mechanism is to imagine oneself having it. But this is a long way short of saying that explanation just *is* imagining oneself in another person's place. From the functionalist point of view, the limits of our imagination erect only a practical barrier to explanation, not a principled boundary.

Of course those committed to the hermeneutic tradition are unlikely to have much sympathy with functionalism in the first place. In particular, they would no doubt have dug their heels in at the point in the last chapter (5.4) where I argued that once we accept the principle of humanity we can scarcely avoid full-fledged functionalism. My argument, remember, was that, since humanity forces us to recognize that we can explain beliefs by *some* circumstances other than their truth conditions, why not allow the idea of *all* the possible causes of a belief? But the hermeneutician will complain that this argument begs the question. For, as I observed at the time, it takes it for granted that we explain false beliefs by identifying their non-truth-conditional *causes*. According to the hermeneutician, however, we explain such beliefs by showing how it could *make sense* to accept them in the relevant circumstances. The hermeneutician will deny that the principle of humanity brings in non-truth-conditional causes, and will thereby block the move to the idea of a full causal role: humanity only shows that it can make sense to accept a belief even though it is false, and this tells us nothing about causes at all.

Whether *verstehen* or causal explanation is the appropriate model for understanding mental life has long been a matter of fundamental philosophical debate. I can scarcely hope to resolve it in a few brief comments. However it does seem to me that the whole idea of *verstehen* as a distinctive mode of understanding loses its appeal once we reject the idea of incorrigible private access to mental 'givens'. To many people, I know, it seems obvious that we have a special way of knowing about our own mental states. And then it is natural enough to suppose that a proper appreciation of somebody else's beliefs comes from imagining what those beliefs are like for them: we need to recreate their beliefs from the inside, so to speak, and in particular to grasp the way they appear to be rational to the subject. But the original idea, that we have a distinctive mode of access to our own mental states, is part of believing in 'givens'. Once we reject givens, we ought to accept that our non-inferential knowledge of our own mental states derives from a fallible perceptual mechanism (introspection) of the same status as our other sensory mechanisms (cf. 7.6 below). And then we ought also to reject the idea that other people's mental states need to be explained in a way different from the way we explain anything else.

We shouldn't think of the identity of beliefs as constituted from the inside, by the phenomenology of what it is like to be persuaded that a given belief is true. Rather beliefs can perfectly adequately be identified from the 'third-person' perspective which presents them as normal items in the natural world. And, then, given this third-person perspective, there is no need to think of their explanation as requiring some distinctive mode of *verstehen*. If they are normal items in the natural world, mental states can adequately be explained by being located in the causal structure of that natural world.

Let me briefly sum up the argument of this chapter. Methodism needs not only to show that the deliverances of rationality cannot but be true (I've yet to consider Dummett's and Putnam's arguments on this point), but also needs to show that in some sense rationality is universal. This requirement of universality obviously means that not all methods of perception, memory, and interference can be counted as canons of rationality. On the other hand, any set of methods that are universal threatens to leave us with a widespread suspension of belief. Worse, methodism needs to find some principled reason why divergence on such methods is impossible. The only candidate seems to be the argument from *verstehen*. But the idea of *verstehen* as a distinctive mode of explanation seems to presuppose a metaphysics of 'givens'.

7

Naturalized Epistemology

7.1 THE EVALUATION OF METHODS

What happens if we reject methodism, and accept divergence of methods? What happens if we abandon the attempt to identify underlying universals of thought which can be considered to constitute 'reality', and accept, as seems natural, that patterns of human belief-formation vary from time to time and place to place?

The obvious question which then arises is: how can anybody ever assure themselves that their habits of thought are correct? By rejecting methodism we allow that 'truth' means something more than deriving from authorized canons of rationality. And so we allow that for any given method of belief-formation there is a substantial question about its suitability for delivering truths. But how can we ever find out about such suitability?

Compare the situation with that which arises from the rejection of anti-realism of belief. When we allowed that alternative beliefs are possible and therefore need deciding between, there was an obvious recourse: we could appeal to principles of rationality, to standards of belief-evaluation, to show us which amongst the alternatives were to be accepted. But what are we to do once we allow that alternative standards of rationality are themselves possible, and so have to be decided between in turn? How can thought possibly step outside itself to adjudicate on the standards which govern it? Who is going to judge the judges?

I suspect the real attraction of methodism lies not so much in the positive arguments (such as they are) in its favour, but rather in the difficulty of seeing how to proceed if we reject it. Surely, one feels, there must be some point at which we will no longer be able to *show* that our ways of thinking are the right ones. Justification has to stop somewhere. And once we get to that point, hadn't we better insist that the conceptual gap between thought and reality has closed? Otherwise it seems inevitable that we will be stuck with questions we cannot answer.

But in fact this difficulty is more apparent than real. Some of the ideas developed in earlier chapters indicate a perfectly straightforward way of evaluating alternative methods of belief-formation.

In chapters 3 and 4 I developed what we could call a *naturalized* approach to belief and truth. Beliefs were explained as functional states individuated by the causal role they played in the natural world. And then truth itself was explained naturalistically, as the obtaining of that state of affairs that it was the biological purpose of any given belief to occur in the presence of.

Once we have naturalized belief and truth in this way, then we can also naturalize the notion of a belief-forming habit. That is, we can work with the notion of a person's dispositions to form beliefs of given types in given natural circumstances. And then, still in a naturalistic spirit, we can raise the question of the reliability of those habits for truth. That is, we can ask, of any given belief-forming habit, whether or not the beliefs it gives rise to are usually true.

Now, there is nothing to stop somebody asking such questions about their own belief-forming habits. They can consider what belief-forming habits they themselves actually engage in, and they can consider whether or not those habits are reliable for truth. And the answer to this last question will then have obvious evaluative implicatons. For people will generally want to continue with just those habits that are reliable for truths, and to eschew those which aren't.

Let me illustrate with a simple example. Many naïve observers are visually disposed to form the belief that they are viewing something green if they view certain red objects (London buses, say) in sodium lighting. But such people are also generally quite capable of discovering that sodium lighting is deceptive in this way (I can remember discovering this) and then ceasing to form the relevant beliefs automatically in the relevant circumstances (I no longer end up believing that red buses are green when I see them in sodium lighting).

This, then, is my general model for the evaluation of belief-forming methods. People can reflect on the dispositions that give rise to their beliefs. Moreover, they can reflect on whether those habits are such as to give them true beliefs reliably. And then they can endorse or reject those habits accordingly.

I trust that the initial idea of such evaluations is clear. Much more will be said about the epistemological significance of such reliability-evaluations in what follows. But, first, lest it be thought that the sodium lighting example just given is essentially trivial, I want to show how some entirely analogous evaluations of perceptual processes have been important in the evolution of human thought.

The kind of case I have in mind arises in connection with the 'theory-dependence of observation' in science. A number of recent writers (Hanson, 1958, Kuhn, 1962, and Feyerabend, 1975) have argued that observation is 'theory-laden', in the sense that scientists from different theoretical camps 'see' different things when looking at the same microscope slide, photographic plate, or section of the heavens.

In the first instance such claims raise as many philosophical questions about the nature of perception as they answer. Are the 'observations' that are supposed to vary across theoretical communities the most basic form of cognitive contact with the natural world? Or are they merely differing 'interpretations', with a more basic level of cognition ('pure experience', 'sense data') remaining constant across communities? More generally, how should we think of basic perception in the first place? Does it consist of cognitive judgements, or sensory images, or what?

I shall have some detailed things to say about the infra-structure of perception in the digression in 7.6 below. But rather than pause at this point, let me simply stipulate for the time being that perception is the *non-inferential adoption of beliefs* in virtue of the operation of the sense organs. After all, our concern here is with *belief*-forming processes: while there is certainly more to say about the structure of perception, our primary interest is the status of processes by which we arrive at beliefs. And from this point of view the relevant feature of perception is simply that it delivers us beliefs that are not inferred from other beliefs.

Consider now the following example. In the sixteenth century Copernican heliocentrism was vulnerable to the 'tower argument': observation shows that a stone dropped from the top of a tower falls straight down and lands directly below where it is dropped; but if Copernicus were right, and the earth were spinning around, the stone ought to land some distance to the west of that point; so Copernicus is wrong.

Galileo argued that despite appearances such a stone is not falling straight down in an inertial reference frame. He pointed out how a body in fact falling at a slant might be mistakenly taken to be falling vertically if viewed against a moving background, as for instance on a moving ship. And he maintained that this was in fact the situation with respect to falling stones: since the earth is itself moving, people get misled into thinking that slanting stones are falling straight. (Galileo, 1632. See also Feyerabend, 1975, chs 6–11.)

In effect we have here a dispute about the reliability of a perceptual habit. The geocentric opponents of Copernicus were naturally inclined, when confronted with a falling stone, to judge that it was falling *straight down*. But the Copernicans repudiated this practice and advocated that in such cases we should judge that the stone was in fact falling on a slant.

Consider now the thinking that led Galileo to reject the perceptual habit in question. He didn't just repudiate it on the grounds that it gave him observational beliefs which contradicted his favoured astronomical theory. If that were an adequate warrant then anybody would be able to uphold any thoery they liked, by tailoring their observational dispositions *post hoc* to give the desired results. But of course Galileo did better than that. He put forward a detailed account of the perceptual processes involved (we arrive at our perceptual judgements about the direction of fall by comparing the moving body with the background) which implied that the naïve, geocentric perceptual habit was unreliable for truth, by comparison with the more sophisticated Copernican alternative which took the movement of the background into account. So Galileo exemplifies the general pattern for evaluating perceptual habits that I mooted above – identify the relevant habits, and consider their reliability for truth.

Incidentally, I think that this now shows what should be said about 'theory-dependence of observation' in general. It is true that theoretical developments in science can lead to changes in perceptual habits, and in particular to the rejection of naïve past practices. But this doesn't mean that all science is relative. For we aren't entitled to change perceptual habits just because some new astronomical (or biological, or geological, etc.) theory implies that certain apparently non-existent phenomena ought to be observable. If that were enough to justify a new perceptual practice, then we would indeed have complete relativism. However, we need in addition some independent account of the way our sense organs detect the relevant phenomena, an account which implies that the new alternative habit is reliable, where the old habit was unreliable. And the need for such an independent account places a substantial constraint on the revision of perceptual habits, and blocks the door to untrammelled theoretical relativism.

In effect my suggestion here is that we should regard ourselves in the way that we regard measuring instruments. In evaluating the worth of a certain kind of thermometer, say, we consider how reliable it is as an indicator of temperatures. Given our general understanding of such thermometers, is it indeed n°C when such a thermometer reads n°C? So, according to the current proposal, with the evaluation of a given perceptual practice. Given our general understanding of people, is a moving body indeed falling straight down when someone who engages in the perceptual practice in question judges so? And just as we should trust a given kind of thermometer precisely in so far as we know it to be accurate, so we should rely on a given perceptual practice only in so far as our general theories of human perceivers imply that it is reliable.

In the next section I am going to consider how such evaluations of perceptual practices relate to the general problems of epistemology. But before proceeding it will be worth while clarifying one important point. At first sight it might seem as if my suggested strategy for evaluating perceptual practices commits me to 'givens'. Am I not suggesting something along the following lines? When one is unsure about an observation, one should first look into one's mind to note how things appear (the stone *looks* as if it is falling straight down, the bus *looks* green); one should then appeal to the generalizations of perceptual psychology which say how it must be 'out there' for things to be appearing as they are; and one should then infer from these two premises how it in fact is 'out there' (the stone is actually moving rapidly to the east, the bus is actually red). But then am I not taking it for granted that observers are 'given' knowledge of how things *seem* to them?

But this would be a misconstrual of my suggestion. I am not proposing that we should use the generalizations of perceptual psychology in order to license inferences from knowledge of how things appear to conclusions about the way they are. This would indeed require us to take for granted our introspective ability to know how things appear. But, as I say, this is not my line. I do not want to attach any special status to our beliefs as to how things appear.

As I shall explain in 7.6 below, our ability to introspect our sensory experience is best viewed as just one amongst a range of fallible abilities that deliver us beliefs directly without need of inference from other beliefs. We should think of ourselves as having six senses, with introspection playing its part alongside our more familiar sensory abilities to judge 'external', non-mental matters, such as the motion of bodies, the colours of nearby objects, the makes of cars, the identity of people, the sex of chicks, etc. The distinctive feature of all these abilities, the 'external' as well as the introspective, is that the processes leading *up to* the delivery of the beliefs in question lie outside the realm of conscious belief: the *outputs* of these processes form the *starting-point* for our conscious reasonings about the world.

Though qualifications will be needed, for the moment we can usefully think of these processes as simply dumb habits: we simply *find* ourselves with beliefs in response to non-conscious stimuli. And it is *as* such dumb habits that I want to vindicate our perceptual processes, the 'external' world-registering ones along with the introspective mind-registering ones. (In particular, I do not want to vindicate 'external' perceptual abilities merely by replacing them, in the way suggested above, by a conjunction of supposedly 'given' introspections with inferential, non-perceptual processes of thought.)

So my idea is not that our general understanding of how we work as perceivers should be used on particular occasions as premises for arriving at particular conclusions about the observed scene. Rather the suggestion is that they should inform our deliberations when we stand back and reflect on the reliability of the perceptual practice in question, just as we might stand back and reflect on the reliability of a given kind of instrument. Thus, for instance, we might consider whether alcohol thermometers are accurate at temperatures near the boiling point of alcohol. In just the same way we can wonder whether people are to be trusted when they 'register' that an observed stone is falling straight down.

And the upshot of such reflection will not be a theoretical move within our corpus of existing beliefs (such as: since the stone appears to be falling straight down, and since such stones are in fact moving to the east, the stone is moving to the east). Rather it will be the *practical* conclusion that, in so far as we are unreliable, we should reconstruct ourselves as observers. If we decide that alcohol thermometers are unreliable in a certain range, we will redesign them, or replace them by some alternative device. Similarly, if we conclude that certain of our perceptual habits are unreliable, the moral is that we should change ourselves as observers. The practicalities of such changes will be discussed in 7.3 and 7.4 below.

Let me sum up. We embody a set of perceptual belief-forming habits. These deliver beliefs to us in response to non-conscious stimuli. But we can investigate what is going on when these processes operate, and we can thereby reach conclusions on whether these processes are unreliable or not. And if we decide that such a process is unreliable, we should reconstruct ourselves as belief-formers.

7.2 TWO KINDS OF EPISTEMOLOGY

The rejection of methodism left us with a puzzle as to how to judge the judges, how to arrive at reasoned decisions as to which habits of human thought are correct. In response I have introduced the idea of evaluating belief-forming processes with respect to their reliability. And I have produced a couple of cases which I hope provide initially plausible examples of such reliability-evaluations of perceptual habits. In due course I hope also to produce similar examples of reliability-evaluations of memory, inductive and deductive habits. (Henceforth we may as well take 'habits of human thought' to include all perceptual, memory, inductive, and deductive dispositions. Now we have lost interest in 'universals of thought' there is no need to look for anything more complicated or fundamental.)

My eventual aim, however, is not just to suggest that reliability-evaluations provide an initially cogent sense in which the belief-adjudicating judges can be judged, but, more ambitiously, to show that such reliability-evaluations can lead us to solutions to the overall problems of epistemology. That is, I want to show that by concentrating on such reliability-evaluations we will be able fully to understand how we can avoid doxastic error. But showing this will take some time, and, in particular, will involve some re-examination of traditional epistemological preconceptions. Let me make a start in this section by introducing some general considerations about the nature of epistemology.

Let us continue to assume that the primary aim of epistemology is to tell us how to get the right beliefs: epistemology is the science of how to avoid doxastic error. Then we can think of an epistemological *theory* as specifying, at the most general level, a certain kind of *technique* for acquiring beliefs, and as then making the normative *recommendation* that anybody concerned to avoid error should acquire all their beliefs from that technique. When an actual belief derives from the preferred technique, the theory will say it is *justified*. And when a justified belief is also true, then it will be said to be *knowledge* (provided its truth is not an accident relative to its coming from the preferred technique).[1]

Let me now contrast two general epistemological theories of this kind, which I'll call the 'Cartesian' and 'naturalized' theories. The

---

[1] For the general conception of epistemology as a strategy for avoiding error, see Bernard Williams's *Descartes* (1978), pp. 37–48. The clause about knowledge not being an accident is necessary to deal with Gettier cases: a belief can be true, and come from a recommended technique, and yet can fail be to knowledge because in the particular case its truth isn't due to the worth of the technique. (Cf. Gettier, 1963.) Given that I am bypassing the concept of knowledge, I can avoid the difficult task of making this idea precise. But see Peacocke, 1986, ch. 9.

Cartesian theory is both familiar and seductive. But I want to show that the naturalized theory is a preferable rival.

According to the Cartesian theory, the right technique for acquiring beliefs is *inference*. The concerned believer ought to assent only to those beliefs that have been generated by valid steps from secure premises. An actual belief is justified just in case it issues from such an inference.

This Cartesian theory goes hand in hand with 'givens' and the idea that the conscious mind is transparent to itself. According to the Cartesian theory, we are to assent only to those beliefs that follow validly from secure premises. But how are we to select those secure premises? And how, for that matter, are we to ensure that the steps leading from them to the conclusion are indeed valid? In order to avoid the regresses threatening here, the Cartesian theory needs some beliefs whose truth is ensured without inference, and some inferential steps whose validity is immediately apparent. From Descartes on these have been provided by the conscious mind's supposed privileged awareness of its own ideas and the relations between them.

Now for the naturalized theory. According to this theory, the right technique for acquiring beliefs is simply to be a *reliable belief-former*, that is, to have belief-forming processes that generally produce true beliefs. Concerned believers should try to ensure that all their beliefs come from belief-forming processes that are reliable in this sense. An actual belief is justified just in case it issues from a reliable process.[2]

The difference between the naturalized and the Cartesian theory is best brought out by considering how the naturalized theory will deal with perception and memory. According to the naturalized theory, perceptual beliefs and memories will be justified if they

[2] Alvin Goldman's (1976) defends the reliabilist theory of knowledge, and his (1979) defends the more specific view that justification is itself a matter of reliability. An obvious question is *how* reliable a process needs to be to yield justification and knowledge. Goldman discusses this issue in detail in his *Epistemology and Cognition* (1986), chs 3.2 and 5.5. For my purposes the way to decide this issue is not by appeal to existing intuitions about knowledge and justification, but by general reflection on what kind of reliability is needed for the avoidance of error. For more on this see 10.5 below.

come from reliable processes, and will be unjustified if they come from unreliable processes. So a good example of an unjustified belief would be the belief of an observer who judges the direction of falling bodies without being sensitive to the motion of the background: for the process behind this belief is unreliable, in that it characteristically generates false beliefs. Similarly, to take a memory example, people who naïvely succumb to *déjà vu* experiences, and take themselves genuinely to be seeing things for a second time, will have unjustified beliefs, for, again, the process behind their beliefs is unreliable. Of course not all the perceptual and memory processes embodied by human beings are unreliable in this way. In cases where our beliefs do come from reliable processes, the naturalized theory implies straightforwardly that those beliefs are justified.

This now should make it clear that the naturalized notion of justification doesn't necessarily involve conscious inference. The naturalized theory distinguishes perceptual and memory beliefs into justified and unjustified beliefs. But this difference can't be a matter of the former having a superior provenance in conscious inference, for, after all, the distinguishing characteristic of perception and memory is that from the perspective of consciousness they are non-inferential: our perceptual and memory processes deliver beliefs into consciousness, but the processes leading up to those beliefs lie outside consciousness.

Of course Cartesians will analyse the above examples rather differently: since conclusions about the colours of physical objects, or about past occurrences, aren't themselves givens, the Cartesian will represent the careful believer as somehow inferring them from incorrigible knowledge of current sensory or memory experiences, and will distinguish justified and unjustified such conclusions on the basis of the soundness of the inferences involved. (Cf. the idea, dismissed at the end of the last section, that 'external', world-registering perceptual practices should be replaced by a conjunction of givens and inferences.) But the important point here is not that Cartesians will tell a more complicated story, but that epistemological *naturalists* don't have to. Since their notion of justification doesn't demand incorrigible inferences from givens, they can regard a corrigible belief about the external world as justified even if it isn't inferred from anything, provided only that the process generating it is reliable for generating truths.

Some psychologists argue that perceptual beliefs about the external world are the 'conclusions' of 'inferences' which take retinal stimulations as 'premises' and are carried out by various sub-personal non-conscious processes. (Cf. Gregory, 1974.) I don't want to dispute that this is a useful way of analysing the processes by which our cognitive systems generate perceptual beliefs, and indeed I would allow that the terminology of 'conclusions', 'inferences', and so on, can be legitimated by reference to the teleological properties of the processes involved. But we need to be careful with such terminology in the present context of argument. In particular we need to be clear that, since the 'premises' and the 'inferential steps' of such sub-personal processes aren't available for authentication by consciousness, such processes aren't Cartesian justifications. (For more on perceptions as 'inferred' judgements, see 7.6 below.)

I don't want to create the impression that naturalized epistemology has no room for the idea of justification by inference at all. For inferences are themselves belief-forming processes. Given existing beliefs as premises, inference is a process that moves us to new beliefs as conclusions. So, as part of the general recommendation that our belief-forming processes should be reliable, the naturalized approach will recommend that our inferential habits should be reliable too. (Though of course here the appropriate notion of reliability is conditional rather than categorical: the conclusions should be true *if* the premises are.)

So the naturalized approach will certainly allow that a belief's justification can depend on its inferential provenance: if the premises of an inference are themselves reliably generated, then the conclusion of that inference will be justified just in case the inferential habit in question is conditionally reliable for truth.

But note that the naturalized attitude to inference is quite different from the Cartesian attitude. It is not because inference is a conscious phenomenon, transparent to the mind, that inference is good for justifying beliefs. The point is simply that certain kinds of inferential habits reliably generate true conclusions given true premises. Consciousness doesn't come into it. From the naturalized perspective, if a completely non-conscious being had mental states sophisticated enough to be called 'beliefs', and if those beliefs were reliably generated, then they would be justified.

7.3   CAN NATURALIZED EPISTEMOLOGY BE NORMATIVE?

I want to have it that epistemology is a subject with practical implications: it advises us on how to avoid error. However, it might be unclear from the above remarks how the naturalized theory, as opposed to the traditional Cartesian approach, could possibly contribute to this practical enterprise.

The naturalized theory urges that we should get all our beliefs from reliable processes. But if we try to follow this recommendation we seem to face an awkward dilemma. We can either read the recommendation that we seek naturalist justification 'externally', with justification depending on the objective reliability of belief-generating processes, or we can read it 'internally', as placing a requirement on believers' beliefs about where their beliefs come from.

Suppose we read it 'externally'. Then justification depends on facts about the reliability of processes some of which lie outside the domain of consciousness. But how then can such 'justification' be of any significance to a believer concerned to avoid error? Such a believer won't necessarily know whether or not the processes involved are reliable. So how can the fact of their reliability or unreliability possibly influence the concerned believer in deciding what to believe?

Alternatively, we can read the naturalized recommendation 'internally', as recommending that for any given belief we need to have a further belief to the effect that the original belief was reliably produced. But then we face a particularly obvious version of the familiar regress. (What about that further belief about reliability? Do we need to believe that *that* was reliably produced? And so on.)

But this dilemma only seems damning because the grip of the Cartesian approach is so strong. The very posing of the dilemma takes it for granted that what the concerned believer needs is *inferences*: the trouble on the 'external' horn is supposed to be that, since the relevant facts are unknown, they can't enter into the concerned believer's conscious inferences; and the trouble on the 'internal' horn is supposed to be that we end up with a regress, as soon as we try to get the relevant facts into the concerned believer's inferences.

The naturalized theory, however, denies that concerned believers need to seek out inferences in the first place. It recommends instead that they should simply aim to be reliable belief-formers. So it straightforwardly begs the question against the naturalized theory to read it as putting forward a recommendation as to how better to perform inferences. That's the very point at issue between the naturalized and Cartesian approaches.

Perhaps it still seems unclear how the naturalized approach can be of any practical help. But once we free ourselves from the Cartesian idea that better inferences are the only way for concerned believers to improve themselves, nothing could be simpler. You want to be a reliable belief-former? Well then, you'd better do what has to be done to bring this about. In particular, you'd better investigate what belief-forming processes you embody, and you'd better consider what alternative such habits you might adopt. And then you'd better investigate which of those habits, actual and possible, are reliable for generating truths. And having done all that, you should take steps to rid yourself of any bad, unreliable habits you already have, and take steps to instil any good, reliable ones that are open to you.

Recall the discussion of Galileo's evaluation of the pre-Copernican perceptual habit at the end of 7.1 above. I argued there that Galileo's critique shouldn't be thought of as giving rise to new theoretical conclusions *within* our body of beliefs, but rather as having the practical consequence that we ought to *reconstruct* ourselves as belief-formers. This general idea now turns out to be crucial to an appreciation of the normative import of naturalized epistemology. Given the naturalized theory, the appropriate discipline for concerned believers isn't to be more careful about the theoretical inferences they make within their body of existing beliefs. Rather they should do what they can to make sure they are suitably constructed for arriving at the right beliefs in the first place.

The naturalized idea is that you should think of yourself as a system for generating true beliefs. You want to be as reliable such a system as possible. So you should consider ways of redesigning the system, and should implement those that promise an improvement.

In so far as you succeed in so making yourself a reliable belief-former, there will be no further need for any Cartesian introspections into the soundness of your mental moves. For a reliable belief-former is *per se* someone whose initial beliefs are generally true and whose further inferences are generally truth-preserving. And so once the work of reconstruction has been carried out, you can retire from epistemological endeavour and lie back and enjoy the fruits of your labours.[3]

Let me finish this section by using these last remarks to help with a couple of general objections to the idea that knowledge and justification depend on reliable processes. Alvin Goldman and Christopher Peacocke have both argued that having a reliable process isn't in itself enough for knowledge, for it might just be a matter of luck that the process is reliable (Goldman, 1986, pp. 51–2; Peacocke, 1986, p. 140). To take Goldman's example, suppose that Humperdink, the gullible student of Elmer Fraud, the bad mathematician, generally used Fraud's defective algorithms to find answers to mathematical questions. However, one of the algorithms Humperdink learns from Fraud just happens to be correct. This algorithm is a reliable belief-forming process. But surely Humperdink's belief in the answers it produces isn't justified knowledge.

Peacocke suggests a neat solution: not only do you need to have a reliable process, but your having it needs to be due to its being

[3] The normative import of the reliabilist approach to epistemology is discussed in some of Goldman's recent papers (1978, 1980, 1985). Much of what he says there is consistent with my arguments. But at the same time it seems to me that Goldman has not fully freed himself from the Cartesian perspective: see p. 30, (1980), where he argues that the inputs to 'doxastic decision principles' must be *'available'* to the cognizer, and also p. 40, (1985), where the same claim is implicit. In *Epistemology and Cognition* (1986) Goldman mentions the possibility of revising belief-forming processes in the Introduction (p. 3) and on the last page (p. 380); but apart from that he ignores the possibility, and treats our mental mechanisms as effectively immutable. Michael Devitt touches on the normative aspects of naturalized epistemology in his (1984), ch. 5.8.

reliable (1986, p. 141).[4] Peacocke is here thinking primarily of the fact that natural selection has given us certain mental mechanisms because they are reliable. But the point can be expanded. For instance, certain kinds of trial-and-error learning can also be argued to 'select' processes in virtue of their reliability (cf. 4.2). And, more generally, the argument of this section shows how subjects might consciously recognize that a certain process is reliable, and so come to adopt it for just that reason. I shall take Peacocke's point as read from now on: a reliable process won't yield justified beliefs unless its adoption is somehow due to its reliability. (Note that this *doesn't* mean that you aren't justified unless you have consciously reflected on the reliability of your processes. The point is simply that such conscious reflection, plus subsequent action if necessary, is one way, along with genetic evolution and unreflective learning, in which Peacocke's requirement can be satisfied.)

The requirement that a justificatory process's adoption must be explainable by its reliability helps with a further issue, namely, the *individuation* of processes. What counts as a single process for the purposes of assessing reliability? Is 'visual perception', say, one process? Or does visual perception include many different processes, such as 'recognizing magenta', 'recognizing heptagons', 'recognizing my aunt', etc.? Clearly, without some constraints on how processes are to be individuated, assessments of reliability will be radically underdetermined. In particular, it looks as if it will be too easy to get high reliability, simply by cutting very broad ('visual perception'), or by cutting very fine ('recognizing my aunt').

I suggest that we appeal here to the requirement that if a process is to yield justification its adoption must be explainable by its reliability, and stipulate that the properties used to individuate reliable processes should be ones that play a role in such explanations. I take it that this will rule out 'recognizing my aunt'

---

[4] Goldman's solution is that our first-order processes need to be acquired (or sustained) by second-order processes which are themselves reliable for producing reliable (first-order) processes. This is roughly a corollary of Peacocke's requirement. But Goldman's way of putting it makes it seem that a regress threatens. (It is worth noting that Peacocke is not himself a reliabilist about knowledge. He thinks that reasons are also necessary for knowledge. Cf. 1986, Ch. 10.)

as a reliable process, for surely the explanation of my having this ability won't be that *it* is reliable, but rather that it is an instance of a more general process ('face recognition', say) which is explained by its reliability.

In addition, we need to require that we cut as finely as is consistent with the constraint of the last paragraph. There's a perfectly good sense in which our having *visual perception* is explainable by its reliability. But that's not enough to make every true visual judgement justified: consider somebody who truly believes that x is a duck as a result of looking, but can't in fact tell ducks from geese. They way to block this is to recognize that there are various subdivisions within visual perception ('face-recognition', 'shape-perception', 'colour-perception', and, in some people, 'bird-recognition') each of which is explainable by its reliability, and which should therefore be considered separately. Once we make these divisions, the bird-blind person's belief won't count as the product of a reliable process. (The idea of cutting as finely as certain properties allow is in Goldman, 1986, p. 50, though his way of picking out those properties is somewhat different).

7.4 MENTAL HABITS

Let me now say something about belief-forming *habits*. The Cartesian approach presupposes minds capable of some kind of incorrigible inner authentication of beliefs. Naturalism, on the other hand, leads us to think of minds as simply having habits of forming certain beliefs in certain circumstances. But this in itself might seem to raise difficulties for the idea of a naturalized epistemology with normative force. For doesn't the picture of mental operations as mere habits lead to a kind of epistemological quietism, to a denial of the possibility of epistemology, rather than to a programme of *evaluating* habits? Both Wittgenstein (and, in a less general context, Hume) seem to suggest that demands for further justification are inappropriate, once we recognize that our beliefs are forced on us by mere mental habits.

However, there is nothing in the idea of a habit as such to imply that habits can't be evaluated and changed. Certainly in other areas we regard our habits as things we might alter. People decide that it is bad to smoke, or to split their infinitives, and they try to get rid of these bad habits. Why shouldn't I similarly decide that it is a bad thing to judge people's characters by first appearances, or to jump to conclusions about political issues, or, indeed, to succumb to *déjà vu*, or to judge direction of fall without sensitivity to the motion of the background, and so similarly set myself to get rid of these undesirable belief-forming habits?

Of course you can't get rid of a habit just at will: that's part of what it means to call it a 'habit'. But that doesn't mean you can't get rid of it indirectly, by adopting a course of action which will result in the habit disappearing. Getting rid of a linguistic habit offers a good model here. When I set myself to stop splitting my infinitives, I start by consciously monitoring my behaviour, and correcting myself, either privately or publicly, when I notice myself inclined to transgress. After a while my unsplit infinitives become automatic and this monitoring process becomes unnecessary: at which point I have altered my linguistic habits as desired. We can monitor and change our mental behaviour in just the same way. People who succumb to *déjà vu* have a habit, a disposition of mind, which on occasion leads them to form certain beliefs about the past. But when they learn about *déjà vu*, and realize that this habit needs changing, they start to monitor this aspect of their mental behaviour, and correct themselves when they find themselves forming those beliefs. And as a result they end up with their mental disposition changed: where they used to form beliefs to the effect that they were seeing something for the second time, they now no longer do so.[5]

If all our mental habits were inescapably dictated by our genes and early training, then perhaps such reshaping would be

[5] A note on terminology. In his (1986), pp. 93–5, Goldman distinguishes 'processes', which are somehow innate and basic, from 'methods', which are somehow secondary and acquired. I think this distinction is neither clear nor useful. I prefer to think of all belief-forming dispositions alike as mechanisms which govern thinking at a given time, but can be altered over time by appropriate courses of action. I shall use 'habit', 'process', 'disposition', 'mechanism', and 'method' interchangeably in what follows (though I tend to avoid 'method', because of the irrelevant connotations of consciousness).

impossible. But, while there may be some respects in which we are so mentally immutable, I see no reason to suppose that we are incapable of transcending any of our *belief*-forming habits. I don't want to pursue this issue at this point, however: it can more conveniently be dealt with at the end of the digression on perception which comes after the next section.

7.5 WILL THE NATURALIZED STRATEGY SUCCEED IN AVOIDING ERROR?

I turn now to a point which will no doubt have been worrying many readers for some time. So far in this chapter I have suggested that the obvious response to divergence of method is to reflect on the reliability of our belief-forming methods and to revise those methods accordingly, and in addition I have argued that from the perspective of naturalized epistemology this is exactly what anybody concerned to have justified beliefs should do. But even if I have thereby shown how we can sensibly *seek* to have justified beliefs, surely I am still a long way off showing how anybody will *succeed* in getting justified beliefs. In particular, haven't I omitted to say anything about the source and status of the assumptions about the reliability and unreliability that are used to evaluate belief-forming methods?

The problem here is that even if reflection on reliability can have a straightforwardly practical conclusion (reconstruct yourself *qua* belief-former), such reflection will invariably itself be informed by various assumptions about the natural world and how human beings respond to it. Thus we have had the assumption that human beings judge the direction of falling bodies by comparison with the background, or the assumption that green things in sodium lighting look red to human beings, or the assumption that certain hazy feelings of recollection are caused by current brain states rather than previous contact with the scene viewed. And, as we shall see when we come on to the possibility of evaluating and revising inferential habits, we are also going to need assumptions about the logical structure of complex judgements, and about the nature of natural kinds. But where do these assumptions come from? What is their authority? If my eventual aim is to show how reflection on reliability will enable us to avoid error in our beliefs in general, surely such reflections oughtn't to be informed by other beliefs which are themselves simply taken for granted.

An initial point to make here is that these assumptions needn't be entirely arbitrary within the context of the naturalized approach. For they themselves might come from belief-forming methods which the concerned believer has checked for reliability. Let us assume that we are dealing with believers whose concern is global, believers who want *all* their beliefs to be error-free. Such believers will then want to reflect on the reliability of all their belief-forming methods, and to make such revisions to those methods as seem advisable. There is no reason in principle why such believers shouldn't be able to carry out this global check. Any believer will only embody a finite number of belief-forming methods, and so, given sufficient time and energy, ought to be able to survey them all and check their reliability. This might involve some amount of iteration, for revisions of methods will give rise to new beliefs, which might then have new implications as to which methods are unreliable and need revision, and so on. But even so, there is no reason why this process shouldn't terminate, with the believer's total body of beliefs then implying that all his or her belief-forming methods are reliable. When this stage has been reached, the endorsement of any given method will still itself be informed by further beliefs, to the effect that that method is reliable for truth. But these further beliefs won't simply be arbitrary, since, by hypothesis, they themselves will have been generated by methods which the believer has checked for reliability.

But this initial response is scarcely much of an answer to the original worry. Even if globally concerned believers are able to bootstrap themselves into a position where all their methods appear reliable in the light of all the beliefs those methods generate, how much will have been achieved? Won't even such bootstrapped-up believers still merely be people whose belief-forming methods *seem* reliable in the light of their existing beliefs, as opposed to people whose methods actually *are* reliable?

This is a central issue. I want eventually to argue that fully bootstrapped-up believers won't just seem to themselves to be reliable, but will indeed *be* reliable. But I certainly don't want to deny that these are different things, and that this eventual conclusion will require further argument. However, now that we have raised this issue, I would like to shelve it for the time being. For the next two chapters I want to continue discussing the possibility and structure of reliability-evaluations themselves. I shall return to the problem that such evaluations are inevitably informed by corrigible background beliefs in the last chapter.

7.6 DIGRESSION ON PERCEPTION

Before continuing with the main line of argument, I would like to complete this chapter with a discussion of the infra-structure of perception. Pretty much everything said about perceptual processes so far could have been said just as well even if sensory perception had no distinctive phenomenology. My model has been one of pre-conscious processes which have conscious beliefs as outputs. But this model could perfectly well be instantiated by a being that had no sensory experience at all. Just as we can *believe* there is a table in front of us when our eyes are closed, so there seems no reason in principle why a being that never saw or otherwise sensed things should not embody processes that delivered beliefs to it. (Think of people with 'blindsight', who can't *see* whether there is a light in front of them, but who can nevertheless judge the matter reliably if their eyes are aiming in the right direction. Cf. Weiskrantz, 1986.)

But, still, there is a phenomenology of sense experience for most human beings. How does this fit into my account? What do I say about the vibrant passing show of shapes and colours that most of us are aware of? (Most of my remarks will be put in terms of vision, but will apply to some degree to the other senses).

In recent years it has become popular to adopt a *judgemental* account of sensory experience. Instead of thinking of sense experiences as introspectible *things* from the apprehension of which we can infer hypotheses about the rest of the world, the idea is that we should think of sensory experiences as themselves amounting to such hypotheses. To see a table is not first to be aware of some mental image, and thence to hypothesize an external object; the seeing is itself a matter of judging there is a table there.

This suggestion is supported by certain features of our perceptual psychology. Illusions, gestalt switches, and the way in which special trainings can lead people to 'see things differently', all make it plausible to suppose that our visual systems extrapolate from retinal input to conscious sensory output analogously to the way in which a person with certain assumptions might infer judgements about the external world from a two-dimensional description of a retinal image. And this analogy then makes it natural to assume that sensory experiences really are a sort of hypothetical judgement. (For an analysis and defence of such views see Craig, 1976.)

What exactly does it mean on this account to say that things *seem* a certain way? If visual experience itself consists of judgement about the external world, then what are subjects saying when they say that something seems so-and-so? Why don't they just report that it is so, if that's what their vision tells them? The simplest version of the judgemental account explains claims about how things seem as simply a diffident way of asserting that they actually are that way. The report that a tomato *seems red* has just the same content as the claim that it *is red*. The difference is merely one of force, with the former report conveying an element of caution, as for instance when the perception is of a less than conclusive character. (Cf. Quinton, 1955.)

But this account has difficulty with *knowingly experienced illusions*. For example, when I see the Muller–Lyer illusion, one line *seems* longer than the other to me. But at the same time I know (since I am familiar with the phenomenon) that the lines are actually the same length. So we can scarcely construe the 'seems' report as a diffident expression of the belief that the lines are different lengths – for I don't believe that they are different lengths *at all*, let alone diffidently. (Cf. Craig, 1976; Papineau, 1979, ch. 1.5; Fodor, 1984b.)

This possibility of knowingly experienced illusions shows that if sensory experience does indeed consist of judgements, they must be judgements made in a different part of the mind (in a different 'module', in the terminology of Fodor, 1983) from the central part containing the beliefs we stand and act by. For while my visual system, so to speak, judges the Muller–Lyer lines to be of different lengths, *I* am in no doubt that they are the same length. What we seem to need is a model of several different judgemental faculties: first there are the various sensory faculties (visual, tactual, etc.) issuing in lower-level judgements about the external world, and then there is the central faculty, which normally simply 'rubber-stamps' these lower-level judgements and embraces them as they stand, but which can if necessary (as when the sensory faculties conflict, or when other relevant informaton is available) reject a lower-level judgement and adopt a contrary view.

On this view, then, we get a somewhat different account of what it means to say that it *seems* to me that p. This report no longer comes out as a half-hearted assertion of the claim that p (since I needn't believe that p at all), but rather as a report to the effect that one of my sensory systems (my visual system, let us say) is of the opinion that p. That is, when I say it seems to me that p, I am expressing a belief *about* an occurrence in my visual system, a belief to the effect that my visual system has judged that p.

This is where introspection comes in. This latter belief, about what is occurring in my visual system, hasn't been *inferred* from any other belief: for, note, the occurrence in my visual system isn't itself a belief embraced by my central faculty, and so isn't available as a premise for an inference. So we need to recognize that amongst the non-inferential processes that deliver beliefs to us are processes that give us information about the goings-on in our own sensory systems – that is, about how things seem to us.

Given all this, the original question of whether sensory experience itself consists of judgements loses some of its epistemological importance. True, the arguments on the side of the judgemental view of experience are still fairly persuasive: apart from those already mentioned, there is also perhaps the point that the judgemental view allows a natural explanation of the 'rubber-stamping' operation by which our central faculty normally embraces sensory findings. On the other hand, there are reasons for thinking there are aspects to experience other than the judgemental. (Cf. Peacocke, 1983, ch. 1.) But, either way, since sensory experiences aren't themselves beliefs in our central faculty, and so aren't themselves the kind of item on which our basic epistemological concern is focused, it won't matter for my arguments how this issue is decided. The important thing, for our purposes, is that sensory experiences *cause* beliefs (about the external world, when they are 'rubber-stamped', or about themselves, when they are 'introspected'), not the extent to which they themselves are analogous to beliefs.

If the claim that it seems to me that p is a belief *about* an occurrence in one of my sensory systems, oughtn't it to be possible for me to be mistaken about how things seem to me? As I pointed out back in 1.2, when I first mentioned the rejection of 'givens', we ought always to allow the conceptual possibility that any judgement (any belief) that lays claim to something other than itself might be mistaken. Yet is there such a possibility in this case? Can we really be mistaken about how things seem to us?

I don't see why we can't be. Imagine I am looking at a disordered array of a few dots on a piece of paper. When asked how many dots there seem to me to be there, I sincerely reply 'eight'. But when they are actually counted (on the paper) there turn out to be seven. It seems quite possible that in this case it is not my visual system that is awry, but my ability to introspect my visual system. The most plausible analysis here is surely that my visual system has succeeded in representing seven dots (that's the kind of thing visual systems are good at), but that my introspective sense has misinformed my central faculty about the number of dots represented in my visual system. Which is to say that while it did seem to me (visually) that there were seven dots, I mistakenly believed that there seemed to be eight.[6]

---

[6] Cf. the similar example in Evans, 1982, pp. 228–9. Evans, however, is making the contrary point that while such mistakes are conceivable where complex counting operations are involved (in his example there are ten dots, which are too many to be surveyed instantly), they aren't conceivable with simpler judgements about sense experiences. Accordingly he aims to explain the infallibility of such simpler judgements. However, it seems to me that his initial explanation (pp. 227–8), that we make judgements about our experiences by determining what we would judge if we had no extraneous information, (a) makes such judgements implausibly counterfactual, and (b) doesn't make it obvious why such judgements should be infallible. And his further explanation (p. 229), that it's constitutive of concepts of sense experience that we be disposed to apply them in response to those experiences, requires 'disposed' to be read in a very strong sense if it is to yield infallibility.

Perhaps this example seems contrived. For a convincing example of introspection generating a false belief about experience, don't I really need a case where I am aware *internally* of the experience, am aware that things seem p, even though I *believe* that the experience is different, even though I believe things seem not-p? Isn't it cheating if the only way of finding out how many dots appear to me to be there is by counting them on the paper?

I don't think so. Consider what is now being asked for here: a case where we can somehow tell internally that things seem p, even though we believe they seem not-p. But how are we supposed to 'tell internally' how things seem, if this is supposed to mean something more than merely *having* the experience, as I arguably had the experience of seven dots? Surely only by exercising our introspective faculty, and getting a belief about the matter. So to get to 'tell internally' that things seem a certain way while believing the opposite, would seem to require that introspection simultaneously delivers the belief that our visual system is judging that p and the belief that our visual system is judging that not-p. Maybe that's not impossible. But it's scarcely surprising it doesn't happen. I am committed to the view that introspection can generate the belief that things seem p, when in fact they don't seem p. But that doesn't commit me to the unlikely further possibility of introspection simultaneously delivering the contradictory beliefs that things seem p *and* that they don't.

Our everyday language rather lets us down here. There is a sense in which if I am in pain, then I can't but 'know' that I'm in pain. And if something seems green to me, then I can't but 'know' that it seems green. And perhaps in this sense, if I visually experience seven dots, then I can't but 'know' that there seem to be seven dots. But in this sense 'knowing that I am in pain', or 'knowing that it seems green', or 'knowing that there seem to be seven dots' shouldn't be taken necessarily to imply that I have any beliefs about my experience. It simply conveys the fact that there is a phenomenology of pain, and of visual experience: there is *something that it is like*, in Thomas Nagel's phrase (1974), for me to have a pain, and for things to seem green or sevenfold to me.

Of course if I'm in pain then, in this phenomenological sense, I 'know' all about it. But why assume that its being 'like something' in this sense for me to experience x, necessarily carried with it my having a propositional belief to the effect *that I am experiencing x*? Mightn't I have the phenomenology of a certain experience (as of seeing seven dots) and yet believe that I am having a different experience?

Wittgenstein took it, quite rightly, that any judgement, properly so-called, had to admit the possibility of error. But he didn't think you could doubt whether you were in pain. So he concluded that the report 'I am in pain' ('It seems to me green', etc.) didn't in fact express a proper judgement, a claim that could be true or false, but merely evinced an experiential state, as a groan or a scream would (Wittgenstein, 1953, especially 244–6). It seems to me that he would have done better to distinguish a phenomenological sense of 'knowing you are in pain', in which it is true that you must 'know' about it if you are in pain, and a judgemental sense, in which it is conceptually possible for your judgement as to whether you are in pain to be mistaken. (See also Dennett, 1978a, for the inability of our everyday concepts to cope with the complex psychology of pain.)

Let me now return briefly to a question left up in the air in 7.4: to what extent are our mental processes immutably fixed by our genes and early training?

It seems to me crucial here to distinguish between the processes which give rise to sensory experiences themselves, and the processes which give rise to beliefs. The argument of this section indicates the following model. Peripheral sensory stimulation leads in the first instance to sensory *experiences*. In the normal ('rubber-stamping') course of events, there is then a further process whereby the experience causes a *belief* about the external world. There is also the other possible further process in which the experience is introspected and this leads to a belief about the experience itself.

Let us first address the question of the immutability of *experience*-producing processes. This is itself a topic of much recent debate. Many of the advocates of the 'theory-dependence of observation' stress that it is not just the beliefs about the external world ('interpretations') of different scientists that vary with their theories, but the very experiences themselves. And certainly many of the examples, of X-ray tubes, of cell recognition in microscopes, and so on, make a plausible case for just this conclusion. But at the same time it is clear that some of the more extreme recent claims to the effect that scientists always experience things in accord with their theories are over-ambitious. No amount of theoretical indoctrination enabled phlogiston theorists to *see* beam balances tilting in directions that would indicate that 'dephlogisticated' substances lose weight, or enabled Galileo to *see* bodies falling on a slant, or indeed, *pace* Hanson (1958), enabled Kepler to *see* the earth rotating. So we need to recognize that there are probably some experiential responses that are not mutable by adult re-education.

But – and this is the central point I want to make here – this leaves the question of whether our *doxastic* responses are so mutable entirely open. Even if things go on *seeming* the same way, it by no means follows that humans will go on believing they are the same way. We Copernicans believe that the earth is rotating and that freely falling bodies are moving on a slant in any inertial reference frame, even though it doesn't look like it. And in general it seems to me that one of the reasons we human being are so clever is precisely that we are always capable of suspending any given *belief*-forming habit and replacing it with another, even if we're stuck with the experience involved. (Which, incidentally, shows that the non-mutability of experience itself is irrelevant to the relative worries raised by the 'theory-dependence of observation', *pace* the argument in Fodor, 1984b. If we always have room to alter our doxastic responses to fit in with our theories, what consolation is it that brute non-doxastic feelings are constant across theoretical camps? The appropriate response to the theory-dependence of observation was outlined in 7.1 above, and was quite independent of questions of phenomenology.)

8

Naturalized Realism

8.1 COHERENCE AND CORRESPONDENCE

I have now argued that, far from being prisoners of our existing belief-forming processes, we are quite capable of evaluating and adjusting those processes. We can take active steps to make our belief-forming processes reliable and our beliefs thereby justified (even if it yet remains to be shown that such attempts will actually succeed).

In the last chapter I dealt mainly with perceptual processes, and, to a lesser extent, with memory. I haven't yet explained how the idea of evaluations for reliability might apply to deductive and inductive inferential processes. But rather than tackling this topic directly, it will be more convenient to go off at something of a tangent, and first try to bring out the way in which the reliability-evaluation strategy commits us to an essentially *realist* view of the relation between thought and the world. I shall return to inferential processes in the next chapter.

The above claim about realism might at first sight seem somewhat surprising. I suggested in the last chapter that believers with a global concern to avoid error will achieve intellectual stability when they have a set of belief-forming *processes* which give them a body of *beliefs* which imply in turn that those processes are reliable. But isn't this just to say that globally concerned believers are aiming for a kind of *coherence* within their intellectual stance? And isn't coherence a quite different aim from the realist goal of correspondence with reality?

But this is much too quick. I do indeed want to say that concerned believers ought ideally to reach a state where the beliefs delivered by their belief-forming methods imply in turn that those belief-forming methods are all reliable. If somebody's intellectual position lacks this kind of coherence, with the beliefs generated failing to vindicate the methods involved as reliable, then that person should adjust those methods, until such time as the adjusted methods do deliver beliefs which vindicate those adjusted methods as reliable.

But the coherence so required for such epistemological stability should not be confused with the coherence notion of *truth* which is an alternative to the correspondence notion.

The 'coherence theory of truth' is the anti-realist doctrine that the ultimate aim of belief is to be part of a maximally coherent set of beliefs. Reality, on this doctrine, just *is* the picture presented by this maximally coherent set. (In my terms this is a version of anti-realism of method, in which the central methodological prescription is to make your beliefs coherent.)

The kind of coherence I am interested in differs from the notion we get from the coherence theory of truth in a number of respects. In the first place, my coherence is a coherence between processes *and* beliefs, not just a coherence within a corpus of beliefs alone. And, consequently, it isn't achieved just by adjustments within the realm of mental judgement, but by our acting in the world, by our changing the way that we react as natural beings to natural facts.

More pertinently, the kind of coherence I am interested in, far from competing with the correspondence notion of truth, itself embodies a concern with that notion. What we want of our corpus of beliefs is that they should imply that our methods are reliable for producing *truths*. And truth here means truth as correspondence to an independent reality.

Remember the teleological theory of representation. This gave us a conception of beliefs being true or false depending on how the world independently is. It is this notion of truth as correspondence that our evaluation of belief-forming methods aims at. Belief-forming methods generate beliefs as 'outputs' from perceptible circumstances (or other beliefs) as 'inputs'. What we want of those methods is that they should generate beliefs as outputs only when things are independently such as to make those outputs true. (In particular, what we want of non-inferential methods is that they should be causally triggered to produce their output belief only by

the truth condition of that belief, or by some condition which
reliably causes that truth condition.)

From this point of view coherence isn't *per se* the aim of
epistemologically concerned believers. What such believers want is
beliefs which correspond to the facts. Coherence, in the relevant
sense, only comes in because the way to achieve this is to attempt to
ensure that your processes are reliable, and since such attempts will
inevitably be informed by certain beliefs, concerned believers will
not be able to rest until their beliefs and processes fit each other
appropriately. Coherence is thus a necessary corollary of
epistemological success, but it is not itself what epistemology aims
at.

8.2 THE INELIMINABILITY OF REALIST TRUTH

Some readers may remain unconvinced. Maybe I can formulate the
idea of reliability-evaluations in a way that makes mention of a
realist notion of truth as correspondence. But is the realist notion of
truth doing any real work here? Perhaps the relevant ideas can be
alternatively formulated without bringing in realist truth.

After all, how *could* realist truth possibly play an essential part in
epistemological evaluations, given that we have no independent
access to the putative reality which is supposed to stand at the
other end of the truth relation? Surely our epistemological
predicament means that any suggestion as to how to revise our
intellectual stance has eventually to collapse into the comparison of
some beliefs with others for coherence.

I think that this is a bad line of thought. It rests on the old
Cartesian picture of internal viewing rooms with inaccessible
exteriors. That is, it presupposes that we have direct access to our
own beliefs, and so can compare them for coherence, but have no
such access to the objects of those beliefs.

Still, the idea that only a coherence theory of truth can possibly
be relevant to epistemology, and that the notion of correspondence
can do no real work, has exerted a powerful hold on many thinkers,
and it will be worth exploring the possibility of an epistemology
based entirely on a coherence theory of truth in some detail. My

aim will be to show that such a coherentist epistemology will inevitably suffer certain deficiencies, which deficiencies can only be remedied by the introduction of a realist notion of truth.

The aim of a coherentist epistemology is not that our beliefs should correspond to the facts, but rather that we should have as large as possible a body of beliefs which also satisfies the requirement of internal coherence. Suppose we start with the particular perceptual judgements made by human beings about the natural world, judgements about the shapes and sizes of particular objects, about the motions of stones and stars, and so on. The issue of coherence arises because in addition to such particular perceptual judgements, people can also formulate inductive generalizations, like the assumptions of astronomy, and of dynamics, and many more familiar common-sense generalizations, which can 'bind together' the particular judgements into a *coherent* theoretical system.

Sometimes new perceptual judgements contradict established general assumptions. One way of restoring consistency in such a case is simply to drop the contradicted general assumption. But this would then reduce the overall coherence of the system. So from a coherentist point of view it can sometimes be preferable to keep the generalization and *reject* the anomalous perceptual judgement instead.

So this then gives us a possible coherentist alternative to the supposedly realist approach to epistemology introduced in the last chapter. In particular, this alternative seems to allow for the possibility of evaluating and rejecting perceptual judgements, in something like the way discussed in the last chapter, but without any mention of any realist notion of truth.

But let us look a bit more closely. According to the suggested coherentism, perceptual judgements get rejected if they fail to cohere, modulo our general theories, with other perceptions. But note now that there is nothing in this as it stands to motivate the revision of perceptual *processes* as such. The focus of the coherentist story, as told so far, is the acceptability of particular perceptual judgements, not the worth of the processes behind them. So far the coherence requirement has been imposed on the output of perceptual processes, rather than on the processes themselves.

So it seems as if the coherentist will be faced with an everlasting supply of bad perceptions. For if the underlying processes remain unchanged, then what is to stop new, incoherent perceptions keeping on coming in, just as fast as the old ones are thrown out?

But perhaps this is unfair. It is true that traditional versions of anti-realism, such as phenomenalism, find it difficult to give any serious analysis of where the deliverances of the senses come from. If the whole world consists of mental images, then what space is left to locate the processes that produce those images? Which is why from the point of view of traditional anti-realism the only way of evaluating perceptions does seem to be the *post hoc* disqualification as 'unreal' of those images that don't cohere with the rest.

But there doesn't seem to me any real reason why a modern coherentist anti-realism should be constrained in this way. Provided coherentists steer clear of the mental metaphysics of 'givens', why shouldn't they take an interest in the (fallible) processes that produce our basic judgements? After all, why shouldn't coherentists accept, along with their other generalizations about the workings of the world, psychological generalizations about the way humans respond perceptually to circumstances? And what is this except to say that coherentists recognize the existence of processes giving rise to our perceptual judgements? And so why shouldn't coherentists be able to advocate the practical alteration of those processes themselves? If they recognize that such processes exist, and indeed that some of them persistently give rise to unwanted perceptual judgements, then why aren't they as well placed to recommend that we change those processes as anybody else?

But now let us focus on the grounds on which such changes will be recommended. For the coherentist a perceptual process will need changing if the particular perceptual judgements it gives rise to fail to cohere with the rest of our beliefs. Contrast this with the realist motivation for such changes. Realists want perceptual processes to be changed when the particular perceptual judgements they give rise to are *false*.

It mightn't seem as if there is much in it here. Or, rather, it might seem that at this point the realist story does indeed collapse into coherentism. After all, how are realists ever going to tell that a particular perceptual judgement is false, except by comparing it for coherence with the rest of our corpus of established beliefs? Do they think that we can somehow step outside the world of belief, and judge truth and falsity by direct inspection of the real world? Maybe realists can *say* that what they dislike in perceptual processes is the production of 'false' judgements. But what can this mean, except that those judgements fail to cohere with the rest of what we believe?

These might look like a damning objection to my insistence that we can't avoid realism. But it is not a good argument. Think back to some of the earlier examples of perceptual processes which were argued to be unreliable for truth. For instance, consider the naïve disposition to judge that London buses seen in sodium lighting are green. Now, one way of finding out that this disposition is unreliable is indeed to note that it yields particular judgements to the effect that such-and-such buses are green, and then to note that these judgements are incoherent with certain other of our particular beliefs (such as that the buses in question are red in the daytime), modulo the generalization that buses don't change colour without being painted.

But there are other ways of concluding that the process is unreliable, which don't require us to investigate whether or not its particular output judgements are coherent with the rest of our beliefs. Thus, for instance, we might find out that the wavelengths emitted by sodium lighting are such as to make red things reflect a wavelength profile very much like the one produced by green things in normal lighting. And this then would suggest that unreconstructed observers will believe that red things seen in sodium lighting are green. And all this could be discovered by people who had *never made a particular judgement about a particular red object in sodium lighting*, and so had never been in a position to compare that particular judgement with the rest of their beliefs for coherence.

To take another example of an unreliable process, consider the pre-Copernican tendency to judge that dropped stones are falling straight down. Again, one way of finding out that this process is unreliable would be to note that it issues in particular judgements that such-and-such stones are falling straight down, and then to note that these judgements are incoherent (modulo the general assumptions of heliocentrism) with other of our beliefs, and in particular with beliefs about particular stones landing directly below where they were dropped. But we could also discover that people judge movement by comparison with the background, and this would in itself tell us that naïve observers will be unreliable about falling stones, even if we ourselves had never seen a falling object.

Let me spell the point out. I want to think of humans as natural beings interacting with the natural world. And I want to think of truth in the way indicated by the teleological theory of representation, that is, as a relation between belief states and circumstances in the world. But this then means that the degrees of reliability or unreliability of our perceptual processes are themselves natural facts, as much within the scope of our general theories of the world as any other natural facts. And so there is no need to rely on direct inductive inferences from past incoherences of output to decide whether or not a given perceptual process is reliable. For we can well figure this out indirectly, from our more general theories of the workings of the world, whenever such theories tell us whether or not the relevant perceptions are usually caused by their truth conditions (or by reliable causes of those truth conditions). Thus our theories of colour perception and the sodium spectrum can tell us that naïve observers will judge red things to look green in sodium lighting; and similarly our general theories about perception of movement can tell us that naïve subjects will judge falling bodies to be falling straight down. In both these cases we can conclude that these naïve processes are not in general triggered by the truth conditions of their output beliefs, and are thus unreliable, even if we've never had any opportunity directly to compare particular outputs for coherence with other beliefs.

But perhaps the coherentist isn't beaten yet. I've been assuming that any conclusions about unreliability of processes for *coherence* have to be inferred directly and inductively from the incoherence of specific outputs of those processes with other beliefs (and thus I've argued that only realists can accommodate the possibility of inferring unreliability indirectly from more general theories). But why so? Why can't coherentists themselves appeal to general theories of how humans respond to the world, in order indirectly to reach conclusions that certain perceptual processes characteristically produce results that are incoherent with the rest of our beliefs? Indeed why can't coherentists appeal to just the same theories that realists appeal to in this context? Thus they might argue that since green objects viewed in sodium lighting produce the same reflectance profiles as red objects viewed in normal light, and since falling bodies do not move with respect to the terrestrial background, the perceptual processes behind naïve observations of sodium-lit colour, or behind naïve observations of direction of terrestrial fall, will generally produce outputs which are incoherent with other beliefs.

But let us look more closely at the details of the proposed coherentist reasoning here. Coherentists will appeal to the fact that in sodium lighting naïve observations, to the effect that something is green, will generally be caused by a red object, and will thence conclude that such judgements will fail to cohere with other independently derived judgements bearing on the colour of the object in question. But having come this far, why not just say that in general the naïve observational judgements are *false*, in that they fail to correspond to the facts, and admit that it is only via this realist claim, plus the assumption that further independently derived judgements bearing on the matter will tend to be *true*, that we conclude that the naïve observations in question will tend not to cohere with such further judgements? For surely what is really going on here, when coherentists argue that the process in question is unreliable for coherence, is that they implicitly recognize that the output judgements (*x is green*) get made in circumstances other than the circumstance they are supposed to be made in, and so conclude that such output judgements won't generally fit in with our other beliefs, which by and large only get made in the circumstances where they are supposed to be made.

By this stage coherentists are thinking of humans as organisms that interact causally with an independent natural world. They have moved beyond the picture that originally gave coherentism its appeal, the picture of human subjects trapped within mental rooms in which they are impotent to do anything except compare beliefs for consistency with each other. Which means that it would be perverse, given the availability of a theory like the teleological theory of representation, to continue to insist that what is wrong with unsound perceptual processes is that their outputs fail to cohere with other beliefs. The more fundamental fault with such processes is that their outputs aren't triggered by their truth conditions, and are therefore generally false.

Of course it is true that processes which are unreliable in this realist sense will also, as it happens, tend to be processes whose output beliefs don't cohere with other beliefs. For (assuming, as above, that the general run of beliefs tends to be true) a process that produces false beliefs is *per se* a process that produces beliefs that won't cohere with related beliefs. And to this extent it is also true that the incoherence of a given process's outputs can be good evidence for thinking that the process is unreliable in a realist sense. But all this is quite consistent with unreliability for coherence merely being a symptom of the more fundamental failing, unreliability for realist truth.

Simon Blackburn (1984, ch. 7.6–7.8) emphasizes the importance of our supposing that our beliefs about the natural world are caused by the facts that make them true. But, while allowing that 'these are deep waters' in which 'nobody . . . has ever swum very far' (p. 247), he suggests that this still leaves room for a coherentist 'gestalt switch', which preserves the idea that the aim of judgement is to be part of a coherent system: the coherentist simply incorporates the requirement, that we should believe our beliefs about the natural world to be caused by their truth conditions, as a kind of 'extended coherence' that our overall system of beliefs has to preserve.

In effect I have shown, in this section and the last, that Blackburn's 'gestalt switch' ceases to be possible once we attend to the normative implications of our beliefs about the provenance of our beliefs. Somebody who believes that their belief-forming processes are unreliable for truth will *act* so as to alter those processes. This means that the 'extended coherence' which is really needed for epistemological stability is not just a coherence amongst beliefs, but a mutual adjustment between beliefs and *processes in the world*. And as such this 'extended coherence' is not a possible basis for a coherence theory of truth, or at least not for a theory that bears any resemblance to traditional coherence theories. It involves real non-conscious processes, as well as beliefs about such processes, and so can't possibly satisfy the coherentist, whose underlying motivation, after all, is to reduce the aim of belief to something that involves only beliefs and relations between them.

Moreover, once we realize that epistemological reflection leads to actions in the world, we can focus on the question of what end those actions are aimed at. This is what I have done in this section. I have argued that it makes little sense to deny that this end is truth as correspondence.

In short, the 'coherence' of mutual adjustment between our processes and beliefs isn't any good for a coherence theory of truth. And the notion of truth that does the work *within* that 'extended coherence' is undeniably a correspondence notion of truth.

8.3 MATHEMATICS AND MORALITY

The way in which the reliability-evaluations discussed so far are realist can be brought out more clearly by contrasting our beliefs about the natural world with our mathematical and moral beliefs.

I want to argue in favour of a kind of anti-realism about mathematics and morality. That is, I don't think that there is an independently existing reality for our mathematical and moral beliefs to answer to. Mathematical and moral 'reality' doesn't have any existence beyond the picture painted by human thought.

And because of this I don't think moral or mathematical belief-forming methods can be evaluated for their reliability at generating beliefs which correspond to an independent reality. In so far as we want to speak of mathematical or moral truth at all, truth comes down to a matter of provenance, a matter of beliefs being derivable from authorized methods. And in so far as there is evaluation of methods, it won't be a realist matter of evaluating them for producing beliefs which correspond to an independent reality, but rather (though this would apply more to morality than mathematics) evaluation for the coherence of outputs with related beliefs.

Let me go a bit more slowly. One complication here is that on some philosophical accounts of mathematics and morality, mathematical and moral beliefs reduce to species of beliefs about the natural world. Thus reductionist utilitarians argue that moral rightness is simply a matter of ensuring the greatest happiness of the greatest number, where happiness is taken to be an ordinary natural property. And similarly Millians about mathematics argue that arithmetic relations are simply normal empirical generalizations about what occurs in certain counting operations.

Clearly, if such reductionist views were correct, then there would be no contrasting moral and mathematical beliefs with beliefs about the natural world. In particular, realism about natural beliefs would carry with it realism about mathematics and morality, for mathematical and moral beliefs would answer straightforwardly to a certain sub-class of natural facts.

However, I take it that reductionism is false for both morality[1] and mathematics.[2] Whatever else is true of the worlds postulated by moral and mathematical thinking, moral and mathematical statements need to be understood as laying claim to facts involving non-natural entities and properties, such as justice and wickedness and numbers and sets, which cannot be equated with anything existing in the natural world. (Which is not of course to deny that the *importance* of mathematical and moral judgements rests on the way that they relate to natural facts. I shall return to this in the next chapter.)

But while I think we have to allow that mathematics and morality lay claim to non-natural facts, I don't think that we should allow that such facts have an independent existence. The reason is this. Suppose we did accept the independent existence of

[1] Here I am treading rough-shod over much recent work. Blackburn (1971, 1985a) and Baldwin (1985) are concerned with the precise sense in which moral facts are not equatable with natural facts. Wiggins (1976) and MacDowell (1978, 1985) use the analogy with secondary qualities to question the distance between moral and natural facts. This analogy is criticized in Blackburn (1985b); see also Dancy (1986), Hookway (1986).

[2] Philip Kitcher defends a post-Millian naturalism about mathematical facts in *The Nature of Mathematical Knowledge* (1983). But in order to get the requisite structure he has to construe mathematics as about the operations of *ideal* counters, categorizers, etc. I think that Kitcher ought to be rather more worried than he is about the epistemological accessibility of such ideal facts. (Cf. Papineau, 1976.) The advantage of Kitcher's approach is that it yields an immediate explanation of the utility of mathematics. But other explanations are possible, as in 9.3 below.

mathematical and moral facts. Given that they are non-natural, such facts wouldn't be part of the causally interacting natural world of space and time. (That's what it means to call them non-natural.) But how then are we supposed to find out about them? As natural beings in the natural world, we lack access to any such Platonic realm of non-natural facts. Which is why, I argue, there is no alternative to the conclusion that mathematics and morality do not answer to any such independent realm, but merely to intentional worlds created by our own ways of thought.

Let us be clear about the logic of this argument. I am not just arguing that because mathematical and moral facts are outside space and time, they can't have any independent existence. Simply to assume that natural reality is the only independent reality would beg all the interesting questions. The argument is rather that *if* we accepted the independent existence of mathematical and moral facts, then we would be unable to account for our ability to find out about those facts, and that for *this* reason we should deny their independent existence.

We can put it the other way round. Clearly there is something worthwhile about mathematics and morality. (About mathematics, anyway. Let me stick to mathematics for the moment to avoid irrelevant controversy and having to say everything twice.) There is clearly some sense in which competent mathematicians give correct answers to mathematical questions. But this ability would be entirely mysterious if (a) the correctness of mathematical judgements consisted in their corresponding to independently existing facts, while (b) we had no account of how mathematicians succeeded in responding reliably to those facts.[3] And so the only way of sustaining our respect for the beliefs of competent mathematicians is to recognize that those beliefs don't answer to any world outside the realm of human thought.

A central theme of this chapter and the last has been that part of what we believe about the natural world is that certain belief-forming methods allow us to respond reliably to natural facts. Natural science contains its own epistemology, so to speak, in that it explains how humans find out about natural facts. But there is

---

[3] The difficulty involved here is spelt out in Benacerraf (1973).

nothing corresponding in mathematics. Mathematics certainly doesn't itself explain how humans discover mathematical facts. And even philosophers can't come up with any satisfactory story of how natural being might respond to non-natural facts. (Maybe such stories used to be possible. Maybe the word of God, or the light of reason He gave us, were means by which humans could plausibly have access to non-natural facts. But I take it that such stories are no longer available.)

If we are to uphold the judgements made in a certain area of discourse, we have a choice. We can maintain that those judgements are characteristically caused by their truth conditions, and that this is how they manage to inform us accurately about an independent world. Alternatively we can accept that in this area there is no rightness 'but that thinking makes it so', and that therefore the judgements don't have to be responsive to an independent realm in order to be correct in the first place. But there is no third way. Given that we are causal beings responsive only to the causal world, the only way to respect judgements which aren't caused by their truth conditions is to recognize that they don't have independent truth conditions at all.

And so we should see the worth of mathematical judgements as in effect self-sustaining. We do want to accept that in general competent mathematicians only believe that p when that claim is correct. But we can't explain this generalization by saying that mathematical beliefs are caused by independent mathematical facts. Instead we should account for the success of competent mathematicians as due to the fact that there really isn't anything more to 'p obtaining' than that competent mathematicians can be moved to the belief that p.

These last remarks should make it clear that my denial that mathematical judgements correspond to an independent reality isn't intended to suggest that mathematical judgement is somehow subjective or arbitrary. On the contrary, I am denying an independent reality precisely in order to preserve the authority of mathematical judgement as more than the expression of individual whim. Of course individuals aren't free to choose their mathematical beliefs. There are objective constraints which make some such beliefs correct and others wrong. Somebody who asserts an incorrect mathematical belief, or who actively denies a correct one, must either be incompetent or in some other way be failing to conform to the principles of mathematical practice (the principles of the mathematical 'language game').

How does this insistence on the objectivity of mathematics tally with my professed anti-realism about mathematics? Doesn't anti-realism imply that the abstract objects of mathematics don't really exist? On the other hand, if certain mathematical beliefs are objectively correct, doesn't it follow that certain mathematical entities do exist? If it is objectively correct to hold, say, that $2 + 2 = 4$, then doesn't it follow that we ought to accept that the number two exists?

But there isn't any formal contradiction in accepting both anti-realism about mathematics and the existence of mathematical entities. Anti-realism about mathematics is the denial that mathematical facts have an *independent* existence. But this just means that correctness, for mathematical judgements, consists entirely in their having an authorized provenance, in their having been derived in an authorized way, rather than in their correspondence to some set of facts, a correspondence to which our actual ways of deriving mathematical judgements might or might not conform. That is, anti-realism about mathematics is in the first instance a thesis about the epistemological underpinning of mathematical claims, not a rejection of those claims. So anti-realism about mathematics does leave us room to accept that mathematical objects have a kind of existence.

However, even if anti-realism about mathematics is in this way formally consistent with the existence of mathematical objects, there is still, it seems to me, some tension between them. This is a somewhat delicate matter, and in the end I'm not sure much hangs on it, but it will be illuminating to pursue it for a while.

If we were anti-realists across the board, holding that the only acceptable account of correctness for judgements about the *natural* world was in terms of authorized provenance, just as I have argued is the case for mathematical judgements, then there would be no issue: mathematical beliefs would be as good as any others, and numbers as real as tables and chairs.

But I have argued that we *shouldn't* be anti-realists across the board. While the only way to uphold mathematical judgements is to take an anti-realist attitude to them, we can think of the justification of natural judgements as a matter of their being reliably caused by their truth conditions.

I think that this difference between mathematical and natural judgements provides some reason to deny the existence of mathematical reality outright. At its simplest, this denial would just be a matter of contrast: one way of marking the difference between mathematical correctness (authorized provenance) and natural correctness (conformity to causally efficacious truth conditions) is to say that natural objects exist and mathematical entities don't. But we can dress this thought up a bit by appealing to the apparent univocality of 'exists': whatever existence comes to, surely it's the same for all existents; so I can't say both that natural facts exist, where this means being part of the causal world of space and time, and that mathematical entities exist, where this doesn't come to anything more than the mathematical acceptability of certain judgements mentioning those objects.

As I said, I'm not sure that anything substantial hangs on the existence of mathematical entities. Once we recognize that there is some difference in status between mathematical discourse and natural science, what does it matter whether or not we elevate it into an ontological contrast? But, even so, I think it is probably more straightforward, from the point of view of the exposition of my overall argument, to opt for the outright denial of mathematical existents. It might seem somewhat paradoxical that we end up denying mathematical entities only because of our realist views about *natural* judgements. But that just serves to emphasize that there isn't much more to this issue than a matter of argumentative contrast.[4]

Of course, a number of consequences follow if we deny that mathematical entities exist. If mathematical objects don't exist,

[4]Blackburn expresses similar sentiments about moral facts (1984, p. 257). He says he does not 'greatly commend the question' of whether moral facts really exist, or are merely a useful fiction. But he does allow that, *if* we could block the coherentist 'gestalt switch' which makes truth about the natural world a matter of coherence, as I say we can, *then* this would give us reason to consider the moral world imaginary. Cf. my remarks at the end of 8.2 above.

then any mathematical statements which imply the existence of such objects (that is, nearly all normal mathematics) will be false. Moreover, we can't believe things we take to be false. So it follows from my position that we ought to stop believing the claims of mathematics.

It might seem like a *reductio ad absurdum* of my suggestion that it implies that $2 + 2 = 4$ is false and therefore to be disbelieved. But I think we can come to terms with this, and indeed in a way which remains consistent with the objectivity of mathematics, by adopting a *fictionalist* account of mathematics.

The idea here is that our attitude to mathematical propositions should not be *belief*, but rather the attitude that we have to occurrences in a fictional narrative. When I read that Sherlock Holmes lived at 221B Baker Street, I don't *believe* this, for I know full well that Sherlock Holmes never existed. But at the same time, and especially when I am engrossed in the story, my attitude is very like belief.

Let us call this attitude 'pseudo-belief'. Some philosophical positions would make pseudo-belief a problem: if we thought of the identity of propositional attitudes as given in essential part by the objects in the real world that they referred to, then the identity conditions of such fictional 'pseudo-beliefs' would obviously present an awkward puzzle. (Cf. Evans, 1982, ch. 10.) On the other hand, if we take the line adopted in earlier chapters, and regard such 'extrinsic' identifications as posterior to 'intrinsic' identifications in terms of causal roles, there is no special reason to be suspicious of 'pseudo-beliefs'. No doubt the philosophical psychology of pseudo-belief would be an interesting subject in its own right, with things to be said about the precise causal roles of such attitudes, and about their similarities and differences to the causal roles of real beliefs. But rather than pursue this topic here, let me simply rely on the example of reading fiction. Whatever conceptual complexities lie hidden, the analogy with fiction does at least show how one could have an attitude of non-belief to mathematical propositions, and yet still get caught up in them, so to speak, when engrossed in the activity of doing mathematics.

More remains to be said. The analogy with fiction only goes so far. Mathematics and narrative fictions are both important to human beings, but they aren't important for the same reasons. I still owe some account of why mathematics is important. A related question concerns the objectivity of mathematics. The analogy with fiction breaks down here as well. Even if the reader of a fiction is constrained by the text as to which pseudo-beliefs to adopt, the author of a fiction isn't constrained by anything but the conventions of narrative and the limits of his or her imagination. The mathematical author, on the other hand, seems to have no freedom at all in choosing mathematical pseudo-beliefs. What is the source of these objective constraints on mathematical judgement? It is no good waving the phrase 'language game' about, for there are obvious questions about variant language games. I shall return to these questions about the importance and objectivity of mathematics, and to some similar questions about morality, later on in the next chapter.

9

Inferential Processes

9.1 THE EVALUATION OF DEDUCTIVE LOGIC

Earlier I divided belief-forming processes into non-inferential processes (perception and memory) and inferential processes (deduction and induction). So far I have illustrated in some detail how our *non*-inferential processes can be evaluated for reliability and adjusted accordingly.

My eventual aim is to show that any process-adjuster who reaches a fully 'self-vindicating' state (that is, whose totality of processes yields beliefs that imply that those processes are all reliable) will have succeeded in avoiding error. But I still want to postpone this issue until the next and final chapter. In this chapter I want to do for *inferential* processes what has already been done for non-inferential ones: that is, I want to show in detail how it makes sense to evaluate our deductive and inductive processes for reliability and adjust them accordingly if necessary.

Inferential processes differ from non-inferential processes in that they take us from beliefs already accepted to further beliefs. Where non-inferential processes can generate beliefs on their own, so to speak, inferential processes can only get going after non-inferential processes have done some work. What we require of non-inferential processes is that they reliably produce true beliefs. Correspondingly, what we require of inferential processes is that they should be conditionally reliable, that is, that they should normally produce true conclusions given true premises.

Let me start with deduction. The question is whether we can make sense of the idea of evaluating deductive processes for conditional reliability in some way that might inform decisions about which such processes to adopt, analogously to the way in which we can evaluate perceptual and memory processes and adjust accordingly.

Recall the discussion in 4.5 above, where I talked about the presence of structure in beliefs (considered as bearers of causal roles) and the presence of a corresponding structure in their truth conditions, and where I pointed out that the existence of such co-ordinated structures meant that the truth of some beliefs was guaranteed by the truth of others. In effect this is just the kind of evaluation of deductive logic we are looking for.

Recall the example. I argued that beliefs labelled 'p and q' were biologically supposed to be present just in case both the belief labelled 'p' and the belief labelled 'q' were supposed to be present. Which, given the teleological theory of representation, meant that beliefs that p and q will be true just in case the belief that p is true and the belief that q is true. And I pointed that this then validated the habit of moving from any belief of the form 'p and q' to the corresponding belief 'p' (or to 'q'). Somebody adopting this habit would invariably be taken from truths to truths.

I take this to be an evaluation of the inferential pattern 'p and q' ⊢ 'p', quite analogous to the kind of evaluation of perceptual processes discussed in chapter 7. On reflection we see that anybody who moves from true beliefs that p and q to beliefs that p will move from truths to truths.

Note in particular that this isn't just a coherentist validation, based on the fact that the outputs of the inferential pattern in question fit with what we otherwise believe. (Cf., for example, Goodman, 1954, pp. 66–7.) On the contrary, I have appealed to a detailed picture, of beliefs answering to truth conditions, and structured beliefs answering to structured truth conditions, which *explains* why the inferential move in question is reliable for preserving truths.

The point can be put in more familiar terms. Let us talk, not of the truth conditions of beliefs with structured causal roles, but of the truth conditions of sentences with certain syntactic forms. From my point of view, of course, sentences have truth conditions because they express beliefs, and beliefs have truth conditions because of their biological purposes. But if we take all this as given, then we can transpose the above story about conjunctive *beliefs* to the claim that the word 'and' gives rise to sentences 'p and q' which are true just in case 'p' is true and 'q' is true. And we can see how similar conclusions would apply to the other propositional connectives: 'p or q' is true just in case 'p' is true or 'q' is true; 'not p' is true just in case 'p' is not true; and so on. (We can generate similar explanations of the constants of the predicate calculus by starting with satisfaction rather than truth. I shall omit these extra complexities.)

Given all this, the validity of various inferential moves between sentences follows. Corresponding to the earlier example, there is the inference rule: from the sentence 'p and q', infer the sentence 'p'. Or, to take one further case, since the sentence 'p or q' is true just in case 'p' is true or 'q' is true, and since the sentence 'not p' is true just in case 'p' is not true, if both 'p or q' and 'not p' are true, 'q' must be true – that is, it is valid to infer 'q' from 'p or q' and 'not p'.

Despite appearances, the above explanations of the workings of the propositional connectives are not empty. It is true that as stated they would be no good for introducing the English propositional connectives to people who didn't already understand them, for the obvious reason that they would need to understand the words in question in order to understand the explanations. But, even so, they convey something substantial, as is seen by considering the equivalent English explanations of, say, German connectives like 'und', 'nicht', etc.: English people who don't speak German need to be *told* that 'p und q' is true just in case 'p' is true and 'q' is true.

Analogously, although the vindications I have given for certain inferential moves will scarcely *persuade* anybody who doesn't already make deductive inferences to start making them, since the vindications themselves proceed via deductive moves, it doesn't follow that the vindications are worthless, that they lack all normative substance. Think of the situation in negative terms. Suppose that our understanding of how language related to reality, and in particular of how the logical constants made new statements out of old ones, implied that certain of our existing inferential habits were *un*reliable. Clearly this would give us reason to change those habits. (Nor is this just an idle thought experiment. There *are* people who habitually affirm the consequent, or who commit the fallacy of the missing third. And the natural response in such cases is to try to show, by appeal to the semantics of the logical terms involved, that the deviants' habits are bad ones, that they are in danger of starting with truths and ending with falsehoods.)

No doubt the feeling persists that there is *something* circular about using certain methods to arrive at beliefs which vindicate those selfsame methods as reliable. But for the moment we can simply note that this is a special case of the general worry about the significance of 'self-vindication', to which I have promised to return in the next chapter.

9.2   DIGRESSION ON DUMMETT ON THE JUSTIFICATION OF DEDUCTION

The general notion of a 'justification of deduction' in terms of a semantic account of the workings of the logical constants will be familiar to many readers from the writings of Michael Dummett (see in particular Dummett, 1974). Dummett's interest in the possibility of such 'justifications' is rather different from mine: whereas I am concerned to show how a realist might vindicate belief-forming processes in general, and deduction in particular, as reliable for truth, Dummett's primary concern is to contrast the way in which realist semantics and anti-realist semantics respectively vindicate classical and intuitionistic logic. But it will be helpful at this point to digress somewhat and discuss Dummett's own views on these matters.

Dummett holds that there are two possible candidates for 'the central notion in the theory of meaning': namely, truth and assertibility. Truth is the option taken by the realist. Realists think of the correctness of a statement as a matter of its corresponding to the facts, and therefore of the content of a statement as given by its truth condition. Anti-realists, on the other hand, take assertibility as the central notion. They think of correctness in terms of provenance, in terms of a statement having been arrived at by proper methods, and therefore of the content of a sentence as given by the conditions (having a proof, having observable evidence) which will warrant us in asserting it.

We explain the meaning of the logical constants, according to Dummett, by explaining how they work in making new sentences out of old. That is, we explain them as functions which take us from the contents of the constituent sentences to a content for the complex sentence.

Thus I explained 'and', for instance, as giving rise to sentences 'p and q' which are true if and only if 'p' is true and 'q' is true. This of course, along with the other explanations offered, was a realist explanation, given in terms of truth.

Consider now the alternative anti-realist explanations, in terms of assertibility: 'p and q' is assertible if and only if 'p' is assertible and 'q' is assertible; 'p or q' is assertible if and only if 'p' is assertible or 'q' is assertible; 'not p' is assertible if and only if it is assertible than 'p' is not assertible.

Dummett points out that these alternative explanations of the logical constants will justify a different logic from the classical logic justified by a realist semantics. Thus consider the law of the excluded middle: ⊢ 'p or not p'. Given realist semantics, 'p or not p' is true if and only if 'p' is true or 'not p' is true, which holds if and only if 'p' is true or 'p' is not true, which will always be the case, for any 'p', and however things are. But with an anti-realist semantics, 'p or not p' is assertible if and only if 'p' is assertible or 'not p' is assertible, which holds if and only if 'p' is assertible or it is assertible that 'p' is unassertible, which needn't always be the case, for nothing guarantees that, for every sentence 'p', we will always either have grounds for asserting it, or have grounds for asserting it is not assertible.

As this example makes particularly clear, the logics justified respectively by realist and anti-realist semantics diverge in particular on the question of whether the world determines the correctness of either a positive or a negative answer to every meaningful question. If we could somehow be assured that for every sentence 'p', either we will have grounds for asserting 'p', or grounds for assering 'not p', then anti-realist anxieties about the excluding of middles would dissolve. But, as Dummett points out, for any but the most restricted parts of language, such decidability is extremely implausible. On any reading of 'assertible', it seems inescapable that there are questions (about the distant past, about unrealized dispositions, about unsurveyable infinities) that are simply not decidable either way. The realist, by focusing on correspondence to how things objectively are, and not on the availability of grounds for asserting them to be a certain way, can recognize such undecidability and still insist that, for all 'p', either 'p' or 'not p' corresponds to reality. But the anti-realist has to accept that, for some 'p's, it may well be that neither 'p' nor 'not p' is assertible.

Thus for Dummett the interest in the 'justification of deduction' is the way it focusses the conflict between realists and anti-realists. The realist, happy to start from a conception of the world as 'out there', independent of human thought, maintains the law of the excluded middle. But anti-realists, by identifying correctness with legitimate provenance, forfeit their right to the schema 'p or not p'. They equate 'reality' with the picture that authorized ways of thought lead us to, and since there is no reason to suppose that our ways of thought must answer all questions, they have therefore to allow that reality itself can fail to decide between 'p' and 'not p'.

In the next section I· shall show that even in the context of mathematics (where Dummett's analysis is generally thought to be most plausible) one can accept anti-realism and yet resist the non-standard logic which Dummett claims to follow. But let me devote the rest of this section to a different issue. Dummett doesn't just draw attention to the contrast between realist and anti-realist semantics and their respective implications for logic. He goes on from this contrast to outline an argument for anti-realism. (Whether Dummett actually endorses anti-realism isn't always entirely clear. But certainly he takes the argument to support it.)[1]

For Dummett, the distinguishing feature of realism is the claim that there are sentences whose correctness depends on circumst-

---

[1] In my terms the anti-realism in question is a version of anti-realism of method. But note that Dummett's concern to *evaluate* deductive habits by means of semantic analysis makes it a somewhat idiosyncratic kind of anti-realism of method. Even though Dummett does use anti-realist semantic notions for this evaluative purpose when wearing his anti-realist hat, more thoroughgoing anti-realists, such as Lear (1982), argue that we shouldn't go in for such evaluations at all, and should simply accept that classical logic is constitutive of our human 'mindedness'.

ances beyond our epistemological grasp. It is precisely because realists countenance such 'verification-transcendent' truth conditions that they differ from anti-realists on the law of the excluded middle. But, asks Dummett, is it possible for a sentence in a human language to have such a 'verification-transcendent' content? If the meaning of a sentence was given by a truth condition the presence or absence of which was not detectable by human beings, then how could anybody ever *learn* from other people what that sentence meant? Or, to make the same point from the other side, how could anybody ever *manifest* their understanding of such a sentence, if that required that they display sensitivity to circumstances they were incapable of recognizing? (See, for example, Dummett, 1976, p. 101.)

Thus, to take a favourite example of Dummett's (originally used in his 1958), a realist understands the term 'brave' as standing for a certain property, a property that everybody either has or lacks, whether or not they are ever put to the test. An anti-realist, on the other hand, will understand 'brave' by grasping its assertibility conditions, by grasping that *if* somebody is put to the test, then he or she is to be deemed 'brave' or 'not brave' according as he or she does or does not discount danger, avoid panic, etc. But, Dummett now asks, what could possibly show that 'brave' had the former, realist, meaning, rather than the latter, anti-realist, one? After all, by the nature of the example, everybody learns what 'brave' means by learning what its displays are, and everybody manifests their grasp of the term by responding to those displays. As soon as we look closely at the kind of case that distinguishes realism from anti-realism, it is difficult to see how our words could possibly have realist contents.

Recall that in 6.2 I said that anti-realism of method needs to establish two claims: first, that the answers produced by rational methods of thought cannot but be true, and, secondly, that human beings do not diverge on such methods of thought. As I observed at the time, Dummett's focus on assertibility conditions for specific sentences means that he never really addresses the second, divergence-denying claim. But the argument currently under consideration can be construed as an attempt to establish the first claim: it aims to show precisely that truth cannot be something different from the answers our verification procedures deliver, on the grounds that if it were we would be committed to crediting people with a grasp of judgements that they couldn't possibly manifest.

There are various possible objections to Dummett's argument. I shall mention two. First a relatively technical one. It seems to me that Dummett has his own difficulties with the supposed anti-realist understanding of dispositional terms such as the pair 'brave' and 'not brave' (b, ~ b). Dummett has it that we understand these in terms of test conditions (c, say) and decidable display conditions (d, ~ d). But note that we don't want 'b' just to be equivalent to 'c & d', and '~ b' to c & ~ d'. For then 'b' and '~ b' would only be contraries, not contradictories. Rather 'b' should be understood as equivalent to '*if* c, *then* d', with '~ b' as equivalent to '*if* c, *then* ~ d'.

But now suppose we ask: 'What entitles us to understand *these conditionals* as something more than just contraries?' I know the correct interpretation of conditionals is a difficult subject. But my objection is that on Dummett's account it's not clear why it isn't a simple one. Why doesn't 'if c, then d' just mean the same as 'c & d', and 'if c, then ~ d' just mean the same as 'c & ~ d'? After all, by Dummett's own argument the former pair have just the same assertibility conditions, and so do the latter pair.

Couldn't Dummett reply that we don't deny 'if c, then d' just on the basis of 'not c', as we ought to on the suggested understanding? But for Dummett accepted patterns of inference can't decide questions of content, for they are themselves answerable to such questions (1976, pp. 102–3). Our exclusion of middles doesn't show that 'not' must mean the absence of truth; rather, since 'not' doesn't mean that, we oughtn't to exclude middles. Similarly, it seems to me, Dummett isn't in any position to argue that our refusal to infer 'not, if c, then d' from 'not c' shows that 'if c, then d' means something different from 'c & d'. For it might mean precisely that, and it might be that our eschewing the inference was just due to our misguided realism about bravery. (Nor can Dummett say that 'not' is *per se* a construction that makes contradictories rather than contraries. What about 'bald'/'not bald', 'tall'/'not tall', etc.?)

Now for the second and more fundamental objection to Dummett's argument for anti-realism. It seems to me that Dummett's argument depends on an implicit premise that we have every reason to reject: namely, that the only way we can possibly make sense of a truth condition is as a condition that believers in some sense *respond* to epistemologically.

Note that Dummett's argument is that people couldn't possibly grasp judgements that answer to verification-transcendent truth conditions, since this would imply, absurdly, that they would have a grasp that they couldn't manifest. But for this argument to go through we have to assume that the truth condition of a judgement relates directly to the way believers are *led* to that judgement. For without something like this assumption Dummett couldn't argue that to ascribe verification-transcedent truth conditions is to credit a believer with some unmanifestable *ability* (the ability to recognize that truth condition).

In a sense Dummett's argument begs the case against anti-realism. It simply assumes that the notion of a truth condition has somehow to be understood in terms of epistemological tendencies. Given a properly realist account of truth conditions, Dummett's argument loses its force.

Thus consider the approach to truth developed earlier in this book. I took the basic representers of reality to be beliefs. Beliefs had causal roles. Because of these causal roles, they fulfilled certain biological purposes, namely, to be present when certain circumstances obtained. These circumstances were then their truth conditions.

Given this approach to truth, Dummett's argument gets no grip. The quite proper demand that a grasp of some judgement should always be manifestable is respected in the idea of belief's *causal role*. The causal role of a belief involves precisely such discriminations amongst external circumstances as believers are responsive to: if believers can't tell trees from papier-mâché trees, then trees and tree replicas are rightly counted together in the relevant causal role. But it doesn't follow from this that the presence or absence of *truth conditions* can't transcend recognitional abilities. For, as the tree example shows, the biological purpose of a belief can well be to represent some circumstance which transcends the recognitional abilities of believers.

The difference between my position and Dummett's is that I have a more full-bloodedly realist notion of truth. My approach to truth allows that people can have certain beliefs, and manifest that they have them, without imposing any *a priori* requirement that their methods for acquiring such beliefs should lead them to the truth. Dummett, on the other hand, even when he is contemplating the possibility of 'verification-transcendent' truth conditions, still doesn't free himself from the idea that truth is *per se* what people's judgemental methods relate them to. So it is scarcely surprising that he finds the idea of epistemologically inaccessible truth conditions incoherent.

Of course these last comments don't engage directly with Dummett, for Dummett takes linguistic representation to be more fundamental than mental representation, and so might well object to an argument that had as a premise the presumed ability of *beliefs* to have verification-transcendent truth conditions. But I don't think that this affects the underlying issue. Even if we were to start with sentences rather than beliefs, Dummett could still be accused of begging the question by implicitly assuming that the truth condition of a sentence must be something that competent users of the sentence relate to epistemologically.[2]

9.3 MATHEMATICS AND THE NATURAL WORLD

At the end of the last chapter I argued, in general terms, against a realist view of mathematics and morality. We are now in a position to be a bit more specific about these topics. I shall deal with mathematics first, in this section and (after a digression) in 9.5, and with morality in 9.6.

In the first instance we can think of mathematical truths as generated by an underlying deductive logic applied to specific sets of assumptions. These sets of assumptions implicitly define the subject matter of each mathematical speciality. Thus Peano's

---

[2] For related criticisms of a recent attempt to find space for 'verification-transcendent' truth conditions within a broadly Dummettian framework, see my (1987) discussion of Peacocke (1986).

postulates define the integers, Euclid's axioms define Euclidean space, the axioms of group theory define what it is to be a group, etc. ('Mathematical truths' aren't real truths: think of them on the model of truths about Sherlock Holmes.)

The assumptions specific to each mathematical topic can be thought of as conventions. They answer to no independent reality, but simply 'fix' a notional subject matter. They define their subject matter as that mathematical structure which satisfies the assumptions in question.

To call these assumptions conventions is not to say that they are purely arbitrary. For some conventions can be better than others. Particularly important here is the fact that mathematics can be of help in describing the natural world. For example, countable physical objects conform to the arithmetic of the natural numbers. Empirical quantities like distances, temperatures, masses, are isomorphic to the real numbers. Physical space has the geometry, not of Euclidean space, but of a non-Euclidean space with variable curvature. Quantum mechanics represents physical systems as vectors in n-dimensional spaces. And so on.

These empirical applications give us an obvious sense in which certain mathematical conventions can be more significant than others, and the notional structures they implicitly define of more than technical interest. Indeed I would say that it is these empirical applications (or at least the possibility of such applications) that make mathematics more than a formal game. But, even so, we shouldn't equate mathematical truth with truth in such empirical applications.

The easiest way to see why this equation is wrong is to note the difference between criticizing a mathematical structure for its lack of empirical relevance, and criticizing it in mathematical terms. Maybe physical space doesn't conform to Euclidean geometry, and maybe physical triangles therefore don't contain 180°. But it is still a perfectly good mathematical truth that Euclidean triangles contain 180°.

I don't necessarily want to deny here that the 'folk' notion of triangle is that of a physical triangle (a figure bounded by three rigid rods, say), and that therefore the 'folk' thought that triangles contain 180° is downright false. (Cf. Putnam, 1962.) My point is only that according to our everyday conception of mathematics and our intuitive notion of a mathematical truth, anything that follows from conventions by logic qualifies as mathematical truth, even if it is empirically irrelevant (or trivial, or otherwise uninteresting). Which is why it is still true that Euclidean triangles contain 180°, even if folk triangles don't.

This difference between pure mathematical truth and applied mathematical truth corroborates the point, noted in the last chapter, that mathematical claims present themselves as having a distinctive content: mathematical claims are naturally understood as referring to such abstract entities as numbers and shapes and sets and groups, entities which have no place in the natural world of space and time.

Let us now consider the question of applied mathematics in its own right for a moment. Even if *pure* mathematics is free of reference to *natural* objects, it certainly seems as if *applied* mathematical statements refer *inter alia* to abstract objects. Thus the easiest way to read the claim that 'This ruler is three feet long' is to see it as saying that the ruler bears a certain relation (the length-in-feet relation) to the number three. Similarly, to assert that 'This water is at three degrees centigrade' is to claim that the water bears the temperature-in-degrees relation to the number three. And so on. But this now presents a problem for my overall position. I say that abstract objects don't exist, and therefore that all beliefs laying claim to such objects are strictly speaking false. But then it seems to follow that applied mathematical statements are strictly speaking false too, and therefore that we oughtn't to have any full-fledged beliefs about such things as lengths or temperatures.

Here I would like to appeal to some ideas developed by Hartry Field (1981). Field indicates how applied mathematical statements, like the above statements about length and temperature, can be given an alternative 'nominalist' reading, according to which they refer solely to structural features of the natural world, and are free of any reference to such 'platonist' entities as the number three itself. In practical contexts it is often convenient to bring the platonist numbers in, because then we can 'plug in' to the pure theory of numbers in order to facilitate the making of inferences from given data. But such references to platonist entities are in principle always dispensable, and when we are concerned with what we ought strictly to believe we should stick to the nominalist structural claims which avoid reference to abstract entities. In effect Field is suggesting that we can view pure platonist mathematics in the way that 'instrumentalists' view scientific theories about unobservables: the platonist mathematics (like theories about unobservables) helps to generate nominalist (observable) consequences, even though those nominalist consequences themselves make no reference to abstract (unobservable) entities.

Field's approach not only shows how we can manage without abstract objects in our full-fledged beliefs about the natural world (as opposed to the fictional pseudo-beliefs about abstract objects it is often convenient to indulge in), but it also makes clear *why* those ficitional pseudo-beliefs are so convenient, that is, why the game of mathematics is so especially important to human beings. By having an intellectual practice which is specifically directed at the investigation of implicitly defined abstract entities, we can simplify empirical arguments by relating them to abstract structures which can be pressed into service in any number of different empirical applications. (Consider the number of different physical quantities that the real numbers help to describe.)

In 8.3 I said that mathematical judgements aren't caused by independent mathemetical facts (it is closer to the truth to say that mathematical judgements themselves create the mathematical facts). We now see, however, that there are independent nominalist natural facts which, so to speak, exemplify platonist mathematical claims. The nominalist fact that two bodies each of mass 2 grams together have a mass of 4 grams exemplifies the platonist fact that $2 + 2 = 4$. Now, there is a sense in which such nominalist natural facts do cause mathematical beliefs: for instance, it is no doubt because of such natural facts that humans are interested in numbers to begin with. But note that the nominalist natural facts which in this sense cause mathematical beliefs aren't themselves platonist mathematical facts. And the 'real' platonist mathematical facts, involving abstract objects like the number 2 and the number 4, don't themselves do any causing.

9.4 DIGRESSION ON MODALITY, POSSIBLE WORLDS, AND TRUTH CONDITIONS

Because platonistic mathematical facts can't do any causing, we are forced to a fictionalist view of platonist mathematical beliefs. But at the same time Field's approach indicates how we can be realists about the nominalistic mathematical beliefs that we do need for describing the structure of the natural world.

The need for this kind of analysis is not restricted to mathematics. There are other kinds of beliefs which turn out on examination to involve commitment to causally impotent abstract entities. In this section I want to look at some of these further platonist beliefs, and to consider how far their work could be done by nominalist substitutes which are susceptible of a realist interpretation.

The remarks in this section will be sketchy and programmatic. This is a complex area, and one in which I feel my overall argument is stretched to its limit. What I shall say will have revisionary implications for many of our most familiar beliefs, and it is possible that I am here overloading my underlying ideas with more philosophical weight than they will bear. For those who share these doubts, it is worth pointing out that, just as in the case of mathematics, there is an alternative to the fictionalist response that relegates platonist beliefs to the status of pseudo-beliefs and replaces them with others. This is the more moderate kind of anti-realism that I discussed in connection with mathematics in 8.3 above, which doesn't reject beliefs about abstract entities, but simply contents itself with observing that the notion of correctness applicable to such beliefs is different from that applicable to natural beliefs.

Let me start with causal beliefs. I take it that our everyday causal beliefs commit us to literal claims about what would happen in possible worlds other than the actual, namely, in the nearest possible worlds in which the cause is absent. This kind of interpretation of causal claims has been defended by David Lewis (1973). In my (1986b) I consider the issue from the perspective developed in this book. I point out that our causal beliefs cannot be causally responsive to facts involving other possible worlds, and so suggest a fictionalist attitude to such beliefs. Pseudo-beliefs about what would and would not happen in other possible worlds are extremely useful to us, in virtue of the fact that reflective decision-making works by considering what would happen given various alternative courses of action. But such beliefs should not be thought of as anything more than useful fictions, and our full-fledged beliefs should be restricted to claims about what does follow what in this world.

If this is the right line for causal beliefs, then we ought also to adopt a similar line for beliefs about what is logically necessary or possible. For such judgements also commit us to claims about worlds other than the actual, and so ought also to be viewed as useful fictions. Our full-fledged beliefs ought again to be restricted to the this-worldly consequences which can be distilled out of such logical truths.

These points about causally and logically modal beliefs are of course significant for the arguments put forward in this book. Causal notions permeate such ideas as that of a belief-forming *process* being triggered by the truth condition of its output beliefs. And the notion of logical necessity is implicated in the idea that deductive processes *guarantee* the preservation of truth. For full rigour I ought to purge such claims of commitment to possible worlds, and to restrict myself to the assertion of their this-worldly consequences. But this would be a lengthy and tiresome task, and one which would serve no good purpose once the general idea of distilling realistically acceptable consequences from claims about possible worlds is conceded.

Another notion which calls for possible worlds (or something equivalent) is the notion of a truth condition itself. A truth condition can be thought of as a subset of the totality of possible worlds, namely, as that subset in which the belief in question is true. Truth itself then comes out as one of those possible worlds actually obtaining. We can see why it is natural to think of truth in this way. As with causal beliefs, thinking in terms of possible worlds fits with the structure of our reflective decision-making: if reflective decision-making is a matter of comparing the attractions of different possible worlds, then accepting a judgement as true has the effect of imposing a restriction on such comparisons, namely, a restriction to the set of possible worlds contained in that judgement's truth condition. But even if the notion of a truth condition is for this reason a natural one, it too should be avoided in strict contexts, for claims about sets of possible worlds cannot be upheld except under a fictionalist interpretation.

This was why I said, way back in 2.6, that I wanted to avoid any ultimate commitment to truth conditions as sets of possible worlds, and consequenctly wanted an alternative to the idea that truth is a matter of the actual world being a member of such a set of possible worlds. I pointed out at that stage that one possible alternative would be to think of truth as the higher-order property of satisfying the Tarski truth predicate for the appropriate language (or repertoire of beliefs), and that this alternative would still entitle us to think of truth as a matter of correspondence to the facts, not in the ontologically burdened sense of the actual world being one of a set of possible worlds, but simply in the sense that a judgement's being true depends on how the world is.

Of course since then I have often eased my exposition by using phrases which imply commitment to truth conditions. But again I don't see that any useful purpose would have been served by excising such phrases, once the general possibility of realistically acceptable replacements is allowed.

9.5 WHAT IS THE RIGHT LOGIC FOR MATHEMATICS?

In this section I want to say something about the deductive logic that underlies our mathematical practice. I suggested earlier that mathematical truth can be equated with derivability from conventions by deductive logic. But we can't equate this logic with any axiomatizable system of logic, such as the first-order predicate calculus, for then Godel's incompleteness theorem will force us to recognize the existence of mathematical truths not derivable by logic from the relevant subject-specific axioms, and this would then discredit the suggested equation of mathematical truth with deductive derivability from conventions. However, this equation can be maintained if we settle instead for some *semantic* characterization of logic, as those inferences guaranteed by the semantic structure of the judgements involved. On ony but the most restrictive notions of semantic structure this will give us an unaxiomatizable logic, which is how we escape the Godel difficulty, but there is no particular reason, in the present context of argument, why such unaxiomatizability should be thought undesirable.

But this still leaves it open which 'central semantic notion' is appropriate in the context of mathematics, and consequently what *kind* of logic should be adopted. Recall Dummett's contrast between a realist semantics based on the notion of truth and an anti-realist semantics based on the notion of assertibility. Dummett argues that where a realist semantics gives rise to classical logic, an anti-realist semantics gives rise to something like intuitionistic logic, in which, for instance, the law of the excluded middle is not a logical truth. I have argued that we should decide to uphold a fictionalist rather than a realist view of mathematics. Does it then follow that the underlying logic used by mathematicians should be intuitionistic?[3]

It is not clear to me that it does. Certainly, as a fictionalist about mathematics, I want to have it that the appropriate notion of correctness for mathematical judgements is assertibility, rather than truth as correspondence to an independent reality. But I don't think it follows that mathematics should have intuitionistic logic.

Dummett assumes that the logic adopted in any realm of discourse has to be *vindicated* by independent appeal to the central semantic notion appropriate to that realm. If judgement aims at truth, then we ought to adopt that logic which is guaranteed to take us from truths to truths. And, correspondingly, if correctness in judgement is a matter of assertibility, then deductive inferences ought to answer to the demand that the assertibility of the conclusion is guaranteed by the assertibility of the premises.

But, while this kind of derivation of logic from semantics makes good sense if we are assuming realism, it is far less compelling in the context of a fictionalist view of mathematics. If we are realists

---

[3] Orthogonal to the general question of whether our logic should be classical or intuitionistic, there is a more specific question of *how much* semantic structure should count as logical. See Evans (1976), Peacocke (1976), Hacking (1979).

about a given subject matter, then our notion of correctness is fixed independently of our choice of deductive practice. We want our judgements to correspond to reality. Such correspondence isn't a matter of provenance, of how the judgement has been arrived at, but of how it stands with respect to the world. Which is why we want our ways of arriving at judgements to respect this notion of correspondence, and in particular why we want our deductive inferences to ensure that our conclusions so correspond if our premises do.

But with a view like our fictionalist view of mathematics, our notion of correctness is itself in large part constituted by our choice of deductive practice. It is not as if there was already a world of mathematics, so to speak, in which certain statements were assertible, and others not, and then we wanted our logical practice to respect this world, by only giving us assertible conclusions from assertible premises. Rather mathematical assertibility itself depends on our logical practice: mathematical correctness simply is a matter of being derivable from conventions by *logic*. Which means that the demand that we should get assertible conclusions from assertible premises places no substantial constraint on the logic for mathematics. Given the extent to which mathematical correctness depends on logic, there is no good sense in which a conclusion inferred from assertible premises by an accepted form of logical inference could *fail* to be assertible itself.

We can put the point more simply. If mathematics is a kind of pretence, creating its own world of notional objects, then why shouldn't we pretend that it creates a classical world, in which every statement is either true or false? It's scarcely much of an objection to say that it doesn't really create that kind of world, that there mightn't, for instance, be any mathematical fact to make either Goldbach's conjecture or its negation true. For mathematics doesn't *really* create a world at all. Speaking realistically, there isn't even a mathematical fact to make '2 + 2 = 4' true.

All that the 'realistic pretence' amounts to is our deciding to reason *as if* every statement were true or false. There is no further question, from a fictionalist point of view, of whether bivalence really holds for mathematics, of whether every statement is *really* true or false. Maybe both Goldbach's conjecture and its negation are indeed unprovable by deductive logic from Peano's postulates. This would certainly amount to a real difference between Goldbach's conjecture and '2 + 2 = 4'. But why should this make us opt for intuitionistic rather than classical logic?

Note here that, as normally understood, the possibility that Goldbach's conjecture is unprovable is the possibility that it is left unprovable by classical logic, rather than the possibility that it can't be proved from intuitionistic logic. This classical possibility is the possibility that even after we have adopted the 'realistic pretence', we will still be unable to prove certain statements or their negations. But there is no reason to suppose that this possibility then discredits our adopting the 'realistic pretence' in the first place. Why shouldn't we pretend that we are dealing with a world in which truth outstrips our proof procedures (a world which in this respect is like the familiar natural world)? Since it's all a pretence anyway, which doesn't answer to anything independent, but merely manifests itself in the way we reason, the possibility of incompleteness is not a good reason for mathematicians to shun classical logic.

Of course none of the above shows that mathematicians *have* to reason classically. I haven't been giving a positive argument for classical mathematics, but simply resisting the negative argument from anti-realist semantics. So the substantial question as to whether mathematics ought to be classical or intuitionistic remains open.

At one level, obviously there is room for it to be both. If mathematics is a kind of game, a practice constituted by its own rules of procedure, then what is to stop it having two variants, one embodying classical logic, and another embodying intuitionistic logic? And certainly this seems to be the situation within the mathematical community. Alongside the majority concern with classical mathematics, there is also the perfectly respectable activity of intuitionistic mathematics, with its own theorems and results.

But mathematics isn't *just* a game. Or, rather, if it is a game, it is far more important than most other games. So there remain questions about the relative importance of intuitionistic and classical mathematics. Do the conventions of intuitionistic mathematics give rise to a game that is as much worth playing as the game of classical mathematics?

Some mathematical conventions are better than others because of their empirical applications. Apart from that they can give rise to non-trivial and otherwise intrinsically interesting results. How does intuitionistic mathematics compare with classical mathematics on these counts? (Note that, when in section 9.3 above I raised the question of some conventions being better than others, I was assuming an underlying logic, and interested in comparing subject-specific conventions – Euclidean v. non-Euclidean axioms, say – for relative importance. I am now interested in comparing the underlying logics themselves.)

Clearly intuitionistic mathematics is of some intrinsic interest. But when it comes to the more practical questions of empirical applicability it seems to me arguable that there are good reasons for sticking to classical mathematics. For a start, classical mathematics is more familiar, and therefore easier to work with. And secondly, and more substantially, in so far as we are realists about the natural world, we will want the empirical consequences of mathematical judgements (cf. the observable consequences of scientific theories) to conform to classical logic. Thus, for instance, because I am a realist about space, I take it that meaningful judgements about spatial intervals are all true or false. I also take it that spatial intervals are isomorphic to the real numbers, and because of this I have the practice of distilling consequences about spatial intervals from the theory of real numbers. And so this in itself provides a reason for conducting my real number theory on the basis of classical logic, which embodies the assumption that statements about real numbers are themselves all true or false.

9.6 MORAL TRUTH

Where mathematics aims to refer to numbers, sets, groups, and vector spaces, morality mentions things like justice, duty, obligation, virtue, wickedness, good, bad, right, and wrong. Mathematical judgements present themselves as beliefs answering to a notional world of mathematical entities. And similarly moral judgements present themselves as beliefs answering to a notional world of rights and wrongs.

I suggested at the end of the last chapter that we should reject realism for morality, for the same reason that we should reject realism for mathematics: namely, that if we were to grant moral facts an independent existence, then we would be unable to give any account of how we had found out about them.

Should we therefore say that moral facts don't exist at all, and that all moral beliefs are therefore false and ought to be rejected? In the case of mathematics I argued that we weren't *forced* to this conclusion merely in virtue of rejecting realism: mathematical anti-realism is in the first instance a view about the appropriate notion of correctness for some area of judgement, not a recommendation that we reject such judgements. But in the case of mathematics I argued that it is philosophically more straightforward, if only in the interests of contrasting the different notions of correctness applicable to mathematical and natural judgements, to opt for the view that mathematical facts don't exist and that mathematical judgements ought not therefore to be believed. In this section I want to explore the consequences of adopting a similar view about morality.

At first sight it might seem that this view will inevitably undermine the institution of morality. How can we remain committed to moral views if we deny that moral facts exist? But we don't have to dismiss morality out of hand just because we reject moral facts. In the case of mathematics the corresponding rejection of mathematical facts still left room for a fictionalist attitude to mathematics. And this fictionalism still allowed us to see mathematical claims as objectively correct or mistaken, and the overall activity of doing mathematics as important and useful, even though, strictly speaking, we didn't believe those claims. Why shouldn't we similarly be able to uphold moral claims by adopting a fictionalist attitude to morality?

However, there is a peculiarity about moral judgements which is absent from the mathematical case: namely, that moral judgements present themselves as intrinsically action-guiding. It is supposed to be part of the notion of wickedness, say, that if people accept that a certain action is wicked, then, other things being equal, they will be moved not to perform that action. And so any sense in which moral judgements can be said to be upheld will have to be a sense which carries with it a commitment to action. But now it might seem that pseudo-belief, acceptance of moral claims as a kind of fiction, cannot possibly be enough to commit us to action.

The action-guiding force of moral judgements certainly raises philosophical problems. But I don't see that it provides any argument against the fictionalist view of morality in particular. For the action-guiding force of morality is a puzzle for any 'cognitivist' view of moral judgements, that is, for any view which construes moral attitudes as somehow akin to beliefs, as opposed to those views which simply read moral judgements as some kind of outright expression of the subject's disposition to action. Subjectivist views of this latter kind are manifestly at odds with the intended content of moral judgements, which is why I have taken cognitivism for granted throughout. But cognitivism, precisely because it assimilates moral judgements to claims about putative facts, has a problem with the action-guiding force of morality.

In particular, this is a problem even for a realist version of cognitivism. Suppose, for the sake of the argument, that we thought of virtue as a real property detected by a special power of moral intuition. This would still leave us with a puzzle as to why believing that an action is virtuous should necessarily move us to do it. Of course, if you *want* to do what's virtuous, then you'll perform the action. But then, if we have to add in an independent want, it's no longer clear that there's anything distinctively action-guiding and moral about the belief in question. If we have to add in wants, why not just count such a belief as a straightforward non-moral claim about a property people happen to have desires about?

I'm not sure what we ought to say about this problem.[4] But whatever solutions are available, there is no obvious reason why they shouldn't be as available to the fictionalist about morality as the realist. Indeed it seems possible (though I have no positive thoughts to offer here) that the fictionalist is better off than the realist: perhaps it will in the end be easier to explain how pseudo-beliefs in fictional properties can be intrinsically action-

---

[4] But see McDowell (1978) and McFetridge (1978) for a recent attempt to make progress with this issue.

guiding than to explain how real beliefs in real properties can be.

Maybe, then, fictionalism leaves us *room* to uphold moral judgements as quasi-beliefs with action-guiding force. But then there is a further question: what is the *point* of so upholding moral judgements? If morality is a fiction, why is it a useful fiction? Clearly the answer available for mathematics, that it helps to generate nominalist beliefs about the structure of the natural world, isn't available for morality.

In the first instance we might say that morality is important to us because of its connection with general human welfare. It is pretty much a matter of definition that moral principles are principles which ensure harmonious social arrangements, within which people can live fruitful lives. At which point it is tempting to try to justify morality in terms of the fact that the acceptance of moral principles leads to certain desirable naturally defined results.

However, we can't move immediately from the definitioinal truth that morality is aimed at welfare, harmony, and fruitful lives, to the conclusion that its observance will produce certain natural results. For the essential non-naturalness of moral facts means that we can't equate the relevant notions of 'welfare', 'harmony', 'fruitful' with such social or psychological natural facts as satisfaction of existing wants, longevity, self-esteem, power over one's own affairs, or whatever.

Perhaps this element of non-naturalness is itself important to the importance of morality. By being somewhat distanced from the natural facts, our moral concepts leave us room to develop and change our moral responses to given kinds of actions and situations. This freedom could well be crucial to the institution of morality. If we weren't able to adjust our notions of human welfare and flourishing in the face of new and often unpredictable social and technological developments, morality might long since have lost its relevance to the way we live.

But still, the underlying point remains: if moral concepts don't report on natural facts, then we can't take it as given that morality will lead to certain naturally defined results. But does this really matter? Should we be thinking of the point of morality in this way in the first place? After all, even if we could have shown that the institution of morality was necessarily conducive to some natural effect, the non-naturalness of moral facts would still have left room for a further question, as to why we *ought* to uphold an institution which had that natural effect.

A far better way to think about the point of morality is as itself a moral issue: we shouldn't ask why morality is good for some non-moral end, but rather why it is *morally* good. And of course once we understand this question in this way, then it is open to us to give the obvious moral answer: we should uphold morality because that will better ensure human welfare, where 'welfare' is understood as a distinctively moral notion.

Is this response open to fictionalists about morality? If fictionalists don't accept the existence of moral facts, then how can they appeal to moral facts to justify morality? But the fictionalist will repeat the point that the demand for a justification of morality is itself a moral question. People who deny that there is any point to morality, and who consequently recommend that we *should* eschew moral attitudes, are themselves putting forward a moral claim. Their claim is made from within the moral realm. Fictionalists don't reject morality out of hand, and in particular they don't deny its action-guiding force. They just have a variant view of its status. So they are as well-placed as the next person to discuss the moral question of the justification of morality, and to give the obvious moral answer.

A rather more substantial problem for fictionalism, however, is presented by moral divergence, by the fact that different people in different times and places have incompatible moral views. Recall the original discussion of divergence in 1.3. I argued there that realism was relatively well-placed to accommodate divergence: It could simply see divergence as a manifestation of the fact that human thought wasn't predetermined to get the world right. Anti-realism, on the other hand, was precisely the view that human thought was predetermined to get things right, and so was forced by divergence to the unpalatable conclusion that different people literally live in different worlds.

It might seem that the view of morality I am defending is similarly undermined by moral divergence. Isn't my view a version of anti-realism, and isn't it therefore unable to accommodate the existence of divergent moral views? But this would be too quick. The anti-realism discussed in chapter 1 was anti-realism about the world in general. Which was why it was inconsistent with divergence: it is indeed incoherent to hold that the world in general is different for different people. But we are currently rejecting realism for morality in particular, by contrast with realism about the natural world. This contrast between moral beliefs and natural beliefs provides a motive, I have argued, for an explicitly fictionalist attitude to morality. And it is by no means obvious that there is anything incoherent about holding that different people live with divergent fictions about the moral world.

But, still, the moral fictionalist isn't yet out of the woods. Maybe there isn't anything immediately incoherent in the idea of different people having divergent fictions. But, as we have seen, even if morality is a fiction, it's a rather special kind of fiction: namely, a fiction with action-guiding force. And this action-guiding element means that divergence raises special problems for the moral fictionalist who wants to uphold morality as an institution.

The analogy with pure mathematics is instructive here. Divergent pure mathematical systems don't even look as if they raise problems about the status of mathematics. This is because different pure mathematical systems, like Euclidean and Riemannian geometry, are simply compatible alternatives, rather than competitors. There are, as we have seen, questions about the relative usefulness and interest of different pure mathematical systems. But even if we answer such a question in favour of, say, Riemannian geometry over Euclidean geometry, this doesn't require a mathematical rejection of Euclidian geometry. We can still uphold the pure mathematical truth that Euclidean triangles contain 180°.

Morality is different. A moral system is something to live by. By embracing a given moral world you allow your actions to be influenced in a certain way. And this means that we can't simply view the possibility of alternative moral worlds with the same kind of equanimity with which we view alternative geometries, or, again, alternative versions of a Sherlock Holmes story. We have to choose between moral systems, in a way we don't have to choose between alternative geometries or Holmes stories. You can't simultaneously live by the code of a Roman soldier and by our contemporary morality.

To this extent, then, our moral views are like our views about the natural world, and unlike mathematical or other fictional beliefs. One moral view necessarily excludes another. And this might now seem to show that an acceptance of moral divergence necessarily undermines the institution of morality. If divergent moral views are possible, and if there is nothing to make any particular such view objectively correct, then how can we continue to uphold any moral views? Doesn't the existence of incompatible systems with as much authority as our own show that we have no right to our own moral views?

But even here I'm not sure. Despite these last remarks, perhaps it is possible both to recognize moral divergence and to preserve our own moral views. What I have in mind is this. Our moral commitments are important to us, as important as anything. But, even so, I have argued that they involve a kind of pretence, a postulation of a world of notional moral facts. Why then shouldn't our moral commitments result from a choice, a commitment, which doesn't itself have any basis? If the importance of morality can survive its being a pretence (as does, for instance, the importance of mathematics), then why shouldn't it be a pretence that we embrace in an existentialist spirit, without any further authority, and in recognition of the fact that alternative moral commitments are possible for human beings? We can't, it seems to me, adopt this attitude to our view of the natural world, for we can't think of this as a pretence, and *a fortiori* can't think of it as a pretence to which alternatives are possible for human beings. But if the epistemology of morality forces us to recognize that, by comparison with the natural world, the moral world is an artefact of our patterns of thought, then why should we be obliged to back up our moral commitments with reasons for rejecting all alternatives? We are compelled to choose a moral system if we are human beings (for even the rejection of morality is, as pointed out above, a moral position). But I don't see why those choices should themselves be based on compelling reasons.[5]

[5] Blackburn (1984, ch. 6.3) holds that relativism threatens morality, but that moral conflicts can always be resolved by moving to a position which transcends both sides. However, Blackburn's main concern is to minimize the contrast between moral and natural discourse. It seems to me that once we reject Blackburn's 'quasi-realism' about morality (cf. footnote 4 to the previous chapter), then we need to rethink such issues as moral relativism (and moral consistency, moral bivalence, etc.). Not that there doesn't remain something disturbing about moral relativism. These issues require far more careful discussion than I have been able to give them here.

9.7 INDUCTIVE INFERENCES

In the first section of this chapter I discussed deductive inferences, and showed how it was possible to evaluate our deductive habits for reliability and adjust them accordingly if necessary. However, deduction is not the only way in which we generate new beliefs from old. We also engage in various species of non-deductive inferences, inferences where there is no question of the truth of the conclusion being logically guaranteed by the truth of the premises. Indeed the vast majority of our beliefs depend on such non-deductive inferences to some extent.

In this section I want to concentrate on inductive inferences to universal generalizations. It is disputable whether all our non-deductive inferences can be reduced to or are dependent on such inferences to generalizations. But I take it that if we can give an adequate account of such inferences then we will at least have dealt with a central part of our non-deductive practice.

The task, then, is to consider whether inductive inferences to universal generalizations can be evaluated for their reliability and whether this will allow us to adjust our inductive habits accordingly if necessary. This might seem rather a tall order. Am I not in effect asking for a solution to the traditional problem of induction?

However, the issue comes out rather differently in the present context of debate. As James van Cleve has observed (1984), if we adopt a reliabilist notion of justification, then an enumeratively supported inductive conclusion (from 'All A's so far have been B's' to 'All A's are B's') will be justified just in case enumerative inductions are in fact reliable, whether or not we can show *a priori* that they are. Moreover, he observes, we might also, as it happens, be justified in believing *that* enumerative inductions are reliable. For we may well be able to infer this conclusion by means of a reliable enumerative induction from the past success of just such enumerative inductions.[6]

Van Cleve's analysis is relevant to my overall programme. Van

---

[6] Van Cleve's generalizations are about most A's, rather than all A's, but this does not affect the points I wish to make.

Cleve shows how people who embody certain inductive habits might thereby be led to views as to whether or not those habits are reliable. And in particular he shows how such people might end up in the stable self-vindicating situation where the beliefs their inductive habits give them inform them that those habits are reliable.

It is worth noting that van Cleve does not in any sense *eliminate* the possibility that enumerative inductions might *not* be reliable. He shows that *if* enumerative inductions are reliable, *then* (assuming the reliabilist thoery of justification) their conclusions will be justified, and we can justifiably believe that they are reliable. But he does not offer any way of detaching the conclusion of this conditional.

However, this is allowed for in my overall programme – or at least it will be allowed for later. For it is just a special case of the point that, even if it is rational to seek justified beliefs by taking steps to ensure that your belief-forming processes are reliable, nothing so far guarantees that such steps will succeed, since they will inevitably be informed by the beliefs that those selfsame belief-forming processes give you. As before, I ask readers to shelve this difficulty till the next chapter.

So van Cleve doesn't prove that enumerative inductions are reliable. But he clearly has it in mind that at least they might be. But even here there is a difficulty. Nelson Goodman's problem of grue and bleen (1954) shows that enumerative inductions *can't* in general be reliable. There are far too many ways of categorizing things as A's and B's for it to be possible that all A's are B's *whenever* we find some A going with some B. If we are to see inductive inferences as reliable we need somehow to place limitations on the *kinds* of things whose co-occurrence indicates a general truth. As it is sometimes put, we need to specify which categorizations are *natural* kinds, where 'natural kind' simply means that sort of classification that might be expected to appear in a lawlike generalization, and which might therefore form the basis for an inductive inference. (Van Cleve mentions this problem, but deals with it by simply helping himself to the assumption that all his A's and B's denote natural kinds. I want to show that once we examine the basis for such a delimitation of predicates the issues come out rather differently, and in a way that more plausibly fits the actual practice of science.)

In the first instance we can appeal to our background beliefs themselves to tell us about natural kinds. For common sense and science don't only give us first-order generalizations of the form 'All A's are B's', but also second-order information about what kinds of properties might be expected to go together. We know that bacteria are the kind of thing that can be responsible for infectious diseases, but that the position of the planets is not. We know that mass, and position with respect to other physical bodies, are the kinds of properties that are relevant to changes in motion, but that colour and smell are not. And this kind of information then tells us which observed, finite patterns might well be manifestations of underlying general truths, and which are mere happenstance.

So far, so good. But this only takes us some of the way. For knowing that certain observed patterns *might* be manifestations of laws isn't knowing very much. If we want to arrive reliably at beliefs as to which observed patterns *are* manifestations of laws, we will need something more. (I am assuming here that the outputs of our inductive habits are full beliefs. For more on this, see 10.4 below.)

However, there is no reason to suppose that science only tells us about natural kinds to the extent of indicating that some pairs of properties *might* happen to go together in laws. We can also think of it as giving us more restrictive information about natural kinds, and as telling us, for certain kinds of results, that only a *limited* number of properties could be causing those results. Science doesn't only tell us that bacteria are one kind of thing that can cause infectious diseases: it tells us that microscopic organisms in general are the only possible causes of infectious diseases. It doesn't only tell us that mass and position with respect to other bodies are amongst the candidate causes of changes in motion: it tells us that these and a few other basic properties are the only possible causes.

If we do have this kind of information, then we are in a position to think of induction in terms of elimination rather than enumeration. Given a limited list of possible causes, we can find out which is the actual cause by applying Mill's methods of induction. Appropriately designed experiments can eliminate all but one of the causes, and allow us to be certain of our resulting causal conclusion. Thus, to take the very simplest case, if A and B are the only possible causes of E, we can find out which is the actual cause by engineering a situation where we have A without B, or B without A, and seeing which gives us E. And there are any number of variations on this theme. (See Mill, 1843; and the Appendix to Mackie, 1974.)

It is true that Mill's methods presuppose determinism, in that they take it that every particular occurrence of a given E will have a deterministic cause. (Otherwise E occurring without A, say, wouldn't eliminate A as a cause, for this might just happen to be an undetermined occurrence of E.) Today we believe that the universe is at bottom indeterministic. But then there are statistical analogues of Mill's methods. If the number of factors that might be probabilistically relevant to some outcome is limited, then we can use the techniques of multivariate analysis to infer which are and which are not in fact connected to that outcome. (Cf. my 1978, ch. 3.6–3.7.)

To some readers this appeal to Mill's methods might seem simple-minded. But while further analysis is certainly needed, Mill's eliminative methods deserve to be taken seriously. Apart from anything else, they seem to capture the actual structure of scientific experimentation and inference far better than approaches which concentrate on enumerative induction. Scientists don't just reach highly tentative general conclusions on the basis of repeated observation of instances. The results of their empirical investigations often put them in a position categorically to assert that a certain phenomenon is caused by such-and-such. And this is precisely because only a limited number of things could be the cause, and their experiments or surveys are carefully designed to find out which that is. Thus, for example, there were a limited number of possible structures for DNA, and amongst these only the double helix was consistent with the X-ray diffraction photographs and the other relevant phenomena. There were various possible causes for the spread of AIDS, and medical scientists narrowed it down to the HTLV-III virus. A number of things could have been responsible for the twentieth-century increase in lung cancer, and survey research showed that it was smoking.

From William Whewell onwards the standard criticism of Mill's methods has been that no account is offered of where the A's and B's come from: how are we supposed to find out that there are only a limited number of possible causes for a given effect? (Cf. Whewell, 1849, p. 44.) I have suggested that we can appeal to science itself to deliver this information. Science itself contains natural kind assumptions that tell us which causes could possibly be responsible for a certain effect.

But is this appeal to science legitimate? Such a natural kind assumption is itself a kind of scientific generalization. ('All infectious diseases are due to microscopic organisms.') So presumably it is also arrived at by some kind of inductive inference. But then this inference will in turn have to appeal to some analogous background natural kind assumption. But this too will have to be induced. And so on. I seem to be in danger of making an infinite regress out of every inductive inference.

But we need to go slowly here. I don't want to think of the natural kind assumptions as *premises* to the Millian inductive inferences. That would make the Millian inductions into deductions, and that's unnecessary. The premises to such an inductive inference are simply the experimental data, and the conclusion is that hypothesis which, as it happens, is the only one amongst the possible hypotheses consistent with the data. The natural kind assumption, *that* these are the only possible hypotheses, only comes in on the outside, as it were, when we try to figure out how it is that inferences of this kind are generally reliable. Natural kind assumptions aren't needed when we are actually *making* inductive inferences, but only when we are thinking *about* them, and trying to understand, in terms of our overall picture of the world, how they work.

But this now points to a real problem. Even if we don't need such assumptions *qua* inductive inferrers, we do need them *qua* concerned believers who are reflecting about induction and trying to explain its reliability. And since we need them in this latter capacity, there ought to be a satisfactory account of how we have reliably arrived at them. And this does now threaten a genuine regress.

The trouble is that our explanation of our arriving at any given natural kind assumption seems to commit us to a different, higher-level natural kind assumption. Consider the assumption that all infectious diseases come from microbes. How are we to account for our having this natural kind assumption? Clearly we can't do so by reference to the kind of inference that this assumption itself vindicates, for, while experiments designed to rule out all other microbes can identify, say, the virus responsible for the transmission of AIDS, such experiments clearly won't suffice to establish that all infectious diseases are caused by microbes in the first place. To explain our arriving at *this* assumption we will need to appeal to a yet higher natural kind assumption. So, for example, we might argue that we got to know that all infectious diseases are caused by microbes because only certain kinds of biochemical agents could possibly be responsible for such diseases, and empirical data have ruled out all agents but microbes. But what then about the assumption that only certain kinds of biochemical agents are possible causes? We seem only to be pushing the problem back. Perhaps we could appeal to basic chemistry, and to the central assumptions of physics. But where did they come from?

The best bet here seems to be to appeal at some point to a principle of simplicity. At some point we need to say that it is right to opt for a given theoretical answer because it is the only one amongst the reasonably simple answers consistent with the data. That is, at some point we need to use, as the natural kind assumption which explains the reliability of our inference from experiment, the principle that only the simple answers are possible.

Doesn't this just push the problem one stage further back? How are we to explain our knowing the principle of simplicity which we appeal to in explaining why such theoretical inferences are reliable? But the attraction of simplicity is that it offers some chance of stopping the regress by inferring an assumption from the selfsame form of inference that that assumption vindicates. (That's in effect the trick that van Cleve pulls, which is why he doesn't have a regress, whatever other objections he faces.)

Suppose that we have arrived at a number of answers to high-level theoretical questions in chemistry, physics, astronomy, etc. Think of the pattern of such high-level answers as the experimental data. Then it may be that the only reasonably simple account which is consistent with that pattern is that high-level answers are in general simple. So we arrive at the conclusion, that high-level answers are generally simple, by an inference whose reliability is explained by that conclusion itself. (To see that this trick isn't as empty as it might seem, consider people who generally opted for complex answers rather than simple ones. Then their general run of theoretical answers would be complex. But such people wouldn't be able to bootstrap themselves to the assumption tht the right answer is generally complex, for that wouldn't be a complex account of their pattern of discoveries, but a simple one.)

How can we make this inference, to the meta-assumption that high-level answers are generally simple, if we don't already have it? Indeed, how can we even arrive at the chemical, physical, etc., answers which provide the data for this inference, without that simplicity assumption? But remember once more that natural kind assumptions in general, and the simplicity meta-assumption in particular, aren't supposed to function as *premises* to inductive inferences. Their role is only to account, from the outside, for the reliability of those inferences. So the idea is that we are led to high-level theoretical answers, and thence to the simplicity principle itself, via a form of inference which doesn't need the simplicity principle as a *premise*. And then, since we do get the simplicity principle as a conclusion, we are able to explain the reliability of the inferences that got us there.

I admit there is a strong element of hand-waving about the solution I am offering here. For I haven't said anything substantial about the notoriously difficult notion of theoretical simplicity. So at best I am offering a shell of a possible answer to the problem, rather than a definite resolution. But perhaps that is as it should be. I don't want to appeal to some *a priori* notion of simplicity, but rather to that notion, whatever it is, that characterizes the general run of high-level theoretical answers. So philosophical analysis on its own can't be expected to say anything substantial about simplicity. The appropriate notion needs to be filled out by detailed reflection on the progress of science.

One last point before proceeding. I said at the beginning of this section that I would offer a more plausible acount of scientific practice than would come from an approach in terms of eliminative induction. But, even if I have succeeded to some extent in this, there is one respect in which my analysis so far has been deliberately idealized. In my concern to show how scientific methods might be vindicated without vicious regress, I have emphasized the static logical structure of the situation. In particular, I have assumed a fixed set of inferential practices moving scientists willy-nilly from experimental data to explanatory conclusions, and have then observed that just those practices might deliver beliefs that will explain the reliability of those practices.

But of course scientists aren't just automatic inferrers. They actively reflect on the reliability of their inferential practices, in the light of their existing natural kind assumptions, and make such revisions to those practices as then seem necessary, in just the way I have emphasized is possible for other belief-forming processes. But this now gives rise to the kind of holism in scientific theory-choice that has been emphasized by much recent writing in the philosophy of science. Different high-level theoretical assumptions, and perhaps even different underlying principles of simplicity, will imply different things about what is to be inferred from lower-level experimental data. And so questions at the lower levels (about the chemical composition of various specific substances, say) will not get answered until the higher-level debates (about the nature of the underlying structure of matter) have been resolved.

But while this complicates the picture, it doesn't destroy it altogether. That small questions can't get answered until big questions get answered doesn't mean that nothing ever gets found out. It just means that it takes longer than might be thought. A 'research programme', or a 'paradigm', based on a given high-level theoretical commitment, is under an obligation to develop a set of lower-level natural kind assumptions which will imply that the experimental results confirm the overall programme and discredit its competitors. It might take time to develop such assumptions, and it might also take time to uncover the requisite experimental data, but there is no reason to suppose that it cannot be done.

Note here that while we do need to admit a kind of temporal holism, allowing that certain small questions might not be answered until certain big questions have been answered, this doesn't imply the kind of confirmational holism according to which evidence only bears on whole 'resrach programmes' as undivided units. Even if certain questions only get answered slowly, and in bunches, when we do discover the answers we find out which bits of the experimental evidence lend inductive support to which of our theoretical conclusions. (See Glymour, 1980, ch. II, for the implausibility of the Quinean thesis that confirmation is always holistic.)

This last paragraph, with its talk of 'discovery' and 'finding out', will have made it clear that in my view a 'research programme' which vindicates its own acceptance by developing suitable lower-level natural kind assumptions will be a programme that has discovered the truth. No doubt many readers will be uneasy about this assumption. There are two obvious grounds for suspicion. First, mightn't it be possible for two incompatible research programmes both to pull this self-vindicating trick? And, secondly, doesn't the history of science in any case demonstrate that all scientific theories turn out in time to be false? Both these points will be dealt with in the next chapter.

10

Relativism, History, and Scepticism

10.1 THE DIFFICULTY OF SELF-VINDICATION

In the last three chapters I have shown how a naturalized approach to epistemology recommends that concerned believers should evaluate their belief-forming processes for reliability and adjust them accordingly, and I have tried to illustrate in some detail how such reliability-evaluations are possible for different kinds of belief-forming processes. However, I still need to consider whether the naturalized recommendation will be effective: will somebody who carried out the naturalized recommendation succeed in avoiding error?

The naturalized recommendation might seem unlikely to achieve its intended aim. Maybe I have shown how a concerned believer can sensibly *try* to be reliable. But why suppose that the recommended strategy will *succeed* in making you reliable? In particular, isn't there an obvious difficulty, which I have had occasion to mention a number of times already? Your judgements as to which belief-forming processes are reliable will inevitably depend on your existing beliefs about the world and how you fit into it. So won't the naturalized recommendation at best get you into the state of your belief-forming processes *seeming* reliable, in the light of your existing beliefs, as opposed to the desired state of your *being* reliable?

In the course of this chapter I am going to argue that despite this prima facie difficulty the naturalized recommendation is indeed effective. Anybody who manages to get themselves into the self-vindicating state where their processes all seem reliable in the light of their beliefs will in fact have reliable methods and in consequence true beliefs.

An obvious initial worry is that there will be too many systems of processes and resulting beliefs ('intellectual systems' henceforth) which are self-vindicating. In particular, if there are a number of self-vindicating systems which respectively incorporate *incompatible* beliefs, then the naturalized recommendation can't be generally effective, for only at most one of those systems can in fact have things right.

In this section I want to show that some initial reasons for thinking that there will inevitably be a plethora of incompatible self-vindicating systems are bad reasons.

It is sometimes suggested that if people engage in a certain belief-forming process, then that process will automatically seem reliable to them. (Cf. Putnam, 1983, pp. 233–4.) However, this is a mistake. It is not automatically true that the adoption of a belief-forming process *per se* gives you the belief that that process is reliable.

Let me lay out the situation as follows. Suppose that person X embodies a number of belief-forming processes, $P_1, \ldots, P_n$, and each such process P_i gives X a set of beliefs B_i. The question is whether the beliefs in a given B_i will vindicate the corresponding P_i as reliable. Suppose for the sake of the argument that P_k is a colour perception process. Then B_k will contain beliefs *about the colours of particular objects*. But the kind of belief required to vindicate a colour perception process won't be a belief about the colour of a particular object, but rather a belief *about the reliability of a process*. To take another example, suppose that P_k is some inductive process. Then B_k will contain scientific generalizations, such as that all bodies fall with constant acceleration, say. But the belief that all bodies fall with constant acceleration isn't the kind of belief that will show that a given pattern of inductive inference is generally reliable for truth. The point is entirely general. There is no reason why the beliefs coming *out* of a given process should include beliefs that will *vindicate* that process as reliable.

But, even if self-vindication isn't completely automatic, isn't the following still an easy all-purpose way to get a positive evaluation for any belief-forming process? Suppose we embody a process that delivers judgements that p. Suppose we have enough reflexive self-awareness to know when we have judged that p. Then on each occasion when the p-delivering process operates we will believe (a) that p (from the process) and (b) that we have judged that p (from our self-awareness). Which then, by a straightforward inductive inference, seems to support the conclusion: p is indeed the case, whenever we judge that p. And isn't this exactly the kind of premise required for a positive reliability-evaluation?

But this too is too quick. For one thing, a belief-forming habit with nothing else but such a cheap inductive vindication in its favour is likely to have its output claims overturned because of judgements that p arrived at by alternative routes. Imagine, for example, somebody who had an observational disposition to judge that certain observed people were rich, but where the disposition was triggered by some relatively arbitrary circumstance, such as, say, that the observed people had red hair. Since there are lots of other ways of finding out whether a given person is rich, which will reveal that many red-headed people are not rich, the beliefs generated by this disposition would regularly conflict with other beliefs as to who is and isn't rich.

More fundamentally, the inductive logic of the cheap vindication can itself be questioned. In addition to the argument just given, that the outputs of cheaply vindicated processes won't in general cohere with those of other processes, it can also be argued that the cheap vindication doesn't even provide an initial reason for accepting such outputs in the first place. For, as I pointed out in the last chapter, purely enumerative evidence is not in itself sufficient for inductive support, because of the Goodmanian point that there are far too many ways of categorizing things for all such enumerative projections to be sound. The categorizations involved need to be mutually projectible natural kinds. But there isn't any general reason to suppose that the (a)s and (b)s in the present kind of case will be such natural kinds.

Thus consider agaian the earlier example. We embody an arbitrary process which generates the judgement 'There's a rich person'. We then notice, on various particular occasions, that the judgement 'There's a rich person' occurs when, in our opinion, there *is* a rich person present. Would this now give us any reason at all to suppose that the process is generally reliable? What we have, so to speak, is a finite number of co-occurrences of (a) somebody judging 'There is a rich person' and (b) a rich person being there. What we need in addition is some indication that the (a)s and (b)s in question are mutually projectible natural kinds. Now, such an indication would indeed be provided by anything which suggested that the (a)s, the judgements about wealth, were being *caused* by (some reliable indicator of) the (b)s, the actual wealth of the people observed. But, by hypothesis, we have an *arbitrary* process giving rise to the (a)s, the judgements about wealth. That is, there is no prior reason to expect that the (a)s, the judgements, are generally correlated with the (b)s, the facts. And so there is no automatic inductive path to the vindication of any arbitrary belief-forming method.

So not every system of processes P_i and resulting beliefs B_i is one where the beliefs in the B_i's vindicate the P_i's as reliable. A set of processes can perfectly well seem unreliable even in the light of the beliefs they themselves generate.

But this mightn't seem to take us very far. Even if not *every* intellectual system is self-vindicating, won't there still be a large number of incompatible systems which are? And doesn't this show, as before, that the naturalized recommendation can't possibly be an effective way to avoid error?

Thus suppose your only belief-forming process is to believe everything an oracle tells you. And suppose that one of the things the oracle tells you is that it is infallible. This will give you a self-vindicating intellectual system. But if one oracle system can be so self-vindicating, then clearly many can be, each generating an incompatible set of beliefs. (Cf. Putnam, 1983, pp. 233–4.)

However, an oracle system as just described would suffer from a terrible paucity of belief-forming processes. Its only source of beliefs would be the deliverances of the oracle. Moreover, this blinkeredness would be essential to the stability of the system. The oracle's adherents would succeed in being self-vindicating only because they had closed off all other possible channels of information to the natural world. If they trusted their senses as well as the oracle they would quickly find grounds for believing the oracle to be highly unreliable.

I want to discount such oracle systems from being properly self-vindicating on the grounds that they manage to preserve their stability only by radically restricting their range of belief-forming processes. This might seem *ad hoc*. But note that reliability is not the only desideratum the concerned believer will place on belief-forming processes. If our only requirement were to maximize reliability, in the sense of maximizing our proportion of true beliefs, an easy way to succeed would be to eliminate all processes that were in any way risky. (The surest way to avoid error would be to have no beliefs at all.) But clearly there is little point in insisting that our beliefs are delivered with maximal reliability, if that means that we end up with scarcely any beliefs. We also want our processes to be as *informative* as possible, to tell us about as wide a range of issues as possible, even if that introduces some abstract element of risk. As Goldman has put it, we want to avoid ignorance, as well as error (1986, pp. 26–7).

So there is a principled reason for adopting, as an extra regulative requirement on our overall intellectual system, the requirement that our intellectual system contain as informative a range of processes as is compatible with their being self-vindicating. That is, not only should our overall system contain *only* processes that can be vindicated as reliable, but it should also contain as *many* such processes as is possible. From now on I intend to take this extra rider as read, and to assume that intellectual systems like the oracle-follower's are not adequately self-vindicating.

(But now consider a more sophisticated set of oracle-believers. They embody all the processes that we have, and consequently have all the same beliefs, including ones that vindicate those processes, save on matters where the oracle has pronounced, where they believe the oracle instead, once more on the grounds that it has assured them of its infallibility. This intellectual system can scarcely be faulted on grounds of informativeness, for they have views on all the matters that we do. But perhaps it can be faulted on other grounds. Presumably the deliverances of the oracle will tend to conflict with those delivered by other processes. So, given that they stand by the oracle, they will have to dispute the reliability of those other processes. But, by hypothesis, they have beliefs that imply that those processes are reliable. So they will have to abandon those beliefs as well, and the processes behind them, and so on. And I would suggest that in this way their whole system will unravel itself, until they end up, as in the original example, believing nothing but the oracle. Which is to say that they would be well advised, given that they want informativeness, at some point to question their faith in the oracle instead.)

We might also mention here a further regulative requirement on satisfactory intellectual systems. This relates to the *individuation* of belief-forming processes. I have already touched on this issue. In 7.3 I pointed out that without some restrictions on what count as processes, it would be too easy to present any given belief as emerging from a reliable 'process', and so I suggested some appropriate such restrictions. At that point the issue was simply the objective question of what is required for something to count as a reliable process, and didn't especially involve the idea of a concerned believer actively seeking to make all his or her processes reliable. But a related subjective question arises in connection with the enterprise of a concerned believer: namely, does the believer individuate processes in a way that makes it sensible to count the resulting intellectual system as self-vindicating? For it will be far too easy to end up believing one's belief-forming processes are reliable, if one is allowed to cut very broadly, into, say, 'visual perception', 'memory', 'inference', etc., and to avoid any finer divisions.

I think that the appropriate requirement here is that concerned believers should always aim to cut as *finely* as is relevant to assessments of reliability. If they can divide 'visual perception' into various sub-processes, such that their beliefs about the reliability of those sub-processes will differ, then they should consider those sub-processes separately. At first sight this might seem to make it too easy to get specific processes vindicated as reliable (remember 'recognizing my aunt'). But note that if you *need* to distinguish 'recognizing your aunt' from other cases of face-recognition in order to get it coming out reliably, then this can only be because you are capable of distinguishing other kinds of face-recognition into processes where you are *un*reliable: for distinguishing 'recognizing my aunt' from other cases can only *improve* its perceived reliability if it is thereby dissociated from recognizably inferior processes. Now, clearly, if you are capable in this way of identifying reliable and unreliable parts of existing belief-forming processes, then the aim of avoiding error means that you *should* make those distinctions and adjust your mental habits accordingly. And so there isn't in fact anything wrong, or too easy, about identifying 'recognizing your aunt' as a separate process and thereby vindicating it as reliable, in cases where this distinction indeed makes a difference to your assessment of the reliability of your aunt-recognitional ability. Of course, if that distinction doesn't make a difference (if you think, as most of us do, that you can recognize a far wider category of people just as well as you can recognize your aunt), then there's no point in distinguishing your aunt-recognition as a separate process. But that's all right, since the original suggestion was only that a concerned believer should aim to cut as finely as is *relevant* to assessments of reliability. So from now on let me take it as given that properly self-vindicating intellectual systems don't get their processes to appear reliable just by lumping together sub-processes that would be assessed differently if distinguished. (The idea that a concerned believer might properly individuate 'recognizing my aunt' as a separate belief-forming process might seem to contradict the argument of 7.3, where I explicitly designed criteria of individuation for belief-forming processes to exclude that case. But the aim in 7.3 was to stop an unreliable judger, who luckily had a true belief in a particular case, from counting as justified just because there was *some* description of the particular case such that the judger was generally right in such cases. The suggestion was that we should only allow identifications of processes as reliable if those identifications were relevant to the explanations of subjects having those processes. In 7.3 I took it that 'recognizing my aunt' wouldn't be such an identification. But note now that in the quite specific kind of case we have considered in this section, 'recognizing my aunt' *would* become such an identification. If the process in question came to be adhered to as a result of my reflecting on the matter and realizing that my aunt's face is one of the few I can recognize, then, given the argument of 7.3, it *is* legitimate to individuate it in such terms, for it is specifically the reliability of recognizing my *aunt* that accounts for my having the process.)

10.2   DIGRESSION ON DEGREES OF BELIEF

Further complexities lurk in the idea of assessments for reliability. Thus one might question whether reliability places a substantial demand on processes at all. After all, reliability can range from unity (p is certain if the process delivers the belief that p) to zero (not-p is certain if the process delivers the belief that p). The rational person will presumably have a *degree* of belief that corresponds to the reliability of the process. But can't any process then be a good process, however reliable or unreliable it is, provided it produces degrees of belief proportional to the reliability in question?

But now we should recognize a yet further desideratum on beliefs. We want our *degrees* of belief themselves to be responsive to the facts. For any possible state of affairs p, we would like to end up believing p *fully* if p obtains, and believing not-p *fully*, if it doesn't. True, processes delivering such full beliefs are sometimes *in principle* impossible: for future p's governed by objective chances there is no possibility of getting fully reliable processes for present beliefs as to p. But for all other events (all past and present events, and all determined future ones: all those 'fixed', so to speak, by present circumstances) there is in principle no limit to the degree of reliability of our processes. Indeed, for chance events themselves there is no limit in principle to the reliability of processes for present beliefs about those *chances*, for those chances can themselves be determined by present circumstances. So we can sensibly aim to have all our beliefs delivered by fully reliable processes, save only for beliefs about the actual future manifestations of objective chances (where we will, of course, aim to have degrees of belief that correspond to those chances).

So let us stand by the idea (which has been implicit all along) that what we want (future chance events aside) are fully reliable processes giving rise to full beliefs. This is not to deny that in practice we will often be forced to use processes of less than full reliability, and aim to tailor our degrees of belief accordingly. Nor is it to deny that there are interesting philosophical issues raised by this practical necessity. But in the present context of argument, where our concern is specifically with the significance of being self-vindicating, it will be helpful to prescind from these issues and simply consider the situation of a community which has vindicated all its processes as *fully* reliable.

One further point. A 'full' belief that p, in the above sense, needn't be absolutely indubitable. Its occurrence needn't render the falsity of p unthinkable. Full beliefs need only be almost always true in some sense that warrants giving them a degree of belief indiscernible from one. Full belief requires 'moral certainty', not absolute certainty. This will be of some significance below.

10.3   RELATIVISM OF THEORY

So far I have argued that it isn't as easy to become self-vindicating as you might think. But the basic worry remains. Maybe I have shown that it's not that easy to be self-vindicating. But that still leaves it open that there might be *some* incompatible but equally self-vindicating intellectual systems. To discredit the naturalized recommendation as an effective means of avoiding error you don't have to show that there are *lots* of incompatible self-vindicating systems. Any number greater than one will do.

Recall one of the worries mentioned at the end of the last chapter. Won't two incompatible scientific research programmes sometimes both be able to develop lower-level natural kind assumptions which vindicate their divergent inductive responses to the data? In the nineteenth century the defenders of the atomic theory of matter were able to identify elements and suggest chemical analyses for different substances in such a way as to make it appear that their overall theory was the only possible account of the data. But mightn't the adherents of a different programme, say some version of the eighteenth-century affinity theory, have been able similarly to develop classifications in the light of which their alternative inductive processes would have appeared reliable instead, if only they had persisted with their programme long enough?

Nor does the difficulty stop with natural kind classifications and the inductive processes they underpin. Analogous worries can be raised about the generation of the observational data themselves.

Thus consider once more the Ptolemy–Copernicus example discussed in 7.1. I pointed out there that, from our modern Copernican point of view, the observational habit that uses movement with respect to the earth to judge direction of fall is unreliable and should therefore be abandoned, for the Copernican theory tells us that the earth is moving.

But now consider the situation from the Ptolemaic point of view. *They* didn't think that the earth is moving. And so reflection wouldn't have given *them* any reason to distrust the observational habit in question.

Here again, as with the possibility of divergence of inductive processes, we seem to have alternative intellectual systems each of whose processes appear to be reliable in the light of their own beliefs. The Ptolemaists' geocentric beliefs told them that their naïve observational method was perfectly reliable, while the Copernican's heliocentric beliefs implied that an alternative method was reliable.

I accept that if we focus on this particular aspect of the difference between the Ptolemaists and their opponents, the naturalized recommendation leads to a stand-off. And perhaps the same would hold with the hypothesized conflict between the atomic theory's and the affinity theory's inductive processes. But this still leaves it open that the one of the systems may be in trouble further down the line. What, for instance, about the Ptolemaists' belief that the earth is not moving? Did they exercise themselves about the reliability of the process behind that belief? And, if they did, what then about the beliefs they appealed to in deciding that? And so on. I would suggest that if we continue in this way, it will turn out at some point that one of the two sides have arbitrary methods, which by their own lights they can't vindicate as reliable, or arbitrary beliefs, which don't issue from any such vindicatable method.

More generally, I want to suggest that whenever we have two incompatible intellectual systems generated by alternative research programmes, at least one will turn out in this way not to be properly self-vindicating. Maybe some of its processes will be vindicatable by some of its beliefs, and perhaps most of its beliefs will issue from such authorizable methods. But I want to claim that at some point it will fail to be self-vindicating.

Let me be precise here. I certainly don't want to deny that different people can have different, and indeed radically incompatible, intellectual systems. Most of the first half of this book was devoted to establishing just this possibility. What I want to claim is that two different such systems cannot both be stable relative to the naturalized recommendation. At least one of the systems will not be able to vindicate its processes in the light of the beliefs they generate: if the adherents of that system unreflectively suppose that it is adequate, that can only be because they haven't fully investigated the question of whether their processes are reliable.

It is not essential to this claim that in the case of a conflict between contemporary Western science and some historically or anthropologically distant alternative, it will be the latter system that fails to be self-vindicating. As it happens, I am inclined to suppose that most of contemporary science is true, and will say something more about this in a moment. But the thesis I am currently putting forward is not that we, with our current beliefs, will therefore find fault with incompatible systems of thought (of course we will). It is rather that all but at most one such system is always going to turn out inadequate by its *own* lights.

10.4 TRUTH AND THE HISTORY OF SCIENCE

My underlying thought is that only the *right* system – the system whose processes are in fact reliable and whose beliefs are therefore in fact true – will be properly self-vindicating. But so far I haven't offered any argument for this. I do have an argument of sorts, but I would like to postpone it till the next section.

In this section I want to say something about the contemporary scientific intellectual system. In particular, I want to consider how far this system is self-vindicating and so a possible candidate for the right account of the natural world. Answers to these questions are not really essential to my overall project of answering the abstract question of how error is to be avoided. But the more concrete matter, of which beliefs we might expect to end up with if we do succeed in so avoiding error, and how far those will coincide with current science, is clearly of independent interest.

There is a well-known counter-argument to the claim that contemporary science embodies the correct view of the world. Consider the relation of current scientific theories to past theories. If we want to uphold the current theories it seems we must reject the past ones: if we want to uphold heliocentrism we must reject Ptolemaism. But then we seem to face a meta-induction on past falsity. We accept that all the past products of scientific practice have been false. So present and future products are likely to be false too. (Cf. Putnam, 1978b, p. 25.)

Perhaps we can resist this argument by identifying some relevant difference between current and past scientific theories. Perhaps, for instance, we could claim that contemporary science is properly self-vindicating, whereas past science failed to be so, and that this then blocks the meta-induction from past failure to likely present failure.

However, the claim that contemporary science distinguishes itself from past science by being fully self-vindicating is highly implausible. It is not as if the recommendation that we should reflect on our belief-forming processes and adjust them accordingly were some arcane prescription, which contemporary scientists only lit upon a couple of years ago, and which has suddenly allowed them to unlock the secrets of the universe. On the contrary, I take it that this recommendation has always seemed obvious to rational enquirers.[1]

Perhaps, it is true, efforts to carry out this recommendation have been more energetic at some periods of history than others. Perhaps, indeed, *science*, in the sense of Western, post-Galilean thinking about nature, is distinguished by the inventiveness and iconoclasm with which the naturalized recommendation has been pursued since the beginning of the seventeenth century. But I certainly don't want to maintain that people have only started trying to obey it in the last few years.

---

[1] Perhaps it is worth making it clear that normative naturalized epistemology is not being put forward as an innovatory strategy for active enquirers. First-order enquirers don't need philosophers to tell them that they should try to get their beliefs from reliable sources. The only innovation is on the *philosophical* level, in the offer of an alternative to the traditional Cartesian way of thinking *about* the conduct of first-order enquirers.

Yet, if people have been trying to carry out the naturalized recommendation for some time, isn't it absurd to suppose that they have suddenly succeeded in reaching a stably self-vindicating system only in the last year or two? There seems no obvious reason why contemporary thinkers should suddenly have been blessed with success, where equally virtuous past thinkers have consistently failed.

So we can't avoid the meta-induction from the falsity of past science by appealing to the supposed self-vindication of current science. But what options does that leave us? Should we simply accept the meta-induction and conclude that all current and foreseeable scientific theories are likely to be false?

Some philosophers of science are happy with this conclusion. Karl Popper's whole philosophy of science rests on the idea that the characteristic fate of all scientific theories, including our present ones, is falsity. But this is an uncomfortable resting place. To accept that our theories are false is to stop believing them, and, as we saw in 1.4 above, such sceptical suspension of belief is likely to involve us in a kind of practical inconsistency.

Maybe there is some room to be sceptical about *theoretical science* and yet retain a practically acceptable set of common-sense beleifs. But there are likely to be difficulties about where to draw the line. In particular, note that somebody, like Popper, who wants to take a sceptical view of all inductively generated beliefs, will be left without any beliefs about the future. And that certainly isn't a practically acceptable position.

Perhaps it is worth pausing briefly to say a bit more about the Popperian stance. Popper's underlying scepticism is to some extent obscured by his professed interest in principles governing the 'acceptance' of scientific theories. Although he is against our believing our theories, he does think we ought to 'accept' them. (See, for example, Popper, 1959, p. 108.) However, this notion of 'acceptance' is ultimately obscure. What exactly is one supposed to *do* when one 'accepts' a theory? One doesn't believe the theory. But presumably one does more than just entertain it, devise experiments to test it, etc. For one can do this to two inconsistent theories simultaneously, yet one can't, I take it, 'accept' two inconsistent theories simultaneously.

And even if sense could be made of 'acceptance', it still wouldn't be clear why we should concern ourselves with 'acceptance' rather than belief. After all, it is precisely because belief (unlike 'acceptance') answers to the truth, that epistemology focuses on the legitimacy of beliefs. Popper sometimes suggests that belief, unlike acceptance, is a 'subjective', 'psychological' notion, unsuitable for the analysis of objective scientific worth (for example, Popper, 1972, p. 25). But this is surely just flannel. We can ask serious normative questions about the worth of beliefs, or methods of belief-formation, just as much as about acceptance. Popper dislikes belief, not because it's subjective, but simply because it would force him to face up to the problem of induction: if he allowed that our commitment to theories answered to their truth, he wouldn't be able to maintain that it doesn't matter if the evidence leaves our theories likely to be false. But the tail of the problem of induction shouldn't be allowed to wag the whole dog of philosophy of science in this way.

Let me return to the main argument of this section. The difficulties inherent in Popper's position show that we cannot simply capitulate to the sceptical conclusion that current science is in all likelihood false. But we still face the meta-induction which seems to force us to this conclusion. The only alternative, it seems to me, is to deny the premise that all past scientific theories have turned out to be false. Or at least we want to qualify this premise, and find elements of truth in past theories, by which we can reassure ourselves of the underlying truthfulness of our present ones.

The simplest way to see present truth as emerging from past science would be to see past science as steadily accumulating truths and eliminating falsehoods. No doubt past scientists have believed some false things. But perhaps these falsehoods can all be seen as hangovers from older traditions of thought, which have steadily been corrected as scientific investigation proceeds.

The trouble with this suggestion is that it just doesn't fit the facts. Falsity isn't just found amongst ancient hangovers. Many of the most significant scientific innovations have themselves turned out to be false. Thus Galileo's law of free fall turned out to be strictly false: acceleration in fact increases with nearness to the earth. So also with Kepler's laws of planetary motion: planetary orbits aren't really ellipses, because of mutual planetary attractions. Even Newtonian physics itself turned out to be mistaken: the laws of motion are invariant with respect to all admissible rather than just Galilean transformations.

One familiar suggestion here is that such theories, while strictly false, are at least approximately true. That is, there is a relatively small deviation between what they say happens and what actually happens. Perhaps, then, we ought to think of past science as converging on present truth not just in respect of an increasing *quantity* of past truth, in terms of a simple accumulation of true statements, but also in terms of an increasing *quality*, in terms of an increasing approximation of such statements to the truth.[2]

But there are difficulties here too. One is with the suggestion that the false elements in past theories are approximating *closer and closer* to the truth: for note that it doesn't necessarily follow, from the fact that past falsities all approximated to the truth to some degree, that they are getting *better* at doing so.

And even if we bypass this difficulty, and assume increasing approximation, a further problem remains. Remember our current project. In order to sustain our commitment to the truth of our current beliefs, we want to deny that falsity is the natural condition of past science. But then appeals to approximation are no help. For approximate truth, even increasing approximate truth, is still falsity. Strictly speaking, Kepler's laws, and Galileo's, and Newton's, are just *not* true. And no finite amount of time is going to make a succession of such false views merge smoothly into truth. Maybe those past theories were only a *little bit* false – but then the natural implication seems to be that our theories are probably a little bit false too.

I think the only way out here is to accept that our theories are indeed likely to be a little bit false. If we reject the idea that science has suddenly managed to strike on the truth in the last year or two,

[2] The concept of 'verisimilitude' has been studied in the Popperian tradition (not so much because of worries about *believing* science, but simply in order to articulate some idea of objective progress among false theories). Oddie (1986) surveys this research, in particular the contributions of Pavel Tichy and David Miller, and develops Tichy's qualitative approach to verisimilitude.

the inevitable conclusion seems to be that we ought not to believe our theories as such, but only the weaker claim that our theories approximate to the truth. In order to maintain our beliefs, we need to adjust what we believe.

However, even this concession to the meta-induction isn't enough to resolve all the difficulties presented by the history of science. That past scientific innovations, strictly formulated, only approximate to the truth, isn't the only problem. There are in addition past innovations that diverged wildly from the truth. Take Newtonian dynamics, for instance. Newton's second law states that the acceleration produced by a given force is inversely proportional to the mass of the body, in the sense of amount of matter in the body. But we now know that resistance to acceleration by a given force increases with velocity, as well as with amount of matter. True, the Newtonian second law approximates to the truth for bodies moving with low velocities. But there is absolutely nothing in the Newtonian formulation of the second law to suggest that its application should be restricted to bodies with low velocities. And for bodies whose speeds are significant with respect to the speed of light, the second law, far from being approximately true, is just about as wrong as could be.

Perhaps we could try to argue at this point that past scientists *oughtn't* to have adopted some of their more theoretical assumptions. Perhaps Newton oughtn't to have embraced the second law in unrestricted form. After all, didn't his experimental evidence consist entirely of the observation of bodies with relatively low velocities? So wasn't he unjustified in stating the unrestricted second law, rather than merely claiming that, for relatively low velocities, acceleration was, up to experimental error, inversely proportional to mass?

But there is an obvious problem with this line. Isn't any inductive inference going to have to extrapolate beyond the particular data in some way or other? If we can't assume that the particular data exemplify some general type, if we can't assume that some possible variations of conditions are not going to make any difference to the quantitative relationships under examination, then in the end we won't be able to assert anything on the basis of the evidence except the evidence itself. As we saw at the end of the last chapter, all inductive inferences are underpinned by assumptions about natural kinds, that is, by assumptions about which variations of conditions might, or might not, make a difference to the outcome in question.

So we can't really argue that the failed theoretical extrapolations of past science were simply inferential errors. While in some cases there may have been wanton extrapolations from limited data, we would expect that as a rule past scientists would have had the underlying beliefs about natural kinds required to warrant their inductive inferences. Consider the Newton case again. Given the underlying seventeenth-century assumptions about the structure of space and time, and given the further assumption that the principles governing dynamic action, whatever they were, should not be sensitive to mere motioin (cf. in particular Huygens, 1669), the extrapolation from low velocities to high ones required to induce the second law was impeccable.

If we are to hold past scientists at fault for their inductive inferences, it shouldn't be because they extrapolated irresponsibly, but rather because their underlying natural kind assumptions were themselves arbitrary. (Seventeenth-century physicists had no special basis for assuming Galilean transformations.) But this is scarcely something to *criticize* past scientists for. Maybe their underlying natural kind assumptions were false. And maybe if they had exercised themselves more about the basis on which they reached those assumptions they might in principle have been able to avoid the error. Maybe, that is, if they had tried harder to satisfy the naturalized recommendation they would in principle have been led to different assumptions. But I doubt that such complete and exhaustive searches for error are humanly practicable for any single generation of scientists. And so we can scarcely blame past scientists for failing to achieve it.

And correlatively (given still that we don't want to attribute some special and inexplicable distinction to current science) we ought to admit that we ourselves are in danger of harbouring various false natural kind assumptions, and consequently of making erroneous inductive inferences. The only remedy here seems to me to be to recognize the possible deficiency, and try to identify the sort of natural kind assumption which is likely to come unstuck. And then perhaps we can restrict our tendency to go in for overly ambitious inductive extrapolations.

Once more, the moral of the meta-induction seems to be that we should exercise caution in what we believe. We have already allowed that we need to restrict our commitments to the approximate truth of our theories. Now our analysis of inductive extrapolation seems to indicate that we ought to be chary of what we suspect to be our more speculative inductive steps.

If we do exercise such caution, will we thereby end up with a system which is self-vindicating? I am not sure. One thing that has become clear is the extent to which self-vindication is a holistic business. Scientific beliefs derive from processes that are vindicated by natural kind assumptions which derive from other processes, etc. There is no reason in principle why self-vindication should necessarily degenerate into regress. But in practice we can expect that any actual, historically situated, scientific position will fail to be self-vindicating somewhere. There are many assumptions in any scientific position. Some are buried very deep, and serve to define the questions, rather than themselves being subjects of debate. I would say that, however hard we try, and even if we respond to the meta-induction by suitably truncating what we believe, there will in practice still always be a danger that we have failed to be fully self-vindicating.

But this doesn't mean that we shouldn't view self-vindication as a kind of ideal. We can't, unless we revert to some kind of anti-realism, rest happily in a situation where our overall view of the world, and of how we fit into it, implies that some of our beliefs are arbitrary happenstance, rather than reliable responses to the facts. Maybe it won't always be clear to us when our overall view carries this implication. But the moral then is simply that we should try harder to check the authority of our beliefs.

Let us now leave the question of how close we can get to self-vindication in practice, and turn to the underlying philosophical issues of what would have been achieved if we did arrive at such self-vindication.

10.5   THE AVOIDANCE OF ERROR

From now on I intend to bypass the historical difficulties of the last section, and assume, for the sake of the argument, that it is posible for human beings to develop intellectual systems which are fully self-vindicating. That is, I shall assume that humans are able to satisfy the naturalized recommendation at least to the extent of arriving at a state where all their processes seem reliable in the light of their beliefs. The more fundamental question remains: will such humans satisfy the naturalized recommendation to the further extent of avoiding error? That is, will a fully self-vindicating system actually be the correct picture of the world? The adherents of such a self-vindicating system will *believe* that their processes are reliable and that their beliefs are therefore generally true. But will those processes actually *be* reliable?

This is an issue of some argumentative delicacy. I want to maintain that, as the world is, a fully self-vindicating system will in fact be correct. But I don't want to have it that a fully self-vindicating system *must* be correct. It is central to the overall realism defended in this book that seeming to be right and actually being right are not the same thing: there is no necessary link between things appearing a certain way to human beings and their actually being that way.

But this then means that I won't be able to produce any general *a priori* argument, from the nature of representation or something similar, to the conclusion that a fully self-vindicating system will in fact be correct. However, I deny that we need any such argument.

Consider what is at issue here. The adherents of a fully self-vindicating system will be people who have taken pains to ensure that all their beliefs come from reliable belief-forming processes, and at the same time have tried to ensure that they have as powerful a set of belief-forming processes as possible. And they will thereby have arrived at a set of belief-forming processes, whose reliability they will be able to account for in the light of the beliefs that those processes give them. Wouldn't we expect the resulting intellectual system to fit the actual world, to contain processes that actually are reliable and beliefs that actually are true? After all, its adherents are themselves part of the world, and they have exerted themselves to get epistemologically well-adjusted to the world. Won't this in itself work against their system being a delusion? Won't the world itself act as a rudder, so to speak, which prevents their intellectual system going off in a mistaken direction?

Consider what would be involved in such a mistaken intellectual system. Its adherents would have a battery of belief-forming processes, which processes would then generate a set of beliefs, which beliefs would them imply that those methods were all reliable, *when in fact the methods weren't reliable, and the beliefs were therefore generally false*. This would in effect be to suppose that the world had constructed a kind of conspiracy against those people, making sure that all their mistakes were self-correcting: that their false beliefs were just what were needed to make their unreliable methods appear reliable. To hold that a self-vindicating system is erroneous is to say that the world is conducting a carefully designed conspiracy against its adherents.

These remarks might seem to miss the mark. Despite the rhetoric, they clearly don't *prove* that it is impossible for a fully self-vindicating system to be wrong: perhaps, after all, our world *is* conducting a conspiracy against enquirers. But, as I said, I don't want to produce a general argument to rule this out as a *possibility*. The above remarks are intended rather to shift the onus of argument on to anybody who wants to assert that this possibility is actual.

We need to be clear here that the relevant issue is whether the *actual* world allows erroneously self-vindicating systems, not whether other possible worlds would do so. I shall have occasion to point out shortly that in certain special possible worlds it will seem to enquirers that their beliefs come from reliable processes when in fact they don't. But those who want to deny the efficacy of the naturalized recommendation have to show something more than this: they have to show that the actual world has room for such an illusion.

Let us call this the '*this*-worldy possibility', to distinguish it from the idea of *other* possible worlds generating illusions. It is natural to think in terms of 'this-worldly *possibility*', rather than downright actuality, because we want to know whether the world has space, so to speak, for an erroneous self-vindicating system, rather than whether such a system actually exists. Suppose the Incas would have developed an intellectual system radically incompatible with ours, but equally self-vindicating, if only they hadn't been conquered by the Spanish, or that twenty-second-century science would have developed such a system, if only it hadn't been for the First Nuclear War. Since at most one of the Inca system and ours, or the twenty-second-century system and ours, can be right, I take it that even though these alternative systems never become actual, the potential conflict between them and our system would still show that pursuing the naturalized recommendation isn't in fact an effective means to avoid error.

Does the idea of a 'this-worldly possibility' make sense? Let me go a bit more slowly. The current issue is which possibilities should count as showing that a self-vindicating system can be erroneous. We can cast some light on this issue by digressing briefly, and reverting to a related question which came up in 7.2, before worries about self-vindicating systems came on the scene: namely, the question of which possibilities should count in deciding whether a given belief-forming *process* is reliable for truth. In footnote 2 in 7.2 I suggested that we should approach this question by asking how much reliability is needed in order to avoid error (and further suggested that this, rather than untutored intuition, is the best way to decide what kind of reliability is needed for 'justification' and 'knowledge'). Let me now spend a paragraph saying a bit more about this.

In the first instance we simply want our belief-forming processes to be reliable in this world: a process that always produces true beliefs will never let us down. But from the point of view of somebody actively investigating the reliability of a process, and wondering how to ensure it, this purely actualist conception of reliability is not particularly helpful. For we never know enough about the future to tell directly whether a given process will always give true results. Instead, as with all issues involving future generalities, we need to appeal to our causal knowledge, and to arrive at conclusions about what *will* generally happen by means of an inference from what is causally *possible*. This doesn't mean, however, that reliability should be understood as a matter of producing true beliefs in *all* causally possible worlds. Assumptions about causal possibility aren't the only constraints on the relevant possible worlds. There are also assumptions about what kinds of particular conditions are at all likely to turn up in the future. We won't of course know exactly what conditions are going to turn up (that's why the purely this-worldly conception of reliability is no good). But, even so, in considering whether a given process is sufficiently reliable, we will want to discount outlandish causal possibilities, such as that the earth and everything in it coagulated by accident ten minutes ago, or that 90 per cent of the world's population are robots programmed to mislead the rest of us, and concentrate instead on the kind of circumstance that, for all we know, we might actually run into.[3]

Let me now return to the naturalized recommendation and the idea of a 'this-worldly possibility'. The question being addressed in this section, the question of whether the naturalized recommendation as such is sufficiently effective to ensure that any self-vindicating system won't be erroneous, should not be confused with the question of the last paragraph, the question of whether a specific belief-forming process is sufficiently reliable to avoid producing false beliefs. The former question is on a far more general and abstract level than the latter. But the same considerations about relevant possibilities apply. Thus the significance of the non-existent Inca science, or the non-existent twenty-second-century science, is that these possibilities are close enough to the actual world for the putative failure of the naturalized recommendation in such worlds to give us reason to doubt the naturalized recomendation's effectiveness in this world. Although a world containing these alternative intellectual systems is strictly speaking a non-actual world, it is a 'this-worldly possibility' in the sense that its supposed difference from the actual world lies in some fairly specific particular facts (no Spanish invasion, no nuclear war), not in any outlandish differences. Which is why I am committed to

---

[3]Cf. Goldman's discussion of 'normal' worlds (1986, pp. 108–9). It is no part of my thought, however, that justification should depend on reliability in the worlds we *believe* to be normal. Goldman's suggestion to this effect seems to me an aberration, fostered by an excessive respect for existing (and, I would say, Cartesian-tutored) intuitions.

denying that 'this-worldly possibilities' like the Incas or twenty-second-century science could in fact contain fully self-vindicating intellectual systems incompatible with ours. By contrast I have no such commitment with respect to 'other-worldly possibilities'. Since the non-effectiveness of the naturalized recommendation in some outlandish world is no reason for doubting its effectiveness in this world, I am quite happy to allow that there are other-worldly possibilities in which the naturalized recommendation won't work.

Some readers will no doubt be getting impatient. Why be so delicate about all these different worlds? Doesn't the 100 per cent actual world already contain quite enough evidence of the historical and anthropological diversity of human thought to discredit the naturalized recommendation? But I can only ask readers to think carefully about the precise claim I am making. To repeat, I certainly don't want to deny – indeed I insist – that human beings in this world are capable of incompatible intellectual systems. The issue is rather whether they can have incompatible systems which are fully self-vindicating. And, as the earlier sections of this chapter have made clear, by no means every powerful intellectual system is fully self-vindiating. My thesis is that the historical and anthropological alternatives will turn out on closer examination to fail on this count, and that they therefore provide no reason for thinking that a sustained and thorough pursuit of the naturalized recommendation can lead to an erroneous system.

10.6 THE UNDERDETERMINATION OF THEORY BY EVIDENCE

But what about the underdetermination of theory by evidence? Isn't the possibility of humans adopting incompatible intellectual systems in this world assured by the fact that the choice between divergent answers to theoretical questions is in general underdetermined by the evidence? But we need to be careful here. This is a rather different issue. I don't necessarily want to deny that the best-adjusted intellectual system possible for humans may yet be incomplete, in that inductive evidence might fail to decide between incompatible answers T′ and T″ to certain theoretical questions. In effect this was conceded in the last section, when I responded to the meta-induction by suggesting that we might have to restrict our scientific beliefs. But it doesn't follow from underdetermination in this sense that there could be two incompatible self-vindicating intellectual systems, one containing answer T′ and the other containing answer T″. For the moral of underdetermination isn't that I am entitled to believe T′ and that you are entitled to believe T″. It's that nobody is entitled to believe either.

It will be helpful to be rather more precise about underdetermination. When I say that the choice between incompatible T′ and T″ is underdetermined within some intellectual system S, I mean that S's inductive processes and accepted beliefs lend support to both T′ and T″ to the same degree. This now makes it clear why you would be wrong either to believe T′ or to believe T″ if the choice between them were underdetermined according to your intellectual system. For since they are incompatible, and since, by hypothesis, they are equally well-supported, neither can be recommended for full belief.

If underdetermination were widespread, then we would face a rather different problem. We would be forced rationally to suspend belief on a wide range of issues. But there is no reason to suppose that underdetermination is particularly widespread. Perhaps there are some specific theoretical issues that will inevitably remain undecided by the evidence. But there is no reason to suppose that all questions, or even all theoretical questions, fall into this category.

It is important here not to confuse being equally *well-supported* by the evidence with being equally *consistent* with the evidence. If these were the same, then underdetermination would indeed be widespread, for there will always be incompatible answers to any theoretical question which are both consistent with the evidence. However, they aren't the same.

It is true that if we held, with Popper, that the only way that evidence can weigh in favour of a theory is by not falsifying it, then all theories consistent with the evidence would, in an empty sense, be equally well-supported by it. But we have already seen that there are alternatives to this nihilistic view of inductive support.

Let me give a simple example to illustrate these points. Let T′ be the classical theory that the earth goes round the sun. Then we can easily cook up another theory with the same evidential implications, T″, according to which the sun and everything else go round the earth and there is an extra universal force to explain this. But I would argue, along the lines of the last section of the last chapter, that within our intellectual system T″ is far less well-supported by the evidence than T′, even though it is equally consistent with the evidence, because of the general meta-principle that a complex theory won't be true if a simple theory fits the same evidence.[4] (What should count as 'our' intellectual system in this context? Doesn't 'our' system already include T′? So for fairness shouldn't we also consider the putative intellectual system that endorses T″ instead of T′? Or perhaps we should reason from a base-line of a system that includes neither T′ of T″. But my answer is that it doesn't matter which such system we consider, since all of them, as so far described, are likely to endorse the move from the evidence to T′, and none are likely to endorse the move to T″. The relevant question is not so much which of the two theories is included in the system, but what inductive processes the system has for getting from evidence to theories. Note in particular that the system that differed from ours simply by replacing T′ by T″ wouldn't be self-vindicating, for it wouldn't be able to explain, by reference to any of its belief-forming processes, how it had arrived at T″.)

[4] From the point of view of modern space-time theories, this reasoning would condemn T′ along with T″, since T″'s putative gravitational forces would themselves be 'universal forces'. Cf. Glymour (1980, ch. IX.) I I ignore this point in the interests of a graphic example. But it raises an important issue. In general we don't have to be inventive in order for our belief-forming processes to be reliable. Reliability (as opposed to informativeness, or 'power') doesn't generally require that we be good at thinking up answers, just that we be able to tell which answers are right if they get proposed. However, if high-level theory choice in science involves designing experiments to eliminate all but one among the reasonably simple answers, then scientists will need to think up all those answers. The difficulty of doing this provides a further reason for being wary of inductive inferences, in addition to those mentioned in 10.4.

10.7 SCEPTICAL POSSIBILITIES

Consider once more the normal heliocentric theory, T', and the 'cooked-up' geocentric alternative, T''. At best our understanding of the inductive situation is going to show us that the probability of the heliocentric T', given the evidence, is indiscernible from one, not that it is necessarily true. Thus, if we adopt the approach to inductive inference developed in the last chapter, the inference to the heliocentric T' is sound because in general in this world such inferences to simple explanations of the evidence are successful, not because the evidence makes any alternative to T' logically impossible. And no doubt any other explanation of the soundness of inductive inference would also fail to rule out the geocentric T'' conclusively. It will still be conceptually possible, given the evidence, that the geocentric T'' is true. T'', after all, is *consistent* with the evidence. That's the whole point of cooking it up as we did: even if it were true, things would still look just the same.

It is important that, whilst it is in this sense *epistemologically possible* that the sun goes round the earth, this is no reason to stop believing the opposite. The evidence can leave open the conceptual possibility that T'', yet at the same time imply that T'' is quite improbable. I take it that this is precisely the situation from the point of view of our own intellectual system: we recognize that the geocentric T'' is consistent with the evidence, but reject it as a complex and therefore incredible alternative to the heliocentric T'.

Note that the epistemological possibility that the geocentric T'' might be true is not the same as the 'this-worldly possibility' that would suffice to show that the naturalized recommendation is ineffective. The latter is the possibility that the *actual* world has room for an intellectual system which is (a) fully self-vindicating, but (b) nevertheless erroneous. The fact that the geocentric T'' is consistent with the evidence does not yield this possibility. For, although an intellectual system containing T'' would, we take it, be erroneous in this world, it wouldn't, as pointed out in the last section, be self-vindicating.

Of course if we *were* in a world in which the sun went round the earth, things would be different. Then there would be a fully self-vindicating yet erroneous system, namely, the system involving the heliocentric theory T′. And conversely, and somewhat paradoxically, the system including the geocentric T″ would be veridical but wouldn't be self-vindicating: while people who believed the geocentric T″ would of course be believing truly, they wouldn't be able satisfactorily to explain how they had come by their theory.

This world would be the kind of world I was worried about earlier – a world that conducts an epistemological conspiracy against its inhabitants. It would allow its inhabitants to believe that all their beliefs came from reliable processes, when in fact they didn't. But the goings-on in this world are of no direct relevance to our concerns. Somebody who wants to deny that the naturalized recommendation is effective has to do more than point to the epistemological possibility of such a conspiratorial world. As before, what needs to be shown is that the *actual* world is capable of such a conspiracy. And, as I pointed out a moment ago, the fact that our evidence leaves it epistemologically possible that we are living in a conspiratorial world is no argument at all for thinking that we actually are. I recognize that my evidence leaves open the epistemological possibility of a geocentric world. But at the same time my inductive principles reject this theory as quite improbable.

Consider now the traditional sceptical suggestion that our experiences might be caused by an evil demon, or, again, the modern suggestion that we might be brains in vats whose afferent nerves are being appropriately stimulated by a mad scientist. Even if we were brains in vats, so the argument goes, things would still seem the same. My response to this is the same as to the theory that the sun goes round the earth. It is epistemologically possible that we are the playthings of a mad scientist, and if we were we'd have an erroneous intellectual system. But that's no reason in itself for believing that we are such playthings, and so no reason for thinking that we are actually in error. Moreover, the common-sense theory, that we are in a world of physical objects, is in fact far more likely than the mad scientist alternative, since a mad scientist who precisely duplicates the appearances produced by the physical world is clearly a more complex hypothesis than the physical world itself.

This is perhaps a little bit quick. The notion of 'evidence' relevant to the sceptical argument is rather different from the one I've implicitly been assuming so far. I've been assuming that any non-inferred beliefs can be evidence for an inductive inference, including ordinary perceptual and memory beliefs about the external world. So my 'evidence' is itself incompatible with the sceptical hypothesis. The sceptic, on the other hand, is thinking of the evidence as restricted to the deliverances of introspection. This complicates the picture slightly. I want to argue that the sceptical hypothesis gives us no reason to suppose that the naturalized recommendation will be ineffective. More specifically, I want to argue that it doesn't establish the possible existence in this world of an intellectual system that is self-vindicating but erroneous. I accept, of course, that in this world either our system or the sceptical system is erroneous. But that doesn't bother me, because I think that the system that is in error – the sceptical system – isn't self-vindicating. In particular, it seems to me, adherents of the sceptical system won't be inductively entitled to their mad scientist belief. But this is where the complication bites. I can't reasonably argue this last point, that sceptics aren't inductively entitled to their mad scientist belief, by appealing to standards of inductive reasoning internal to *our* existing intellectual system, with its far wider body of 'evidence', and therefore with a far wider range of theories from which to meta-induce accounts of inductive evidence, etc. Rather the question is whether, within the sceptical intellectual system based on its introspective notion of evidence, you could be inductively entitled to the mad scientist hypothesis. However, now we have spelt these complications out, we can see that they don't really help the sceptic. Having less that counts as 'evidence' is, if anything, going to mean that the sceptic ends up with weaker inductive standards, not stronger ones. And so if *I* can't explain, in terms of my full-blooded inductive standards, how the sceptics are supposed to have found out about the mad scientist, it seems extremely unlikely that the sceptics themselves will be able to explain this from within their more anaemic system.

These last couple of paragraphs might have seemed a bit unfair to the traditional sceptic. No sensible traditional sceptic wants to *assert* that we are brains in vats. A good traditional sceptic will suspend belief on anything but the appearances. The point of the mad scientist hypothesis is merely to make it clear that we might be mistaken, and thereby to undermine our faith in the common-sense theory. But my point remains the same. The mere epistemological *possibility* of the mad scientist hypothesis isn't any reason to think it *likely*, and so shouldn't, contrary to the sceptic's suggestion, undermine our common-sense faith.

Of course there is one sense in which the sceptic who suspensds belief on everything but the appearances is epistemologically better situated than the rest of us: there is less risk of error in the sceptic's position. But we have already seen what to say about that. Avoidance of error isn't the only epistemological desideratum. We also want to avoid ignorance. The sceptic only achieves extra security by adopting an intellectual system with an impoverished battery of belief-forming processes (don't believe *anything* but the appearances). And since we haven't been given any substantial grounds for doubting the general reliability, as opposed to the necessary infallibility, of the belief-forming processes the sceptic eschews, there is no good reason for us to handicap ourselves in the way that scepticism recommends.

Now that I am talking about brains in vats, I would like to return briefly to Hilary Putnam's version of anti-realism of method. Recall that in 6.2 I questioned Putnam's entitlement to the first component in methodism, to the assumption that there are universal standards of belief-evaluation. But now I want to consider his argument for the second component, for the claim that the answers delivered by those standards cannot but be true. Putnam addresses this question by asking whether somebody whose answers do satisfy those standards (whose theories conform to 'all operational and theoretical constraints') could nevertheless be mistaken. Could such a person be a brain in a vat, for instance?

Putnam argues that this hypothesis is incoherent. His argument, at its simplest, is that if we *were* brains in vats, our notion of *tree*, say, wouldn't then refer to real trees, but rather to 'trees' in the 'image' the mad scientist was imposing on us, which would then make our beliefs about trees true. And similarly with the rest of our everyday beliefs: they too should be understood as being about features of the image, and therefore as perfectly accurate. In particular, *vat* should be understood as being about 'vats' in the image, which would make it right to think that we are not brains in vats. In effect Putnam is claiming that the sceptical thought that we are brains in vats undermines itself – if we were right in thinking this, we'd be wrong. (Cf. Putnam, 1981, ch. 1; see also 1978b, part 4.)

I don't think this is a good argument. My underlying objection is that it simply takes for granted something very much like the principle of charity: the only argument for deeming the brain in the vat's tree-concept to refer to trees in the image, rather than real trees, is that this interpretation succeeds in making all the brain's beliefs come out true. It is true that Putnam's use of the principle of charity differs from that discussed in chapter 2, in that he only applies it to the interpretation of the ideal system. It's only a perfect theory, a theory satisfying all epistemological constraints, that cannot but be true. Concepts in a less than perfect theory need to be interpreted indirectly, by imagining that imperfect theory developed to perfection, and then considering how those concepts would need to be ascribed referents in order for that ideal theory to come out true.

So Putnam has room to allow that a less than ideal theory can be false, even radically false, which is why I have counted him as an anti-realist of method rather than of belief. (Thus, for example, even a brain in a vat might have any number of false beliefs about the image, if it hadn't yet had much evidence to go on, or hadn't yet properly figured out the principles which govern vat goings-on.) However, there is nothing in all these refinements to invalidate the objections levelled at the principle of charity in chapter 2. Even when we get to the ideal theory, interpretation needs to appeal to humanity, not charity. And once we acknowledge humanity, we will need to recognize the possibility of intrinsic identifications of beliefs. And then we will need something along the lines of the teleological theory to give us an adequate account of representation. (Not, incidentally, that it's entirely clear what a theory in the style of the teleological theory would imply about brains in vats. The sceptical scenario needs filling out. Are the brains in vats supposed to have a prior evolutionary history, with the mad scientist somehow capturing them for its demonic purposes? Or did the mad scientist construct them from scratch? The two versions will have different implications about the teleology of the brain's states. Roughly, if they are captives, the purpose of their concept will be to be about real trees, while if they are constructs, it will be to represent 'trees' in the image. But either way there will be conceptual room for the brains in vat to be mistaken – although in the latter case, where they are constructs, they won't in fact be mistaken.)

Putnam would object to my using the teleological theory (or any other theory of representation using causal notions) in this context, on the grounds that the issue is how our *total* theory of the world, including any such empirical theory of representation, relates to the world itself. (Cf. 1981, ch. 2.) I am happy to concede that this is the issue. But this does not seem to me a good argument for insisting on a purely charitable approach to interpretation. The suggestion, presumably, is that we should 'bracket' all our natural knowledge of human beings and their workings. But then what position are we left in to do our philosophizing from? That of a pure mind with some kind of *non*-natural knowledge of its interior epistemological situation? Putnam seems at this point to be committed to a highly Cartesian problematic, a metaphysics of thinkers who know about the images on the interior walls of their mental rooms, but don't know about anything else. (And, in any case, why even from that perspective should a charity-based notion of interpretation be taken for granted?)

It is perhaps worth emphasizing the difference between my attitude to the mad scientist hypothesis and Putnam's. We both want to reject this hypothesis. But Putnam, as an anti-realist, wants to reject it on *conceptual* grounds: he wants to argue from the nature of representation that it would be impossible for any being to be correct in surmising that it was a brain in a vat. I don't think that this hypothesis is in any sense impossible: the conjectured situation doesn't violate any conceptual constraints. I just want to claim that we are in fact justified in rejecting this hypothesis, since, as a matter of contingent actuality, the belief-forming process that dismisses this hypothesis on grounds of excessive complexity is a reliable route to the truth.

10.8   TOLERATING THE POSSIBILITY OF ERROR

Perhaps a feeling of dissatisfaction remains. If even full satisfaction of the naturalized recommendation leaves us with the possibility of error, then has anything really been achieved? Aren't we still faced with the worry that seeming to have a system comprising reliable methods and true beliefs isn't the same as actually having such a system?

But why is this a worry? Of course, seeming to have the world right isn't conceptually the same as actually having it right. That's not the present issue. The present issue is whether the naturalized strategy is in fact an effective way to avoid error. Will people who investigate the reliability of their belief-forming processes, and who reconstruct themselves in the interests of improving such reliability, get better at gathering truths? In particular, will people who stick at this strategy of reconstruction until such time as they don't have any belief-forming processes that they don't believe to be good for producing truths, in fact succeed in avoiding error?

I admit that there is no *a priori* guarantee that the naturalized recommendation will succeed. But why demand such conceptual guarantees? Isn't it enough that the naturalized recommendation will lead to success, in practice, in the actual world?

The idea that the conceptual possibility of error suffices for epistemological failure runs very deep. But, as I have had occasion to observe a number of times already in this chapter, there is no immediate inference here. That we *may* be in error does not show that we *are* (nor even that it is the slightest bit probable that we are).

But rather than simply repeating this point, let me try to put my finger on the reason why we feel that the complete elimination of the conceptual possibility of error is so important. As you might expect, I want to attribute this feeling to Cartesian prejudice.

The Cartesian influence operates on two levels. In the first place, the whole idea of avoiding error by making better *inferences* pushes us towards certainty. For, as I observed in 7.2, it is hard to see how we can avoid regresses unless our premises are introspectively incorrigible and the validity of our inferential steps is similarly authenticated by consciousness. It is no accident that most epistemologists from Descartes onwards have rejected beliefs that admit of any possibility of doubt.

But I think there is also a deeper level at which the desire for certainty grips us. Few epistemologists in the latter half of this century still hold out hopes for Cartesian certainty. The discrediting of givens, and the failure of phenomenalist reductions, have made it clear that, whatever basis we find for our beliefs, it is unlikely to be one that rules out all doubts. But despite this there is still another sense in which the Cartesian notion that epistemology is a matter of inference keeps most philosophers committed to a kind of certainty. For even if we recognize that there will always be room for doubts about our beliefs, there is still the thought that we can't be mistaken *about our own epistemological situation*. Perhaps we will always be uncertain to a certain degree about the conclusions of our justificatory inferences. But there is no real room for our being mistaken about the fact that the conclusions are justified to that degree.

On the Cartesian conception of epistemology as inference, justification depends entirely on introspectively available facts. So there seems no serious possibility of a concerned believer being mistaken about whether (or how much) a certain belief is justified. And this, I suspect, is why we feel so strongly that justification about which we are not certain is no justification at all: if we really were justified, then surely we would be certain of *that* at least.

On the naturalized conception of epistemology there is no basis for this feeling. Since naturalized justification can depend on facts not available to consciousness, it is possible for even the most concerned believer to be mistaken about the extent to which a given belief is justified. Perhaps this seems odd. But we should learn to come to terms with it. Once we give up the idea that justification resides in self-transparent minds, and switch to the naturalized idea that justification is simply a matter of being well-adjusted to the world, then it is scarcely surprising that it is in principle possible to be mistaken about our own epistemological situation, just as it is in principle possible to be mistaken about anything else.

References

Baldwin, T. 1985: 'Ethical Non-Naturalism', in I. Hacking (ed.), *Exercises in Analysis*, Cambridge University Press.

Benaceraff, P. 1973: 'Mathematical Truth', *Journal of Philosophy*, 70.

Blackburn, S. 1971: 'Moral Realism', in J. Casey (ed.), *Morality and Moral Reasoning*, Methuen.

    1984: *Spreading the Word*, Clarendon Press.

    1985a: 'Supervenience Revisited', in I. Hacking (ed.), *Exercises in Analysis*, Cambridge University Press.

    1985b: 'Errors and the Phenomenology of Value', in T. Honderich (ed.), *Morality and Objectivity*, Routledge and Kegan Paul.

Block, N. (ed.) 1980: *Readings in the Philosophy of Psychology*, vol. 1, Methuen.

Burnyeat, M. 1983: 'Can the Sceptic Live His Scepticism?', in M. Burnyeat (ed.), *The Sceptical Tradition*, University of California Press.

Craig, E. 1976: 'Sensory Experience and the Foundations of Knowledge', *Synthese*, 33.

Dancy, J. 1986: 'Two Conceptions of Moral Realism', *Aristotelian Society Supplementary Volume*, 60.

Davidson, D. 1967: 'Truth and Meaning', *Synthese*, 7. Reprinted in Davidson (1984).

    1973: 'Radical Interpretation', *Dialectica*, 27. Reprinted in Davidson (1984).

    1974: 'On the Very Idea of a Conceptual Scheme', *Proceedings and Addresses of the American Philosophical Association*, 47. Reprinted in Davidson (1984).

    1975: 'Thought and Talk', in S. Guttenplan (ed.), *Mind and Language*. Reprinted in Davidson (1984).

    1980: *Essays on Actions and Events*, Clarendon Press.

    1984: *Inquiries into Truth and Interpretation*, Clarendon Press.

Dennett, D. 1969: *Content and Consciousness*, Routledge and Kegan Paul.

    1971: 'Intentional Systems', *Journal of Philosophy*, 68.

1978a: 'Why You Can't Make a Computer that Feels Pain', *Synthese*, 38.

1978b: 'Reply to Arib and Gunderson', in D. Dennet, *Brainstorms*, Bradford Books.

1981: 'Three Kinds of Intentional Psychology', in R. Healey (ed.), *Reduction, Time and Reality*, Cambridge University Press.

1982: 'Beyond Belief', in A. Woodfield (ed.), *Thought and Object*, Clarendon Press.

Devitt, M. 1984: *Realism and Truth*, Basil Blackwell.

Dretske, F. 1981: *Knowledge and the Flow of Information*, Basil Blackwell.

1986: 'Misrepresentation', in R. Bogdan (ed.), *Belief*, Clarendon Press.

Dummett, M. 1958: 'Truth', *Proceedings of the Aristotelian Society*, 59.

1974: *The Justification of Deduction*, British Academy Lecture, Oxford University Press.

1976: 'What Is a Theory of Meaning II?', in G. Evans and J. McDowell (eds), *Truth and Meaning*, Clarendon Press.

1978a: 'Realism', in Dummett (1978b).

1978b: *Truth and Other Enigmas*, Duckworth.

Earman, J. and Fine, A. 1977: 'Against Indeterminacy', *Journal of Philosophy*, 74.

Evans, G. 1976: 'Logical Form and Semantic Structure', in G. Evans and J. McDowell (eds), *Truth and Meaning*, Clarendon Press.

1982: *The Varieties of Reference*, Oxford University Press.

Evans-Pritchard, E. 1937: *Witchcraft, Oracles and Magic among the Azande*, Clarendon Press.

Feyerabend, P. 1975: *Against Method*, New Left Books.

Field, H. 1972: 'Tarski's Theory of Truth', *Journal of Philosophy*, 69.

1973: 'Theory Change and the Indeterminacy of Reference', *Journal of Philosophy*, 70.

1978: 'Mental Representation', *Erkenntnis'*, 13.

1981: *Science without Numbers*, Basil Blackwell.

Fine, A. 1984: 'The Natural Ontological Attitude', in J. Leplin (ed.), *Scientific Realism*, University of California Press.

1986: 'Unnatural Attitudes: Realist and Instrumentalist Attachments to Science', *Mind*, 95.

Fodor, J. 1980: 'Methodological Solipsism Considered as a Research Program in Cognitive Psychology', *Behavioural and Brain Sciences*, 3.

1983: *The Modularity of Mind*, MIT Press.

1984a: 'Semantics, Wisconsin Style', *Synthese*, 59.

1984b: 'Observation Reconsidered', *Philosophy of Science*, 51.

1986: 'Banish disContent', in J. Butterfield (ed.), *Language, Mind and Logic*, Cambridge University Press.

Galileo, G. 1632: *Dialogue Concerning the Two Chief World Systems*. Translated by Stillman Drake, University of California Press, 1953.

Gettier, E. 1963: 'Is Justified True Belief Knowledge?', *Analysis*, 23.

Glymour, C. 1980: *Theory and Evidence*, Princeton University Press.

Goldman, A. 1976: 'Discrimination and Perceptual Knowledge', *Journal of Philosophy*, 73.

   1978: 'Epistemics: The Regulative Theory of Cognition', *Journal of Philosophy*, 75.

   1979: 'What is Justified Belief?', in G. Pappas (ed.), *Justification and Knowledge*, Reidel.

   1980: 'The Internalist Conception of Justification', in P. French, T. Uehling and H. Wettstein (eds), *Midwest Studies in Philosophy*, vol. 5, *Studies in Epistemology*, University of Minnesota Press.

   1985: 'The Relation between Epistemology and Psychology', *Synthese*, 64.

   1986: *Epistemology and Cognition*, Harvard University Press.

Goodman, N. 1954: *Fact, Fiction and Forecast*, Athlone Press.

Grandy, R. 1973: 'Reference, Meaning and Belief', *Journal of Philosophy*, 70.

Gregory, R. 1974: 'Perceptions as Hypotheses', in S. Brown (ed.), *Philosophy of Psychology*, Macmillan.

Grice, H. P. 1957: 'Meaning', *Philosophical Review*, 66.

   1968: 'Utterer's Meaning, Sentence Meaning and Word Meaning', *Foundations of Language*, 4.

   1969: 'Utterer's Meaning and Intentions', *Philosophical Review*, 78.

Hacking, I. 1979: 'What is Logic?', *Journal of Philosophy*, 76.

Hanson, N. 1958: *Patterns of Discovery*, Cambridge University Press.

Hookway, C. 1986: 'Two Conceptions of Moral Realism', *Aristotelian Society Supplementary Volume*, 60.

Huygens, C. 1669: 'The Laws of Motion', *Philosophical Transactions of the Royal Society*, 4.

Kitcher, P. 1983: *The Nature of Mathematical Knowledge*, Oxford University Press.

Kuhn, T. 1962: *The Structure of Scientific Revolutions*, Univeristy of Chicago Press.

Lear, J. 1982: 'Leaving the World Alone', *Journal of Philosophy*, 79.

Leeds, S. 1978: 'Theories of Reference and Truth', *Erkenntnis*, 13.

Lewis, D. 1972: 'General Semantics', in D. Davidson and G. Harman (eds), *Semantics of Natural Languages*, Reidel.

   1973: 'Causation', *Journal of Philosophy*, 70.

Loar, B. 1981: *Mind and Meaning*, Cambridge University Press.

McDowell, J. 1976: 'Truth Conditions, Bivalence and Verificationism', in G. Evans and J. McDowell (eds), *Truth and Meaning*, Clarendon Press.

    1978: 'Are Moral Requirements Hypothetical Imperatives?', *Aristotelian Society Supplementary Volume*, 52.

    1985: 'Values and Secondary Qualities', in T. Honderich (ed.), *Morality and Objectivity*, Routledge and Kegan Paul.

McFetridge, I. 1978: 'Are Moral Requirements Hypothetical Imperatives?', *Aristotelian Society Supplementary Volume*, 52.

McGinn, C. 1979: 'An A Priori Argument for Realism', *Journal of Philosophy*, 76.

    1982: 'The Structure of Content', in A. Woodfield (ed.), *Thought and Object*, Clarendon Press.

Mackie, J. 1974: *The Cement of the Universe*, Clarendon Press.

Mill, J. S. 1843: *A System of Logic*, Longman.

Millikan, R. 1984: *Language, Thought, and Other Biological Categories*, MIT Press.

Nagel, T. 1974: 'What Is It Like to Be a Bat?', *Philosophical Review*, 83.

Neander, K. 1984: *Abnormal Psychobiology*, Unpublished Ph.D. dissertation, La Trobe University.

Newton, I. 1687: *The Mathematical Principles of Natural Philosophy*. Translated by A. Motte, 1729. Reprinted 1968, Dawson.

Oddie, G. 1986: *Likeness to Truth*, Reidel.

Papineau, D. 1976: 'Ideal Types and Empirical Theories', *British Journal for the Philosophy of Science*, 27.

    1978: *For Science in the Social Sciences*, Macmillan.

    1979: *Theory and Meaning*, Clarendon Press.

    1981: 'Is Epistemology Dead?', *Proceedings of the Aristotelian Society*, 82.

    1984: 'Representation and Explanation', *Philosophy of Science*, 51.

    1985: 'Social Facts and Psychological Facts', in G. Currie and A. Musgrave (eds), *Popper and the Human Sciences*, Reidel.

    1986a: 'Semantic Reduction and Reference', in J. Butterfield (ed.), *Language, Mind and Logic*, Cambridge University Press.

    1986b: 'Laws and Accidents', in G. MacDonald and C. Wright (eds), *Fact, Science and Morality*, Basil Blackwell.

    1987: 'Discussion of C. Peacocke, *Thoughts: An Essay on Content*', *Philosophical Books*, 28.

Peacocke, C. 1976: 'What is a Logical Constant?', *Journal of Philosophy*, 73.

    1983: *Sense and Content*, Oxford University Press.

    1986: *Thoughts: An Essay on Content*, Basil Blackwell.

Platts, M. 1979: *Ways of Meaning*, Routledge and Kegan Paul.

Popper, K. 1959: *The Logic of Scientific Discovery*, Hutchinson.

1972: *Objective Knowledge*, Clarendon Press.

Putnam, H. 1962: 'The Analytic and the Synthetic', in H. Feigl and G. Maxwell (eds), *Minnesota Studies in the Philosophy of Science*, vol. 3, University of Minnesota Press.

1978a: 'Reference and Understanding', in Putnam (1978b).

1978b: *Meaning and the Moral Sciences*, Routledge and Kegan Paul.

1981: *Reason, Truth and History*, Cambridge University Press.

1983: *Realism and Reason*, Cambridge University Press.

Quinton, A. 1955: 'The Problem of Perception', *Mind*, 67.

Ramsey, F. 1931: 'Theories', in his *Foundations of Mathematics*, Routledge and Kegan Paul.

Rorty, R. 1979: 'Transcendental Arguments, Self-Reference, and Pragmatism', in P. Bieri, R. Horstmann and L. Kruger (eds), *Transcendental Arguments and Science*, Reidel.

1980: *Philosophy and the Mirror of Nature*, Basil Blackwell.

Russell, B. 1946: *A History of Western Philosophy*, Allen and Unwin.

Sainsbury, R. 1979: 'Understanding and Theories of Meaning', *Proceedings of the Aristotelian Society*, 80.

Scheffler, I. 1967: *Science and Subjectivity*, Bobbs-Merrill.

Schiffer, S. 1972: *Meaning*, Oxford University Press.

Sellars, W. 1956: 'Empiricism and the Philosophy of Mind', in H. Feigl and M. Scriven (eds), *Minnesota Studies in the Philosophy of Science*, vol. 2, University of Minnesota Press.

Stampe, D. 1977: 'Towards a Causal Theory of Linguistic Representation', in P. French, T. Uehling and H. Wettstein (eds), *Midwest Studies in Philosophy*, vol. 2, *Studies in Semantics*, University of Minnesota Press.

Stich, S. 1983: *From Folk Psychology to Cognitive Science*, MIT Press.

Stroud, B. 1965: 'Wittgenstein and Logical Necessity', *Philosophical Review*, 74.

Tarski, A. 1949: 'The Semantic Conception of Truth', in H. Feigl and W. Sellars (eds), *Readings in Philosophical Analysis*, Appleton Century Crofts.

1956: 'The Concept of Truth in Formalized Languages', in A. Tarski, *Logic, Semantics, Metamathematics*, Oxford University Press.

Taylor, B. 1982: 'On the Need for a Meaning Theory in the Theory of Meaning', *Mind*, 91.

Unger, P. 1971: 'A Defence of Scepticism', *Philosophical Review*, 80.

Van Cleve, J. 1984: 'Reliability, Justification, and Induction', in P. French, T. Uehling and H. Wettstein (eds), *Midwest Studies in Philosophy*, vol. 9, *Causation and Causal Theories*, University of Minnesota Press.

Weiskrantz, L. 1986: *Blindsight*, Clarendon Press.

Whewell, W. 1849: *Induction, with especial reference to Mr J. Stuart Mill's System of Logic*, Parker.

Wiggins, D. 1976: *Truth, Invention and the Meaning of Life*, British Academy Lecture, Oxford University Press.

Williams, B. 1978: *Descartes*, Harvester.

Wittgenstein, L. 1953: *Philosophical Investigations*, Basil Blackwell.

Woodfield, A. 1976: *Teleology*, Oxford University Press.

Wright, L. 1973: 'Functions', *Philosophical Review*, 82.

Index